CW00921682

School-to-School Collaboration

School-to-School Collaboration: Learning Across International Contexts

EDITED BY

PAUL WILFRED ARMSTRONG

University of Manchester, UK

AND

CHRIS BROWN

Durham University, UK

United Kingdom – North America – Japan – India – Malaysia – China

Emerald Publishing Limited
Howard House, Wagon Lane, Bingley BD16 1WA, UK

First edition 2022

Reprints and permissions service
Contact: permissions@emeraldinsight.com

British Library Cataloguing in Publication Data
A catalogue record for this book is available from the British Library

ISBN: 978-1-80043-669-5 (Print)
ISBN: 978-1-80043-668-8 (Online)
ISBN: 978-1-80043-670-1 (Epub)

Printed and bound by CPI Group (UK) Ltd, Croydon, CR0 4YY

.

 ISOQAR certified
Management System,
awarded to Emerald
for adherence to
Environmental
standard
ISO 14001:2004.

Certificate Number 1985
ISO 14001

INVESTOR IN PEOPLE

Contents

Section 4
Fatalist Systems

List of Figures & Tables

Chapter 10

Chapter 12

Tables

Chapter 2

Chapter 4

Chapter 6

Chapter 12

About the Editors

Paul Wilfred Armstrong is a Senior Lecturer in Education Manchester Institute of Education, University of Manchester. His research interests concern contemporary forms of educational leadership and management, in particular the means by which schools are managed and resourced organizationally. He is also interested in school-to-school collaboration and support. He has worked in educational research for over 15 years on a range of national and international projects across a number of areas of education including school effectiveness, school improvement, school networking, educational leadership, management and policy. He leads and teaches on master's programmes for educational practitioners and aspiring school leaders through which he promotes the development of 'research conscious practice'.

Chris Brown is a Professor in Education and Deputy Executive Dean (Research) at Durham University. He is seeking to drive forward the notion of Professional Learning Networks (PLNs) as a means to promote the collaborative learning of teachers. The aim of this collaborative learning is to improve both teaching practice and student outcomes, not only in individual schools but also in the school system more widely. Alongside his research into PLNs, he also has a long-standing interest in how the collaborative use of research evidence can and should, but often doesn't, aid the development of education policy and practice.

About the Contributors

Isabell van Ackeren, University of Duisburg-Essen, Germany, Faculty of Educational Sciences, Professor of Education and School Development Research and Head of the Working Group on Educational Research. Research topics include reform in the education system, context-dependent school development, education in the digital world and quality development in teacher training. She is currently conducting various research and development projects concerning school networks.

René Breiwe, Dr, University of Wuppertal, Germany, School of Education, is Research associate for the Working Group on Educational Research. Research interests include diversity, racism and critical race theory, school and teaching development in the context of digitalization and inclusion.

Nina Bremm, Zurich University of Teacher Education, Switzerland, Research Professor of School Improvement at the Centre for School Improvement. Dr Bremm's research interests include reproduction of social inequality through the education system, socio-spatial reform, cooperation between research and practice to explore the challenges and potential for reducing social disadvantages through reform in the education system.

Carol Campbell is a Professor of Leadership and Educational Change at the Ontario Institute for Studies in Education, University of Toronto, Canada. Originally from Scotland, she has held education, academic and government roles in Canada, the UK and the USA. Her books include *Teacher Learning and Leadership,* and *Empowered Educators*.

Chris Chapman, Professor, was appointed Chair of Educational Policy and Practice at the University of Glasgow in January 2013 and became the Founding Director (2013-16) of the Robert Owen Centre for Educational Change (ROC). Chris has researched and advised education systems around the world and is the President of The International Congress of School Effectiveness and Improvement (ICSEI) a global organisation that connects research, policy and practice to support the development of high quality and more equitable education systems.

Jordi Díaz-Gibson, Ramon Llull University, Barcelona. He is a Professor and Researcher FPCEE Blanquerna, Ramon Llull University, PhD in Educational Science, co-lead NetEduProject www.neteduproject.org, former physical education teacher and school pedagogist, 24-hour learner, passionate collaborator and weaver. Committed to accelerate the transition into a more equitable and sustainable planet, he inhabits, studies, weaves and supports learning ecosystems that empower people and communities to live for a better world.

Michelle Dibben is the Principal of Manurewa Central School in Auckland. Her research considers the role of principal leadership in and across school collaborations. She is a Member of an Auckland Kāhui Ako (Community of Learning), with previous leadership experience in network learning communities in the UK.

Gavin Duffy is a Lecturer in Education at Queen's University who specializes in research into school collaboration and school networks, education leadership in divided societies and education in custodial settings.

Manuela Endberg, Dr, University of Duisburg-Essen, Germany, Faculty of Educational Sciences, is Research Associate for the Working Group on Educational Research. Research interests include school and teaching development in the context of digitalization, competence and attitudes of teachers in the context of digitalization, digitalization and educational justice, digitalization in the context of teacher training and professional development and structures that support school development.

Tony Gallagher is a Professor of Education Queen's University Belfast who specializes in the role of education in divided societies. His two main research areas are in developing models of collaboration between schools from different ethnic or religious communities and the democratic and civic role of higher education.

Álvaro González is an Associate Professor at the Centro de Investigación para la Transformación Socio Educativa (CITSE) of the Universidad Católica Silva Henríquez, Chile. He studies the processes of educational improvement and change, addressing topics such as leadership, professional and organizational learning, accountability and policy-making.

Toby Greany is a Professor of Education and Convenor of the Centre for Research in Education Leadership and Management (CRELM) at the University of Nottingham. His research is focused on how policy and practice interact to shape educational opportunities and outcomes, in particular across local systems and through networks, and the nature and role of leadership in these processes.

Stuart Hall is a Senior Researcher in the Robert Owen Centre for Educational Change at the University of Glasgow. His research interest include collaborative school improvement, professional learning and research and knowledge mobilisation to tackle poverty-related educational inequity.

Marco Hasselkuß, Dr, University of Duisburg-Essen, Germany, Faculty of Educational Sciences, is Research Associate for the Working Group on Educational Research. Research interests include school networks, school development in the context of digitalization and education for sustainable development. Currently conducting the DigiSchulNet project (*Digital School Development in Networks*) with a focus on a longitudinal, ego-centric network analysis.

Kevin House, Education Futures Architect at Education in Motion (EiM), and an Associate Professor in Practice at Durham University's School of Education. He spent many years in international schools before becoming founding Head of IB World Schools with the International Baccalaureate. Currently, he is leading a design team creating a number of innovative school curricula models, which leverage digital wallets and micro-credentials rather than traditional qualifications. Some of these projects include an online high school called School of Humanity, and an immersive sustainability education at Green School International.

Wenckje Jongstra, PhD, works at the research centre of Hogeschool KPZ University of Applied Sciences in the Netherlands. She serves as the director of the programme Fostering Language and Literacy in childcare and education. She is interested in design-based practical research in interprofessional collaboration focussing on empowering professional competencies.

Hanna Kędzierska, PhD, Associate Professor at the Faculty of Education, University of Warmia and Mazury, Poland. The author of many studies and research papers, her research focusses on teachers' professional lives, career issues and transitions, as well as qualitative methodologies in educational research. As an expert, she coordinates teachers' professional development programmes.

Trynke Keuning, PhD, is a postdoctoral researcher at Hogeschool KPZ University of Applied Sciences in the Netherlands. Her research focusses on the knowledge, skills and attitudes needed by various professionals involved in education and childcare for children (aged 0–14) to implement and continue interprofessional collaboration. With her research, she aims to bridge the gap between academic research and daily educational practice.

Alicja Korzeniecka-Bondar, PhD, Associate Professor and Vice Dean for Research at the Faculty of Education, University of Białystok, Poland. Her research covers the following areas: teacher education, lived experience in education, linking theory and practice, and phenomenographic research. Her most recent book is *Day-to-Day Life at School: A Phenomenographic Study of Teachers' Experiences* (2018).

Marta Kowalczuk-Walędziak, PhD, Vice Dean for International Co-operation at the Faculty of Education, University of Białystok, Poland, and Visiting Professor at the Institute of Sustainable Education, Daugavpils University, Latvia. Her research interests include the policy and practice of teacher education, teacher professional development, evidence-informed practice, and the internationalisation of teacher education.

Anke B. Liegmann, Dr, University of Duisburg-Essen, Germany, Faculty of Educational Sciences, is Research Associate for the Working Group on Educational Research. Research topics include professional development research in the context of diversity and internships in teacher training. Leader of the network project '*Unterrichtsentwicklung in der Sekundarstufe I digital und inklusiv durch RLC*' (UDIN) in Essen.

Jing Liu is an Associate Professor at the Graduate School of Education, Tohoku University, Japan. His research areas include school collaboration for school improvement in China and Japan, small-scale schools and equity of education in rural China and transformation of higher education for sustainability in Asia.

Kevin Lowden is a Senior Researcher in the Robert Owen Centre for Educational Change at the University of Glasgow. His research interests are collaborative practitioner inquiry and equitable educational improvement, teacher professional learning and moving educational innovations to scale.

Romina Madrid Miranda is a Research Associate at the Robert Owen Centre at the University of Glasgow. She has experience on the areas of research, policy and practice partnerships between school–university, teacher professional learning, school improvement and school–family relationships.

Sian May, Head of School at Alice Smith School in Malaysia previously was Director of Senior Schools at Education in Motion, following her tenures as High School Principal at the International School of Lausanne and Head of Middle School at Sha Tin College (ESF), Hong Kong. She enjoys creating innovative professional learning networks, dynamic school improvement cycles and partnering with educators to develop autonomy.

Joanne Neary is a Research Associate in the Robert Owen Centre for Educational Change at the University of Glasgow. Research interests include collaborative practitioner inquiry, whole system improvement, research-policy-practice partnerships, and knowledge translation to improve sustainable system change.

René Peeters had a career as teacher, head of school, policy officer in Amsterdam, school board, chairman school board, alderman education, youth and health in Almere. In 2018, he was asked by 16 organizations to write an advice about the collaboration between the domains of education and youth(care) 'Mét andere ogen' (with different eyes). Rene is a part-time booster of the movement in the programme Mét Andere Ogen and a member of the Advisory Board of the Dutch education inspectorate and chairman of the board of Humanitas, Netherlands.

Mauricio Pino-Yancovic is an Assistant Professor at the University of O'Higgins and Research Associate of the Center for Advanced Research in Education, Institute of Education, Universidad de Chile. His academic and research experience is focussed in educational policy, school networks and evaluation. He currently coordinates the evaluation of the school improvement networks strategy in Chile.

Gareth Robinson is a Research Fellow at Queen's University Belfast who specializes in research into education in conflict and crises, with a particular expertise in the role of social networks.

Sabrina Rutter, IU International University of Applied Sciences Dortmund, Germany, Professor of Social Work. Research topics include reproduction of social inequality through the education system, school improvement and development of educational professionals in the context of social inequality, diversity, and inclusion.

Marta Comas Sabat, is a member of the Educational Consortium of Barcelona. Marta holds a PhD in sociology of teaching associated with the Autonomous University of Barcelona and is also. Head of the Data Analysis and Research Unit of the Barcelona Education Consortium. She has been responsible for educational innovation programmes and undertakes academic. Academic research into social education, young migrants, intercultural education and the participation of families in school.

Rachel Verheijen-Tiemstra is a Lecturer at Fontys University of Applied Sciences and PhD candidate at Tilburg University. In 2019, she was awarded a Doctoral Grant for Teachers by the Dutch Research Council (NWO). Her research focusses on gaining insight into interprofessional collaboration between childcare and primary education providers and the leadership behaviour that is used to strengthen this collaboration.

Andrew Kitavi Wambua is a Kenyan Educator and a Researcher at the Institute of Educational Sciences, University of Heidelberg, Germany. In addition, he is serving on the board of International Congress for School Effectiveness and Improvement (ICSEI) and *Journal of Professional Capital and Community* (JPCC) and is a co-founder of Africa Voices Dialogue. His research interests are in leading for improvement, collaborative professionalism and whole-system change.

Howard Youngs is a Senior Lecturer of Educational Leadership at Auckland University of Technology. His research and leadership development work mainly in schools and across school networks brings together collaborative leadership, distributed forms of leadership, leadership inquiries, critical thinking, emergent processes and leadership-as-practice (L-A-P).

Mireia Civís Zaragoza, Ramon Llull University, Barcelona. Teacher, pedagogue and PhD, tenured professor at FPCEE Blanquerna, Ramon Llull University. Responsible researcher in the PSITIC Research Group. With experience in both the field of social pedagogy and school pedagogy. Her research focusses on the development of educational ecosystems, educational networks and community educational projects. Also, educational co-responsibility and social capital in education is also of nuclear interest. He has written several papers and books related to these topics, has given diverse lectures as well as has carried out research projects and participated in various consultations.

Introduction

Paul Wilfred Armstrong and Chris Brown

Notions of networking and collaboration in education have re-emerged within the popular discourse, often in discussions surrounding solutions to the myriad of issues facing school systems globally. Such ideas are not particularly new. Indeed, there is a history and genealogy of research in this sphere that can be traced back to Kurt Lewin's work in the 1940s (Madrid Miranda & Chapman, 2021). In recent years, however, there has been a renewed interest in this area, resulting in a growing body of literature extolling the virtues of school-to-school collaboration and partnership, and the potential for such activity to facilitate: (1) educational improvement (Brown, 2020; Glazer & Peurach, 2013); (2) equity and inclusion (Ainscow, 2012; Chapman et al., 2016); and, more recently, (3) post-pandemic recovery (Brown & Luzmore, 2021; Harris et al., 2021).

Individual and organizational development and improvement through professional dialogue and partnership is, in principle, a powerful and seductive notion. Yet, in practice, there are pitfalls and barriers that often hinder or prevent purposeful collaborative activity (Chapman, 2019; Gunter, 2015; Huxham & Vangen, 2000; Keddie, 2015). Moreover, as we have argued elsewhere (e.g. Armstrong et al., 2021), this remains a contested area of the wider field of education that is often terminologically vague, theoretically deficient, lacking in critical interpretation and under acknowledging of the wider contextual factors that influence how and the extent to which schools can work together. This has led to what we see as a somewhat superficial empirical foundation that evidences sporadic examples of effective collaborative practice between schools but that often presents such activity in isolation from the contexts in which it takes place.

These issues and concerns provide the catalyst for this edited collection. One which we hope will lead to a more nuanced discussion surrounding collaborative activity between schools, the many forms it can take and the conditions that influence whether, and the extent to which, such activity is meaningful. In particular, we are concerned with the contextual factors that influence school-to-school collaboration, specifically the diverse policy environments that characterize different school systems. We have attempted to throw light on this issue by examining and exploring school-to-school collaboration in 12 school systems (with an additional case study of international schools), stretching across five continents. The 13 cases presented within this book are distinctive in terms of their global locations.

School-to-School Collaboration: Learning Across International Contexts, 1–8
Copyright © 2022 by Paul Wilfred Armstrong and Chris Brown
Published under exclusive licence by Emerald Publishing Limited
doi:10.1108/978-1-80043-668-820221001

At the same time, the cases are tied together through a common structure, in which the authors pay simultaneous attention to the multiple contextual aspects of the education systems in which they locate their chapters. Each author has also drawn on the same conceptual framework to discuss their context: a cohesion/regulation matrix based on the work and thinking of Hood (1998). In addition, we asked the authors to conclude their chapters with policy recommendations based on their insights of these contexts. This structure allows for a comparative analysis of the range of systems represented and the identification of conditions that can drive and restrict collaborative activity between schools across these different systems. At the same time, this book offers some practical implications for policymakers in relation to school-to-school collaboration.

The Cohesion/Regulation Matrix

School systems globally differ, both contextually and structurally, on a range of elements. To help categorize these systems, we invited authors to utilize the cohesion/regulation matrix, shown in Fig. 1, as a way to situate their school systems *vis-á-vis* the main macro- or system-level factors defining them. This matrix follows Hood (1998) and his work on the shifting nature of public service management (with Hood himself influenced by the sociologist Mary Douglas and her use of grid/group cultural theory: Douglas, 1982). In the field of education, the matrix has been used more recently by Chapman (2019) to explore how educational policy reforms of different types were likely to fare in diverse contexts and by Malin et al. (2020) to explore factors affecting teachers' uses of research in different school systems.

The *x*-axis of the matrix, social cohesion, can be understood as follows (adopted from Malin et al., 2020):

- *Social cohesion* refers to the institutions, norms and networks that bind societies together. Systems with high social cohesion have a higher propensity and readiness to engage in collaboration. Threats to social cohesion – which tend to result in low socially cohesive systems – are particularly likely to emerge when such structures and systems (e.g., governmental layers, labor unions, the church, universal services such as health) are dismantled and replaced with policies of deregulation and privatization (Bauman, 2013). These are the types of systematic approaches that generally place greater onus on individual agency than towards collective approaches.

The second axis, regulation, can be understood in this way:

- *Regulation* refers to the institutions that determine control and establish how accountability functions in a system. In a high regulation system, there is typically a dominant, hierarchical culture and associated bureaucratic controls. High regulation systems often also involve establishing 'high stakes' accountability systems associated with 'failure'; that is, systems in which not meeting particular standards can mean major penalties. By contrast, systems displaying

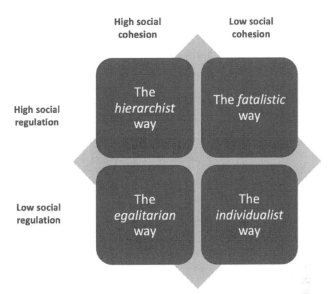

Fig. 1.   The Social Cohesion/Regulation Matrix. *Source*: From Malin et al. (2020; used with permission).

low social regulation typically evidence much flatter, non-hierarchical cultures, with improvement achieved through partnership rather than, for example, top-down accountability.

As shown in Fig. 1, combinations of high/low social cohesion and high/low social regulation result in four system types (Hood, 1998, p. 9):

1. The *fatalist* way (top right quadrant): characterized by rule-bound approaches to organization, with little cooperation related to achieving sought-after outcomes.
2. The *hierarchist* way (top left quadrant): displays social cohesion and coop-eration in order to meet rule-bound approaches to organization. This system is often characterized by bureaucracy.
3. The *individualist* way (bottom right quadrant): atomized approaches to organization, involving bargaining/negotiation between actors.
4. The *egalitarian* way (bottom left quadrant): high participation structures, with all decisions being negotiable, combined with an egalitarian culture and peer-to-peer support.

With the above framework in mind, each of the chapters within this volume provides a detailed, system-level analysis of patterns of collaboration within a particular context. As such, we have clustered our chapters based on their posi-tion within the cohesion/regulation matrix (see Table 1) and have organized them accordingly within this book.

Table 1.   The Organization of Our Chapters.

Hierarchist systems:	*Fatalist* systems:
• New Zealand (although suggest all quadrants feature)	• Chile (with elements of *egalitarian*)
• Scotland	• Netherlands
• Canada (with elements of *egalitarian*)	• Poland
• China (with elements of *egalitarian*)	• Kenya
	• International schools network (with elements of *egalitarian*)
Egalitarian systems:	*Individualist* systems:
• Northern Ireland (with elements of *fatalist*: the shared education agenda only)	• England (with elements of *hierarchist*)
• Catalonia (with elements of *hierarchist*)	
• Germany	

Structure and Contribution

Structuring our book in this way means it can be read from beginning to end, with common threads linking each chapter. Conversely, the chapters can be read as stand-alone pieces for those readers with a particular interest in a specific context or system. As Table 1 indicates, we have tried to facilitate both by organizing the chapters into sections according to the four system typologies from the cohesion/regulation matrix. The first section encompasses systems that are predominantly *hierarchist* in nature with perspectives from New Zealand, Scotland, Canada and China. The second section looks at systems with *fatalist* characteristics and includes chapters from Chile, the Netherlands, Poland and Kenya, with an additional perspective from an international school context. The third section explores systems with *egalitarian* features with reflections from Northern Ireland, Spain and Germany while the final section looks at England from an *individualistic* perspective.

The authors have positioned their contexts within the matrix according to their knowledge of and experience and research in these systems. However, as readers will note, there is fluidity in these cases in respect of the characteristics they share with the four typologies from the cohesion/regulation matrix. We have organized the cases within the matrix according to what the authors perceived to be the dominant features of the systems in which each is located. At the same time, we have acknowledged where cases display elements of one or more of the other quadrants. Accordingly, this book provides a deeper understanding of the system-level factors that influence collaborative activity between schools within these contexts.

Our Own Conclusions

Standing alone, these chapters accordingly present the reader with contextually grounded insights and recommendations. At the same time, it is also useful to consider what can be learnt by comparing across contexts that share similarities, and we encourage readers to engage in wider forms of meaning making and draw comparisons between systems that are similar and distinctive in terms of the policy context in which each operates. We have also engaged in this process, focusing on one key question: *what can we do to achieve effective school-to-school collaboration?* In other words, how we can get educators, globally, to systematically engage with one another to improve how they lead, teach and foster children's outcomes? From our own comparative analysis, we suggest that the factors in Table 2 illustrate points of similarity and difference between systems in driving school-to-school collaboration.

Table 2.   Some Overarching Themes Emerging From Our Chapters.

Quadrant	Barriers to Collaboration	Enablers to Collaboration
Hierarchist	1. A lack of perceived flexibility/balance between top down and bottom up (collaboration subsequently perceived as a threat to autonomy)	1. Adequate provision of resources (in particular time and financial resource)
	2. Perceptions of the usefulness of collaboration (or a lack thereof)	2. The presence of an infrastructure to support collaboration (for instance, the provision of brokers or facilitators)
	3. A lack of time to engage in collaboration	3. Top-down strategies and policies promoting collaboration
	4. Policy overload, which can create situations of 'initiative-itis'	4. Coordination of strategies and policies that potentially impact on collaboration
		5. The intentional cultivation of mutually respectful, trusting relationships
		6. Support for risk taking and innovation

Table 2. (*Continued*)

Quadrant	Barriers to Collaboration	Enablers to Collaboration
		7. A clear purpose and common vision associated with the collaboration
		8. A culture of joint knowledge sharing and the opening up of practices
		9. The recognition of formal and informal leadership of collaboration
Fatalist	1. Perceptions of the usefulness of collaboration (or a lack thereof)	1. Top-down strategies and policies promoting collaboration
	2. A lack of collaborative norms among main stakeholders	2. Coordination of strategies and policies that potentially impact on collaboration
	3. Lack of cooperation skills among main stakeholders	3. The intentional cultivation of mutually respectful, trusting relationships
	4. A lack of time to engage in collaboration	4. A clear purpose and common vision associated with the collaboration
		5. A culture of joint knowledge sharing and the opening up of practices
Individualist	1. The absence of performance/accountability drivers can mean few formal incentives for schools to actively collaborate	1. Top-down strategies and policies promoting collaboration
	2. A lack of collaborative norms among main stakeholders	2. Coordination of strategies and policies that potentially impact on collaboration
	3. Lack of cooperation skills among main stakeholders	3. Top-down strategies and policies promoting collaboration

Table 2. (*Continued*)

Quadrant	Barriers to Collaboration	Enablers to Collaboration
Egalitarian	1. A lack of perceived flexibility (collaboration subsequently perceived as a threat to autonomy)	1. Bottom-up (e.g. teacher, school led or even community led) approaches to promote collaboration
	2. The absence of performance/accountability drivers can mean few formal incentives for schools to actively collaborate	2. The recognition of formal and informal leadership of collaboration
		3. Within school strategies and policies promoting collaboration
		4. Support for risk taking and innovation
		5. A clear purpose and common vision associated with the collaboration
		6. Adequate provision of resources (in particular time and financial resource)
		7. The presence of an infrastructure to support collaboration (for instance, the provision of brokers or facilitators)

What our own findings suggest is that a range of different policy levers and factors are required, depending on the levels of cohesion and regulation within a given system. These factors tackle collaboration from a range of angles: from top-down 'compulsion' to the bottom-up recognition of the need to connect and from norm building to the provision of policies and infrastructure. Such individual factors can also apply to more than one quadrant, and there is likely to be benefit in policymakers drawing up a suite of policy levers that address the issue from a myriad of perspectives. But what is also encouraging (and should quickly become clear from reading through this volume) is that collaboration of some form or other is able to materialize in all systems, regardless of context. What prevents it from doing so therefore is not a lack of appetite for such activity among educators but often a lack of political will and/or understanding from those in power.

This collection therefore attends to the latter: it provides, for the first time ever, a comprehensive, internationally grounded, understanding of the factors that need to be considered to make collaboration a reality. All that is left now is for policymakers and system-level actors to seize the initiative.

References

Ainscow, M. (2012). Moving knowledge around: Strategies for fostering equity within educational systems. *Journal of Educational Change, 13*(3), 289–310.

Armstrong, P., Brown, C., & Chapman, C. (2021). School to school collaboration in England: A configurative review of the empirical evidence. *Review of Education, 9*(1), 319–351.

Bauman, Z. (2013). *Liquid modernity*. Polity Press.

Brown, C. (2020). *The networked school leader: How to improve teaching and student outcomes using learning networks*. Emerald Group Publishing.

Brown, C., & Luzmore, R. (2021). *Educating tomorrow: Learning for the post-pandemic world*. Emerald.

Chapman, C. (2019). *Making sense of education reform: Where next for Scottish education?* Association of Directors of Education in Scotland/The Staff College.

Chapman, C., Chestnutt, H., Friel, N., Hall, S., & Lowden, K. (2016). Professional capital and collaborative inquiry networks for educational equity and improvement? *Journal of Professional Capital and Community, 1*(3), 178–197.

Douglas, M. (1982). *Introduction to grid/group analysis*. Routledge.

Glazer, J. L., & Peurach, D. J. (2013). School improvement networks as a strategy for large-scale education reform: The role of educational environments. *Educational Policy, 27*(4), 676–710.

Gunter, H. M. (2015). The politics of education policy in England. *International Journal of Inclusive Education, 19*(11), 1206–1212.

Harris, A., Azorín, C., & Jones, M. (2021). Network leadership: A new educational imperative? *International Journal of Leadership in Education*, 1–17. https://doi.org/10.1080/13603124.2021.1919320

Hood, C. (1998). *The art of the state, culture rhetoric and public management*. Clarendon Press.

Huxham, C., & Vangen, S. (2000). Ambiguity, complexity and dynamics in the membership of collaboration. *Human Relations, 53*(6), 771–806.

Keddie, A. (2015). School autonomy, accountability and collaboration: a critical review. *Journal of Educational Administration and History, 47*(1), 1–17.

Madrid Miranda, R., & Chapman, C. (2021). Towards a network learning system: Reflections on a university initial teacher education and school-based collaborative initiative in Chile. *Professional Development in Education* (pp. 1–15). https://doi.org/10.1080/19415257.2021.1902840

Malin, J., Brown, C., Ion, G., van Ackeren, I., Bremm, N., Luzmore, R., Flood, J., & Rind, G. (2020). World-wide barriers and enablers to achieving evidence-informed practice in education: What can be learnt from Spain, England, the United States, and Germany? *Humanities and Social Sciences Communications, 7*(99), 1–14. Open access via https://doi.org/10.1057/s41599-020-00587-8

Section 1

Hierarchist Systems

Chapter 1

New Zealand Cases of Collaboration within and Between Schools: The Coexistence of Cohesion and Regulation

Michelle Dibben and Howard Youngs

Abstract

Collaboration is viewed as an essential ingredient for education systems and school improvement. Collaborative leadership has both emergent and intentional components (Woods & Roberts, 2018). Collaborative practices can emerge over time as teachers and schools work together, and intentional interventions and decisions can either support this emergence and/ or work against it. In this chapter, we discuss the New Zealand case of collaboration between schools. The context is situated in policy reform associated with an incentivized and voluntary programme that groups of schools could participate in. The programme, communities of schools (CoLs), was implemented in 2014 and continues at the time of writing this chapter. We draw on critical commentary of the programme, as well as the small number of research studies available. The experienced way of CoLs is replete with tensions. These are illustrated with the help of Hoods' (1998) social regulation and cohesion matrix. Rather than locate the New Zealand case in one quadrant of the matrix, we illustrate how multiple aspects of Hoods' matrix (1998) have been and are currently in play regarding collaboration between schools in New Zealand.

Keywords: Communities of learning; collaborative practices; school principals; school networks; network leadership; incentivization

School-to-School Collaboration: Learning Across International Contexts, 11–25
Copyright © 2022 by Michelle Dibben and Howard Youngs
Published under exclusive licence by Emerald Publishing Limited
doi:10.1108/978-1-80043-668-820221002

Introduction

Collaborative practice is not new to education. Collaboration sits alongside leadership nomenclature such as shared leadership, distributed leadership, collective leadership and teacher leadership (Youngs, 2020a). During the 1980s and 1990s, collaboration was more aligned to school-based management due to the shift to self-managing schools that took place in numerous countries (Youngs, 2020b). It emerged in this period as an 'ubiquitous megatrend' (Brundrett, 1998, p. 307). The focus on collaboration has now broadened beyond management, to include teacher inquiry and professional learning and development (Nelson et al., 2008; Timperley et al., 2014), teaching practice (Drago-Severson, 2016; Moolenaar et al., 2012), teacher professional learning communities (PLCs) (DuFour et al., 2009), inquiry of learning methodology (Drew et al., 2016) and, the focus of this book, networks of schools (Townsend, 2015). Collaboration is claimed to be no longer an option especially when claimed greater gains for individuals surpass isolationist and protectionist attempts (Chapman, 2015; Feys & Devos, 2015). Hence, there has been a shift toward education policies that formalize different forms of collaboration, and in the case of New Zealand, at a system level where schools in a similar location have been incentivized and encouraged to work with each other, and reach out to working with relevant early childhood, and higher education providers.

The New Zealand collaborative school system, *Kāhui Ako*, also known as *Communities of Learning* (CoL), was announced by the National Government in January 2014 as part of a government educational improvement policy, *Investing for Educational Success* (IES) and was met with various responses from teacher unions (for more detail on the union responses, please refer to Thrupp (2018)). Since the Minister of Education's approval of the first 11 CoLs in December 2014, which rose to 180 approved CoLs in 2016, there are, as of January 2021, 220 CoLs

> spread throughout New Zealand, comprised of 1,868 schools (out of 2,536 as of 1 July 2020), 1,551 early learning services, 11 tertiary providers and over 700,000 children and young people. (Ministry of Education, 2021)

However, as of June 2019, the Minister of Education has placed a moratorium on new CoLs being established. Each CoL has a CoL leader (initially called Executive Principals (Charteris & Smardon, 2018)), who is one of the CoL school principals appointed by each CoL, and incentivized roles that did not exist prior to 2014: across schoolteachers (ASTs) and within schoolteachers (WSTs).

The IES policy was in part, a government, Organisation for Economic Co-operation and Development (OECD) endorsed response to New Zealand's declining results in the OECD *Programme for International Student Assessment* (PISA) tests, where Andreas Schleicher, the OECD Director for Education and Skills, promoted the IES policy and proposed spending on the Minister of

Education's National Party political website during an election year (Thrupp, 2018). This illustrates, in the New Zealand case, direct influence from a non-elected perceived neutral source, on education policy in New Zealand. The National Party, when elected in 2008, set about implementing a policy of National Standards in reading, writing and mathematics for primary-aged students, which schools were expected to follow from the start of 2010. The National Standards policy helps provide a backdrop to some of the challenges schools encountered in the early stages of collaboration with each other and with the Ministry of Education. The *Kāhui Ako* – CoL aspect of IES is the focus of this chapter. The system of CoLs across most New Zealand schools is currently a blend of volunteerism, variations of cohesion within and across CoLs and regulations that have shifted since the policy was first implemented. One of the significant shifts was the abolishment of National Standards by the Labour Government at the end of 2017. This blending and shifting means that multiple aspects of Hood's (1998) social regulation/cohesion matrix have been in play and illustrate any reform regarding collaboration between schools cannot be viewed in isolation of other policies. In addition, local research studies that focus on CoL practices illustrate a range of experiences across CoLs. Together, the shifts in regulations and variation in experiences result in multiple tensions across the system as illustrated in Fig. 1 and are a focus of discussion in this chapter.

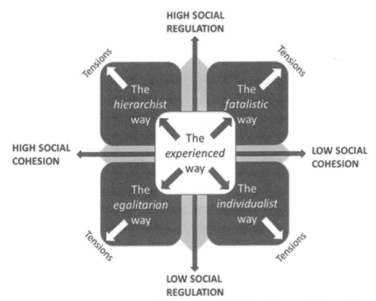

Fig. 1.   The Experienced Way of New Zealand CoLs. *Source*: Adapted from Malin et al. (2020; used with permission).

Shifting Classifications of School to School Collaboration

Hood's (1998) social regulation/cohesion matrix, or what he describes as grid/ cultural theory, was published to illuminate various ways of analysing and under- standing (new) public management. New Public Management (NPM) arose when perceived and real outmoded forms of public management were replaced by 'results-driven, managerially orientated approaches to public service provision with a particular stress on efficient least-cost provision' (Hood, 1998, p. 5). Dur- ing the 1980s, NPM agendas were implemented across OECD member nations. The New Zealand Labour Government (1984–1990) oversaw a rapid deregulation agenda across the public sector (Thrupp, 2018). New Zealand is deemed to be the closest any OECD country came to having 'a coherent NPM "manifesto"' (Hood, 1991, p. 6) with The Treasury's (1987a, 1987b) twin volume, *Govern- ment Management: Brief to the Incoming Government 1987*. Volume 2, which was devoted entirely to education, argued the re-elected Labour Government must be concerned 'with the effectiveness and "profitability" of its expenditure on educa- tion' (The Treasury, 1987a, p. 133) and argued efficiency costs of state interven- tion could be minimized through 'ensuring that management, accountability, and incentive structures cohere and are performance and target related' (p. 139). The government, through the Education Act (New Zealand Government, 1989) regu- lated the introduction of self-managing schools, to be governed by their own local elected Boards' of Trustees, seemingly atomising New Zealand schools at the time into the bottom right quadrant of Hood's (1998) matrix albeit with hoped for greater collaboration between each school and their local community.

New Zealand governments since then have governed at various distances through policies related to accountability and funding, where schools have fol- lowed 'mandated policy stipulations but not roadmaps on how to achieve [state] corporate strategic goals' (Starr, 2019, p. 38). Hierarchist ways were still in play albeit at a distance. Across school collaborations were established, though some have waned, some have been spontaneous, and others have emerged through funded initiatives (Charteris & Smardon, 2018), thus providing a rather eclectic view of degrees of cohesion and regulation among schools. The most significant funded initiative is the $NZ359 million IES policy with the stated aim, provided by the Minister of Education at the time,

> to enable our experienced and talented teachers and school leaders
> to share their knowledge and skills across communities of schools,
> to meet specific achievement challenges within those communi-
> ties and to create better career pathways. (Ministry of Education,
> 2014a, p. 4)

The development of CoLs, as a major aspect of the IES policy, based on this stated intent, seems to indicate a shift was taking place, where collaboration between schools was now officially encouraged, financially supported and had the appearance of being egalitarian. As more details emerged and the coupling of CoLs to the National Standard policy became clear, the development of CoLs also started to reflect aspects of regulation and rules, thus creating tensions across the system and the coexistence of Hood's (1998) quadrants.

Each CoL is expected to set its own Achievement Challenges related to improving student achievement and have these approved before funding is released for the new specialist roles. These additional roles are (at the time of writing this chapter) CoL leader, Across School Teacher (AST) and Within School Teacher (WST). In addition to an extra allowance, CoL leaders' schools and ASTs' schools generate 0.4 full-time release time that appears as part of a school's additional staffing entitlement. WSTs have 0.08 teacher release time and a small yearly allowance which is less than that given to CoL leaders and ASTs. CoL leaders are responsible for leading the CoL as a whole, ASTs work collaboratively across a CoL and WSTs work directly within their own school. Even though 'collaborative inquiry and sharing of effective practices across schools are key drivers for the gains expected for teaching and learning from CoLs' (Wylie et al., 2018, p. 7), the initial requirement for CoLs to narrowly associate Achievement Challenges to National Standards, numeracy and/or literacy resulted in narrow hoops for CoLs to jump through to access funding and contributed to some CoLs taking longer than expected to get underway. Since the abolishment of National Standards, there has been some loosening of criteria from the Ministry of Education, to now include Achievement Challenges, such as those related to improving student well-being. This illustrates how shifts in policy can loosen or tighten regulation.

The two governments, first National and then Labour, have not moved to make CoLs compulsory and take a more regulatory approach to school-to-school collaboration. The CoLs component of the IES policy is possibly heading for reconsideration. In June 2019, the Labour Government put a halt on the formation of new CoLs due to a change in government spending. This example demonstrates the fickle nature of policy and the competing agendas that exist in the system as educators endeavour to adopt and sustain effective school-to-school collaboration. The Education Review Office (ERO) (2019), the government's external evaluation agency, argues there is strong support for building collaborative networks but 'the New Zealand evidence base about the necessary conditions for collaboration is somewhat limited' (p. 4). This provides an additional reason why many CoLs are still in an emergent phase of development despite working together for four years or more (Dibben, 2019; ERO, 2019; Wylie et al., 2018). Dibben (2019) argues that leading a network, formed through a national policy initiative, is complex and challenging, particularly when the Ministry of Education itself is still trying to navigate between two eco-systems – self-managing schools (a product of the 1989 Education Act) and aligning schools in networked communities.

The IES initiative was met by scepticism from the profession in the early stages of design. The New Zealand Educational Institute (NZEI) raised concerns about its lack of application to the New Zealand context (Dibben, 2019). It could be argued that New Zealand has taken a mimetic approach to the development of CoLs, influenced by the international research base considered by the Ministry of Education in their Working Group Report (2014b). Hood (1998) suggests that as public systems modernize they increasingly resemble each other. Observing other nations' educational systems as legitimate and successful gives a perception that 'best practice' can be replicated in a different jurisdiction. The rhetoric of convergence is powerful. However, it would be naive to assume that arbitrary policy transfer from one educational system to another offers a smooth transitional pathway to success. The extent to which New Zealand schools engage in network activity is therefore dependent on the ability of individual Kāhui Ako to work within the system and provide context for their community.

The Extent of School-to-School Collaboration

Collaborative efforts can make slow progress as a result of collaborative inertia caused by the gap between policymakers who see networks as the panacea to educational reform and school practitioners who experience collaborative development as complex (Mifsud, 2020). The New Zealand system of CoLs is no exception. Mifsud (2020) contends that the organic nature of networks takes time to evolve due to their constant reshaping through the actions and interactions of its actors. New Zealand studies reveal a common theme associated with the extent to which schools participate in collaborative CoL activity, namely the time to establish a social infrastructure conducive to effective across school collaboration, which is a necessary prerequisite for sustainable engagement.

In their analysis of five schools within one CoL, Sinnema et al. (2020) found 'low levels of between-school collaboration and advice seeking activity' (p. 1). They concluded that the policy goal of increasing collaboration is emergent as effort is still needed to develop the social infrastructure to support knowledge transfer and increased social capital. Despite resourcing aimed at providing time for those with CoL positions to carry out their roles, and directives on how to work together, the constraints of policy focus on the structure of this enterprise rather than the process of change (Kamp, 2020). This imbalanced approach is highlighted in the findings of the ERO (2019) report focussing on the implementation of CoL collaboration, where one CoL reported gains in building trusting relationships across the school partnership to support the sharing of expertise. On the other hand, another CoL reported a lack of value in participating in collective action as a vehicle for supporting their capacity for inquiry (ERO, 2019). The latter view demonstrates the importance for policy reform to focus on the means by which increased social capital, through knowledge sharing, influences teacher inquiry, which may lead to improved teaching practice and outcomes for students. To date, there is little evidence in CoL research studies that teaching practices have changed as a result of the IES initiative, leading to improved student outcomes through meeting the achievement challenges set by CoLs (Dibben, 2019; Sinnema et al., 2020).

In their nationwide sample of 403 schools, Wylie et al. (2018) found considerable variability between schools. There did seem to be gains for those who had taken on the new CoL roles, and an increased focus on collaborative practices within individual schools, suggesting CoL participation could be mutually supportive. Sinnema et al. (2020) concur and argue that the main actors, such as ASTs, involved in the work of the CoL have more opportunities for collaboration, but this is not filtered down to the majority of teachers within the network.

This filtering through is 'essential to policy achievement and innovation' (Kamp, 2020, p. 187) that is directed from the Ministry of Education and funded by the government. Sinnema et al. (2020) suggest 'the interplay of both relational and technical elements of change may yield the most positive outcomes' (p. 12). If the CoL social infrastructure does not evolve to embody all teachers, the intent of CoLs to encourage 'bottom up' innovation and knowledge transfer may not be fully realized.

The extent to which schools engage in successful school-to-school collaboration is also difficult to discern as impact is subjective (Dibben, 2019). Both ERO (2019) and Smith (2018) recognize that monitoring and evaluation processes are the key to measuring impact, but these are the least developed areas of improvement. Sinnema et al. (2020) concur and state that even when collaboration is unrestricted, there is limited evidence of impact. Mifsud (2020) argues that 'a network's success should be judged on its workings rather than its structures' (p. 7). Collaborative enterprise takes time to establish and develop (ERO, 2019). From inception, the IES initiative and establishment of CoLs has been rushed and lacked consultation (Charteris & Smardon, 2018). Some principals joined a CoL for fear of losing out, particularly where funding was concerned. Others report challenges in finding 'mutually convenient times to participate in meaningful and productive exchanges' (Dibben, 2019, p. 98). This is particularly true when schools try to align their individual school improvement plans with the vision and direction of the CoL. Dibben (2019) asserts that the interplay of existing school structures with the newly created CoL roles requires commitment to the coexistence of hybrid leadership roles and responsibilities. Without this, leadership autonomy exercised at individual school level can disrupt 'the parameters of agreement between CoL members' (Dibben, 2019, p. 96), thus affecting the extent to which collaborative enterprise occurs. Charteris and Smardon (2018) agree and suggest that incentivizing networking activity through newly established roles risks centralizing collaborative actions in a hierarchical structure, where collaboration is possibly centralized to the group responsible for working across schools. This is the polar opposite to the intention of ground up innovation and dissemination of best practice. Hood's (1998) cultural theory framework argues that 'ways of life' are unlikely to converge in the middle because each way of life constitutes a reaction against the disliked alternatives. Viability only occurs when an organizational structure matches a set of values or beliefs. Hood (1998) argues that

> hybridity may itself be a cause of collapse ... triggered by a mixing of organizational ways of life which prevents the matching of attitudes and organizational structure needed to sustain each of the four polar types. (p. 21)

Whatever the barriers are to successful collaboration, Dibben (2019) argues that sustainability is dependent on three key elements 'system leadership, deep learning through engaging the collective in collaborative practices where hybrid forms of leadership exist, and negotiation of the complex and often erratic arena of educational policy' (p. 109). Dibben (2019) suggests that

New Zealand's education system is yet to realise the potential that exists in networks as a reform tool, divorced from mandates and controls, but incentivised by collective norms and collaboration. (p. 114)

Therefore, more time and thinking is needed to achieve greater alignment between policy and the network perspective to maximize collective enterprise for improved outcomes (Dibben, 2019; Wylie et al., 2018).

From the egalitarian viewpoint, empowerment of all teachers is a beneficent change. However, 'different visions of beneficence only seem capable of being reconciled at the most general level' (Hood, 1998, p. 195). Cultural bias can produce barriers as individuals pull back towards the corners of the polar approaches. The next section highlights important tensions that are likely to exist in the CoL system. According to Hood (1998), divergence is common as polar world views often 'produce the opposite of their intended results' (p. 195).

Enablers and Barriers to School-to-School Collaboration

New Zealand's self-managing schools' system has failed to improve achievement, particularly for Maori and Pacific Nation students. The disparity gap is widening and student achievement is not keeping pace with other high-performing nations. Hood (1998) discusses cultural bias and how public management responds to a perceived disaster. In New Zealand, the IES initiative has appeal as its reform agenda is embedded in the discourse that promotes networking and collaboration as a strength-based approach to raising student outcomes. The introduction of CoLs is a construct based on the assumption that collective responsibility for equity and excellence is more effective when professionals see the educational landscape as an interconnected system with the potential for leveraging expertise beyond the confines of their own class or school. This 'near blind belief that networking will solve educational poor performance' sits firmly within an assumed social justice agenda (Mifsud, 2020, p. 16). It is the government's answer to the 'disaster' of dropping down international rankings and sits within Hood's (1998) cultural theory framework as a hierarchist response stressing a focus on developing greater expertise for effective 'best practice'.

New Zealand's self-managing school system is at odds with this shift in thinking and, as a result, tensions exist. There are two key factors emerging from New Zealand research that both enable and hinder inter-school collaboration, namely the challenge of accountability when aligning policy with practice and navigating new co-dependent leadership roles and structures. Findings suggest an interplay between the different characteristics identified in Hood's (1998) cohesion/regulation matrix and highlight the ambiguities that exist when trying to classify the system. Hood (1998) refers to 'cornering' as a limitation on organizational life because cultural dynamics produce mutual antagonism which is a reaction against unsatisfactory status quo and opposing viewpoints. As networks are dynamic in construct, there will always be variables at play dependent on the extent to which individual schools engage and participate. These may shift over time creating tensions in the system. As a result, cornering works against collaboration, the original intent of IES policy implemented through CoLs.

Aligning Policy With Practice – Accountability

There is tension between collaboration and accountability (Mifsud, 2020). CoLs are no exception. It is an incentivized policy framework requiring school principals to lead across a network. Although CoLs are voluntary, leadership positions are resourced with salary allowances to provide alternative career pathways beyond those provided by traditional school structures. As a result, the Ministry of Education policy mandates a degree of prescription to ensure accountability. Charteris and Smardon (2018) suggest that accountability measures, framed as guidelines, can also serve as 'straight jackets'. Their study of nine New Zealand school principals found that some perceive 'the incentivizing process (policy levers) as a mechanism to solicit compliance' (p. 35). In the context of CoLs, the most contentious compliance measure is the introduction of Achievement Challenges. There was a lack of clarity around the process of forming shared goals and engaging the collective. An emphasis on structures and organizational procedures dictated the direction of CoLs and stifled organic innovation, the key to collective endeavours (Dibben, 2019; Kamp, 2020). As a result, many CoLs still find themselves in the 'establishment phase' 12 months or more after beginning their networking journey (Dibben, 2019; ERO, 2019; Smith, 2018). However, there has been a shift at policy level recently with flexibility in the development of achievement challenges and 'less prescriptive settings' (Ministry of Education, 2019, p. 34) partially due to the abolishment of the National Standards policy. Charteris and Smardon (2018) assert that 'far from merely implementing policy, principals can demonstrate agency in their interpretation and recontextualisation' (p. 28).

Contextualization is key to successful alignment of policy with practice. Dibben (2019) suggests that the 'external demands of Ministry of Education policy alongside competing agendas of individual schools create(s) as many barriers as it (does) opportunities' (p. 85). Sinnema et al. (2020) concur and argue that 'the apparent focus on individual schools as opposed to cross school ties may ultimately inhibit the opportunity to address the achievement challenges set for the CoL' (p. 9). Therefore, the growth of the network and the issues it faces are very dependent on 'local realities and local histories" (Mifsud, 2020, p. 12). The speed of implementation and timelines mandated by Ministry of Education policy are also seen to hinder deep engagement (Charteris & Smardon, 2018; ERO, 2019). As a result, de-contextualized goals produce apathy among some principal members and a lack of trust in the very system set up to build collective efficacy (Dibben, 2019; Smith, 2018). Charteris and Smardon (2018) argue that 'policy shift is driven through the compelling rationale of social justice outcomes' (p. 39). However, there is concern that money spent on the IES initiative, particularly on the allowances paid to CoL leaders and ASTs, could be better spent on meeting the needs of individual schools or on initiatives identified at a community level (Dibben, 2019; Smith, 2018). CoL leaders are far more likely to shape their individual contexts and environments for social justice and equity incentives than they are for economic rationality. This has been the case previously. Effective, incentivized networks of schools already existed in New Zealand prior to the inception of CoLs. These networks were generally founded in response to local community needs and provided opportunities for schools with similar aspirations to form professional clusters. Existing collaborations have been reported as beneficial to the success of a CoL (Dibben, 2019; ERO, 2019). However, the CoL initiative requires principals to make fiscal decisions over resourcing distributed at a system-wide policy level that impact directly on the day-to-day working and strategic direction at an individual school level. Charteris and Smardon (2018) suggest that these decisions could impact negatively on existing school-to-school collaborations and potentially undermine the progress of leader agency. Appointment of individuals to the key CoL leadership roles is an example of this tension within the system.

Co-dependent Leadership Roles and Structures

On the one hand, the IES initiative views CoL leadership roles as complementary to existing leadership structures and an opportunity for collaborative practices to positively influence outcomes through shared experience and expertise regardless of power or status (Ministry of Education, 2015). On the other hand, Dibben (2019) argues that 'a lack of clarity about how the two co-exist amplify the difficulties of engagement' (p. 90). Smith (2018) recognizes both CoL roles and existing leadership structures in schools require attention to align expectations. Without this, there is the potential for power plays to detract from the potential for collaboration (Kamp, 2020). Hood (1998) acknowledges that mutuality is difficult to sustain in conditions of competition. He states 'the egalitarian formula of mutuality can be good at providing rich reciprocal surveillance in a culturally homogeneous group but without expulsion cannot cope easily with more heterogeneous groups' (Hood, 1998, pp. 210, 211). He discusses mutuality under the doctrine of groupism, a way of controlling relationships inside organizations, which can be inherently problematic. New Zealand-based studies suggest that the formal structure of CoL roles may limit opportunities for collaborative activity due to the 'level of centralization around a few individuals', thus reducing opportunities for boundary spanning activities that enable meaningful knowledge sharing (Sinnema et al., 2020, p. 12). If system goals are to be realized, the role of the lead principal is crucial in establishing the framework for aligning policy with practice and reducing barriers that conflict with effective networking activity.

ERO (2019) conducted a study of three Kāhui Ako and found the lead principals to have 'high levels of educational leadership and interpersonal skills' (p. 15). Dibben (2019) asserts that CoL leaders in her study viewed themselves as 'leaders of education, not just leaders within their own school – the meso-system' (p. 103). This implies an understanding that the systemic challenges faced by New Zealand education requires a solution beyond self-interest and self-management to a cohesive system where all schools are working as one part of the whole.

Therefore, 'if individual principals do not consider themselves system leaders then the fluidity required to transverse boundaries for increased effectiveness is limited' (Dibben, 2019, p. 105). However, espoused theories of system leadership conflict with theories in use in a number of ways due to the inherent problems of adapting from sole to lateral forms of leadership. ERO (2019) recognizes that non-hierarchical decision-making is key to success, but the appointment of a lead principal has the potential to intensify control and accountability resulting in a top-down hierarchical approach (Charteris & Smardon, 2018). Professional jealousy and competitive activity has the potential to impact negatively on successful collaborative activity (Charteris & Smardon, 2018; Kamp, 2020). For instance, individual principals remain autonomous in their own schools under the current system of education in New Zealand, and there can be difficulties in bridging cultural divides to form a cohesive community (Dibben, 2019). Contrived communities result in individual schools still placing their own concerns at the centre (Charteris & Smardon, 2018; Dibben, 2019; Kamp, 2020). Despite the role of the CoL leader as influencer and facilitator in creating the conditions to strengthen cross-school collaborations, these competing agendas may be a source of frustration and negotiation for CoL leaders (Dibben, 2019).

Conflict is also apparent at times in the appointment of other incentivized CoL roles, namely ASTs and WSTs. Much time has been focussed on applying mandates with little success in implementing effective knowledge transfer processes (Smith, 2018). A lack of interest and slow take up of positions, difficulties associated with learning on the job, insufficient professional learning opportunities, coupled with lack of leadership capability, demonstrates there is still progress to be made in developing professional trust in the system (Dibben, 2019). Furthermore, if trust is absent, individuals are less likely to be responsive to accountability measures (Sinnema et al., 2020). The exclusion of school deputy principals (DPs) and associate principals (APs) in the CoL initiative has created tensions with feelings of dissatisfaction, disengagement and in some cases hostility towards engaging in a culture of collective responsibility as a result of new leadership structures (Dibben, 2019). This is an example of a reverse effect occurring 'when social interventions achieve the very opposite of the desired effect' (Hood, 1998, p. 212). Incentivizing assumes merit in the system being pushed but does not necessarily ensure active participation (Mifsud, 2020). Both fatalist and individualist typologies can be identified in responses to CoL positions from those in traditional hierarchical roles in individual school structures. 'There was a significant level of centralization around a few individuals not necessarily those one might expect given the policy' (Sinnema et al., 2020, p. 12). The incentive for APs and DPs, who are leaders of learning, was not monetary gain but a recognition of their position and skill set, overlooked in the CoL organizational structure due to the requirement that ASTs 'spend 50 percent of their time in classrooms' (ERO, 2019, p. 20). Creating a hybrid approach should be the agreeable norm but 'the elements of mutual repulsion among the basic types are likely to make combinations and hybrids precarious and self-disequilibrating' (Hood, 1998, p. 211). Therefore 'as CoLs navigate new vertical co-dependent relationships, moving between vertical and horizontal forms of leadership become essential to effective team building and growth of social capital' (Dibben, 2019, p. 108). CoL lead principals have responded in a variety of ways to limit the impact as much as possible. DPs and APS have been included in the leadership group of some CoLs and offered roles as mentors to ASTs in others (Dibben, 2019; ERO, 2019). Therefore, redefining their roles is crucial to supporting a shift from a school-centric approach to the adoption of a more systems view (Sinnema et al., 2020). In doing so, the possibility for authentic collaborative activity across a network of schools may be more fully realized.

This section has highlighted the role of Hood's seven reverse-effect mechanisms: functional disruption of traditional roles and responsibilities and bridging cultural divides; some policy oversight of the goodwill of APs and DPs to support the work of the CoL teachers; goal displacement and provocation linked to compliance, accountability and achievement challenges restrictions that were initially too narrow; some antagonism towards the classification involved in the newly created leadership structure of CoLs; overcommitment of resources without time to fulfil objectives; and placation by means of compromise over what is actually achievable in a self-managing system that requires adoption of a networking philosophy.

The enablers and barriers to engaging in school-to-school collaboration are determined by the emphasis on polar approaches and the over reliance on one rather than another. This creates blind spots and unexpected reverse effects (Hood, 1998). As individuals move to the corners of the grid, tensions arise and the 'experienced way' of boundary spanning and collaboration becomes conflicted with the espoused theory underpinning the IES initiative. An effective system

> depends on the extent to which ideas and beliefs of the participants match the institutional structure of any control system. Such congruence cannot be taken for granted, and there are often self-disequilibrating as well as self-reinforcing forces at work in regulation and control. (Hood, 1998, p. 71)

In addition, collaboration 'is often imagined as a "join-the-dots approach" where existing organizations and institutions are better connected' (Kamp, 2020, p. 178). Without direction, beyond the 'joining-of-dots', as to how to collaborate especially through new incentivized roles, New Zealand schools to an extent have been left to work this out for themselves. 'Early implementation efforts have led those working in CoL to realize that educational improvement requires much more than merely establishing such formal structures for change' (Sinnema et al., 2020, p. 3). One of the chapter's authors currently works alongside schools who are in CoLs. Recently in a workshop, one school leader aptly asked the question, 'how do we bring them [i.e ASTs and WSTs] back into the fold [of teacher's classrooms in our school]?'. The challenge before our New Zealand schools is how does CoL activity find its way back into classrooms, so the benefit of collaboration leads to enhanced teaching and student learning. We still have some way to go, as too few teachers say they have sufficient time for collaborative work (Wylie et al., 2018) and a minority of teachers in CoLs are still not sure if their school is in a CoL or not (Wylie & Hodgen, 2020). New Zealand schools have likely experienced all aspects of social cohesion and regulation, to differing degrees and at different times, before the IES policy, and still do as they continue to enhance the conditions of teaching and learning. Tensions in and between the players in the education system continue to take place in what we label as the experienced way (see figure 1), rather than just one of the ways Hood (1998) portrays in his matrix.

Key Lessons for Practice and Policy

The key lesson for practice and policy is that the two are inexplicably linked. If policy is positioned as the driver for reform, then tension will occur along with issues of transference through to practice. The following points outline the interplay of policy reform faced by New Zealand schools as they navigate the complexities involved in working across a network of schools.

- Prior to implementation of an incentivized strategy of reform, there needs to be critical analysis of both the benefits and disruptions likely to occur within the current system.
- Policy reform needs to capitalize on current practices as profession-led initiatives provide the flexibility needed to ensure resources are targeted at what matters most and who already are the key 'point' people in each school, noting this may differ from school to school.
- If external approval processes are in place, then professional accountability needs to develop through a focus on broad goals, rather than narrow measures, that allow schools to 'see their place at the table'.
- Space is required for collaborative leadership to emerge, yet this needs to be coupled to intentionality where decisions are made at a system and local level.
- When a new policy or practice initiative is undertaken, consideration is needed at the system and local school level as to what practices and systems need to be trimmed back and/or stopped, otherwise issues of work intensification and (un)well-being are likely to arise.
- Collaboration cannot be mandated, espoused collaboration does not equate to collaboration-in-use.
- Further emphasis on collaboration between schools must be grounded in evidence that supports enhanced learning conditions for students.

With any system-level reform comes some form of regulation. However, unless there is cohesion between the local school, groups of schools and those overseeing system policy and reform, then a reform is unlikely to become embedded where it matters most, with the students and the teachers who help create and enhance conditions for learning. There will inevitably be tensions during any reform journey as it is experienced across the four quadrants of Hood's (1998) matrix.

References

Brundrett, M. (1998). What lies behind collegiality, legitimation or control? *Educational Management & Administration, 26*(3), 305–316.

Chapman, C. (2015). From one school to many: Reflections on the impact and nature of school federations and chains in England. *Educational Management Administration & Leadership, 43*(1), 46–60. https://doi.org/10.1177/1741143213494883

Charteris, J., & Smardon, D. (2018). Policy enactment and leader agency: The discursive shaping of political change. *Teachers' Work, 15*(1), 28–45. https://doi.org/10.24135/teacherswork.v15i1.237

Dibben, M. (2019). *(Re)locating New Zealand school principals as leaders in school networks: Leadership in communities of learning.* Master of Educational Leadership thesis, Auckland University of Technology, Auckland, NZ. Retrieved from https://openrepository.aut.ac.nz/handle/10292/12981

Drago-Severson, E. (2016). Teaching, learning and leading in today's complex world: Reaching new heights with a developmental approach. *International Journal of Leadership in Education, 19*(1), 56–86. https://doi.org/10.1080/13603124.2015.1096075

Drew, V., Priestley, M., & Michael, M. K. (2016). Curriculum development through critical collaborative professional enquiry. *Journal of Professional Capital and Community, 1*(1), 92–106. https://doi.org/10.1108/JPCC-09-2015-0006

DuFour, R., DuFour, R., & Eaker, B. (2009). New insights into professional learning communities at work. In M. Fullan (Ed.), *The challenge of change: Start school improvement now!* (2nd ed., pp. 87–103). Corwin.

Education Review Office. (2019). *Collaboration in practice: insights into implementation.* Education Review Office.

Feys, E., & Devos, G. (2015). What comes out of incentivized collaboration: A qualitative analysis of eight Flemish school networks. *Educational Management Administration & Leadership, 43*(5), 738–754. https://doi.org/10.1177/1741143214535738

Hood, C. (1991). A public management for all seasons? *Public Administration, 69*(1), 3–19. https://doi.org/10.1111/j.1467-9299.1991.tb00779.x

Hood, C. (1998). *The art of the state: Culture, rhetoric, and public management.* Oxford University Press.

Kamp, A. (2020). Kāhui Ako and the collaborative turn in education: Emergent evidence and leadership implications. *The New Zealand Annual Review of Education, 24,* 177–191. https://doi.org/10.26686/nzaroe.v24i0.6493

Malin, J., Brown, C., Ion, G., van Ackeren, I., Bremm, N., Luzmore, R., Flood, J., & Rind, G. (2020) World-wide barriers and enablers to achieving evidence-informed practice in education: What can be learnt from Spain, England, the United States, and Germany? *Humanities and Social Sciences Communications, 7*(99). https://doi.org/10.1057/s41599-020-00587-8

Mifsud, D. (2020). *School networks.* Euro-Mediterranean Centre for Educational Research. https://doi.org/10.1093/acrefore/9780190264093.013.741

Ministry of Education. (2014a). *Ministry of Education statement of intent: 2014–18.* Ministry of Education.

Ministry of Education. (2014b). *Investing in educational success.* Working Group Report. Ministry of Education.

Ministry of Education. (2015). *Community of schools: Tips and starters working together.* Ministry of Education.

Ministry of Education. (2019). *Supporting all schools to succeed: Reform of the Tomorrow's Schools system.* Ministry of Education.

Ministry of Education. (2021). *Evidence and data.* Retrieved April 15, 2021, from https://www.education.govt.nz/communities-of-learning/evidence-and-data/

Moolenaar, N. M., Sleegers, P. J. C., & Daly, A. J. (2012). Teaming up: Linking collaboration networks, collective efficacy, and student achievement. *Teaching and Teacher Education, 28*(2), 251–262. http://dx.doi.org/10.1016/j.tate.2011.10.001

Nelson, T. H., Slavit, D., Perkins, M., & Hathorn, T. (2008). A culture of collaborative inquiry: Learning to develop and support professional learning communities. *Teachers College Record, 110*(6), 1269–1303.

New Zealand Government. (1989). *Education Act* (Public Act 1989, No. 80). New Zealand Government.

Sinnema, C., Daly, A. J., Liou, Y.-H., & Rodway, J. (2020). Exploring the communities of learning policy in New Zealand using social network analysis: A case study of leadership, expertise, and networks. *International Journal of Educational Research, 99*. https://doi.org/10.1016/j.ijer.2019.10.002

Smith, M. (2018). Effective leadership practices by school principals within CoL/Kāhui Ako that contribute to effective communication, high levels of relational trust and collaboration on shared achievement challenges.

Starr, K. (2019). *Education policy, neoliberalism, and leadership practice: A critical analysis.* Routledge.

Timperley, H., Kaser, L., & Halbert, J. (2014). *A framework for transforming learning in schools: Innovation and the spiral of inquiry. Seminar Series 234.* Centre for Strategic Education.

Townsend, A. (2015). Leading school networks: Hybrid leadership in action? *Educational Management Administration & Leadership, 43*(5), 719–737. https://doi.org/10.1177/1741143214543205

The Treasury. (1987a). *Government management: Brief to the incoming government 1987 – Volume I.* Government Printing Office.

The Treasury. (1987b). *Government management: Brief to the incoming government 1987 – Volume II education issues.* Government Printing Office.

Thrupp, M. (2018). To be 'in the tent' or abandon it? A school clusters policy and the responses of New Zealand educational leaders. In J. Wilkinson, R. Niesche, & S. Eacott (Eds.), *Challenges for public education: Reconceptualising educational leadership, policy and social justice as resources for hope* (pp. 132–144). Routledge.

Woods, P. A., & Roberts, A. (2018). *Collaborative school leadership: A critical guide.* Sage Publications.

Wylie, C., & Hodgen, E. (2020). *Teaching, school, and principal leadership practices survey 2019.* NZCER. www.nzcer.org.nz/research/teaching-and-school-practices-survey-tool-tsp

Wylie, C., McDowall, S., Ferral, H., Felgate, R., & Visser, H. (2018). *Teaching practices, school practices, and principal leadership: The first national picture 2017.* NZCER.

Youngs, H. (2020a). Distributed leadership. In G. Noblit (Editor in Chief), *Oxford Research Encyclopedia of Education* (P. 24). Oxford University Press. http://dx.doi.org/10.1093/acrefore/9780190264093.013.612

Youngs, H. (2020b). Thirty years of leadership in New Zealand education: From the shadows of management to *sine qua non. Journal of Educational Leadership, Policy and Practice, 35*, 60–77. https://doi.org/10.21307/jelpp-2020-008

Chapter 2

Local Authorities and School-to-School Collaboration in Scotland

Joanne Neary, Christopher Chapman, Stuart Hall and Kevin Lowden

Abstract

This chapter explores the Scottish government policy drive for school improvement through processes such as distributed leadership, empowerment and cross-school collaboration to school settings. Compared to other nations, this shift towards collaboration has been relatively slow, but reflects the history of Scottish education, one where there is a reduced emphasis on individualist/competitive cultures and instead focuses on social justice and equity. This chapter discusses two programmes of work that were developed to foster school-to-school collaboration in the Scottish education system. In doing so, we comment on the conflict between national priority setting and the translation of this agenda at the local level by different local authorities.

Keywords: Collaborative enquiry; social cohesion; leadership; regulation; local authorities; Scotland; social regulation; impactful school-to-school collaboration; National Policy

Introduction

Recent policy developments in Scottish education reflect a wider global policy movement to re-professionalize teaching, support the active engagement of teachers in school improvement processes through, for example, empowerment, distributed leadership and cross-school cooperation (Torrance & Humes, 2014; Torrance & Murphy, 2016). Despite this enthusiasm at the policy level, impactful school-to-school collaboration in Scotland remains patchy.

School-to-School Collaboration: Learning Across International Contexts, 27–41
Copyright © 2022 by Joanne Neary, Christopher Chapman, Stuart Hall and Kevin Lowden
Published under exclusive licence by Emerald Publishing Limited
doi:10.1108/978-1-80043-668-820221003

In this chapter, we offer an analysis of the key developments in policy that have influenced this new direction. We then discuss two programmes of work develop by the Robert Owen Centre (ROC) at the University of Glasgow designed to promote more equitable school improvement through school-to-school collaboration. We suggest that the active role of the local authority, and the autonomy they possess to interpret national policy at the local level, has created variation within the system. We explore the impact of this variation in the roll-out and sustainability of the school-to-school collaboration programmes.

Building on the work of Douglas (1982), Hood (1998) and Chapman (2019), we use the two dimensions of social cohesion and social regulation to define sociocultural dimensions of education systems and argue that an egalitarian culture is required to support a self-improving system.

Where social cohesion and regulation are both high, hierarchical cultures prevail, and public service organizations tend to characterize their own cultures as those of hierarchical, bureaucratic, managed organizations. Here we see traditional structures in place, often centrally managed through power and position. Where social cohesion and regulation are both low, an individualistic (competitive) culture dominates. Here the market prevails, and we see the emergence of 'independent' state-funded schools operating outside of school district/local authority control. Where social cohesion is low, but regulation is high, fatalistic cultures prevail. Within these cultures, organizations tend to be unclear about the direction of travel and second guessing what the next initiative or policy is likely to be implemented on them. In systems where regulation is low but social cohesion is high, an egalitarian culture tends to dominate. Chapman (2019) describes in these circumstances:

> mutualistic, self-improving organisations work laterally, often with the support of the middle tier, collaborating with each other in networks to support joint improvement. This interorganisational support for improvement is in stark contrast to the bureaucratic, top-down, and producer-capture arrangements found in hierarchical cultures. (p. 557)

	Low social cohesion	High social cohesion
High social regulation	'Fatalistic culture' *Uncertain nostalgic organisations*	'Hierarchical culture' *'bureaucratic, managed organisations'*
Low social regulation	'Individualistic culture' *'market-based state-funded organisations'*	'Egalitarian culture' *'mutualistic self-improving organisations'*

Fig. 1.   Sociocultural Perspectives on Public Service Reform. *Source*: Chapman (2019).

An Overview of Policy

Scottish education has been a devolved power since the Scotland Act (1998). However, Scottish education has operated independently from Westminster (UK) control since the eighteenth century. This 'independence' is reflected in a number of ways including the Scottish curriculum, the relationship between schools and local authorities. For example, the English and Welsh systems tend to be characterized by 'choice and diversity', where the rise of neo-liberal market-based forms of regulation and competition (Arnott & Menter, 2007) has meant many schools opting out of local authority control. In Scotland, education remains largely homogeneous, with over 95% of schools managed by local authorities. The 32 Scottish local authorities work within a framework set by national policy, although each has their own identified priorities, develop local initiatives and produce guidelines for schools. Therefore, while educational policies are developed at the national government level, the translation and implementation of these policies, along with the responsibility for school improvement, lies with each local authority. This is the so-called Concordat approach (Cairney et al., 2016). While there is a considerable level of autonomy to interpret national policy at the local level, there is also a system of accountability outlined in the form of the National Improvement Framework for Scottish Education (Scottish Government, 2016b). This document details 'Key Performance Indicators', along with associated monitoring arrangements. Her Majesty's Inspectorate of Education (HMIE) inspections help monitor the quality of education within this framework. Although a significant number of schools, 704 out of around 2,500, have not been inspected within the last 10 years. Furthermore, 1,685 have not been inspected for between five and seven years (Scottish Government, 2021).

Compared to other systems, the ideas about who should be responsible for educational change and improvement and the pace of reform have been evolutionary rather than revolutionary as is the case in other parts of the United Kingdom. For example, when the 'self-governing school' was first introduced in Scotland in the early 1990s, there was pushback against the notion of a more competitive market-orientated system (Hartley, 1996; Murphy & Raffe, 2015; Riddel, 2016). Where education districts in Scotland were seen to be delegating responsibility to schools and away from local authorities, there was a distancing of 'Scottish' and 'English' practice:

> fostering cooperating among schools, not competition between them [the Scottish approach], which has been a perceived and regretted result of Local Management Schools in some areas of England and Wales. (Strathclyde Regional Council, 1992, cited in Hartley, 1996, p. 133)

However, the Scottish system is, for a number of sources, typified by more than institutional cooperation. Indeed, many authors have also characterized the history of Scottish education as one with a strong Social Justice strand at least in comparison with other education systems. As Riddel (2009) has highlighted, Scottish government policy, particularly in education, has long stated an adherence to the goals of social justice and equity and inclusion. Riddel rightly argues that these concepts are complex and interrelated. She stresses that while redistributive measures to tackle these issues will continue to be debated, an appropriate evidence-informed discourse in the education system is needed to facilitate more effective policy enactment to promote social justice in schools.

Empowering the System?

Over the course of the current administration, the concept of self-governance has once again become popular in Scottish policy circles with the idea of the 'empowerment', albeit one that remains within the oversight of a local authority. One of the first shifts in education policy was in Devolved School Management (DSM) schemes. While initially rejected in the 1990s, it is now seen as ensuring schools are 'empowered to make the decisions that most affect their children and young people's outcomes, while being part of a collaborative learning community, local authority, and working with others' (COSLA, 2019, p. 7). This commitment to the concept of subsidiary includes control over spending, enabling schools to access a delegated budget that they control (rather than their local authority). This fiscal empowerment is also witnessed in the Pupil Equity Fund (PEF) (Scottish Government, 2017). Introduced in 2017, PEF provides additional funding for students and young people from disadvantaged backgrounds and is calculated using pupil census data relating to free school meal entitlement. It is specifically aimed at closing the poverty-related attainment gap and used to fund resources, activities or interventions that are additional to the existing curricular offer. Importantly, this additional resource is allocated directly to schools from the central government, by passing the local authority. The Educational Institute of Scotland (2017) published guidance suggesting head teachers should work collegiately with teachers within their school and with head teachers from other schools to identify the young people impacted by poverty, address their needs with regard to literacy, numeracy and well-being through the creation of targeted support that would have a positive impact on their learning experience. These cooperative and collaborative activities, driven by professional dialogue, acknowledge the importance of schools using their own knowledge and expertise to drive forward change for the benefit of pupils.

While policies suggest the market is less of a motivation behind recent attempts to regulate school governance (Arnott & Menter, 2007), the ability of schools to access direct funding can enable a more empowered system as decisions can be made closer to learning level. While the local authority maintains much of the control of budgetary decisions, these policies increase the capacity of school leaders and teaching staff to use their professional and contextual knowledge to enact change at the school level. Therefore, the relationship between local authority and school is shifting, albeit slowly in many cases so that schools make decisions based on the identified need of their local communities while the local authority provides support, monitoring and strategic oversight. Put simply, we are moving to a situation where schools are becoming responsible for self-improvement and the local authorities are responsible for ensuring this happens.

Distributed leadership, Professional Learning and Collaboration

Following publication of 'Teaching Scotland's Future' (TSF) (Donaldson, 2010), a review of teacher education spanning initial teacher education, training and development opportunities for qualified teachers and career progression, there has been a significant focus on the need to build leadership capacity within the system. One of the recommendations from the review was the need for 'a clear progressive educational leadership pathway…which embodies the responsibility of all leaders to build the professional capacity of staff and ensure a positive impact on young people's learning' (Scottish Government, 2010, p. 79). This reflected a broader policy consensus, which recognized the potential of teacher leadership to empower teachers (Torrance & Murphy, 2016) and the potential role all teachers within schools could make in empowered decision-making, valuing the knowledge and skills of teachers at all levels.

Over the past decade, there have been a series of policies that strengthen and extend leadership within the Scottish education system, including a discussion of leadership at all levels in the professional standards for teachers (GTCS, 2021), leadership identified as one of the six drivers in the National Improvement Framework for education (Scottish Government, 2016), and the importance of collaborative leadership instilled in head teacher training (Scottish Government, 2016). Despite these developments, there has been criticism of the 'under-theorised' nature of distributed leadership (Mowatt & McMahon, 2018) whereby much of the debate surrounding the concept has focussed on 'the merits of programmes rather than the development of a cohesive leadership system' (Hamilton et al., 2018, p. 73). In order to build a sustainable national strategy that strengths leadership capacity, the authors argue it is important to balance the needs of the education system with the needs of the individuals' professional development needs.

A review of the impact of TSF (Scottish Government, 2016) found that there had been positive steps with regard to staff engaging in professional dialogue and learning suggesting a 'cultural shift' towards a more open and self-reflective practice, as well as evidence suggesting improved training and development opportunities regarding leadership at all career stages. Despite this, the review also described ongoing confusion regarding the different forms of leadership, particularly when staff still equated leadership with career progression and promotion. Linked to this was a criticism of wider leadership strategies of the lack of attention paid to the wider contextual and cultural boundaries within which these activities would be actioned (Harris et al., 2018; Mowatt & McMahon, 2018). For example, head teachers may still chose to task certain teachers with leadership 'tasks' and therefore act as a gatekeeper for opportunities, or junior members of staff may not be perceived by the wider school body as having the 'authority' to carry out certain duties.

Recent curricular changes in Scotland also underline the move towards a system where schools and teachers are more positively involved in developing curricula best suited to the children in their classrooms. The development of Curriculum for Excellence (CfE), as distinct from the previous 5–14 curriculum, represented a move from a more prescriptive, centrally determined curricula to one more locally led and focussed on the pupil as an individual learner. Rather than teaching from textbooks or pre-agreed resources, CfE enabled teachers to move beyond the prescribed methods and address the individual needs and learning styles of pupils. There have, however, been challenges of implementation of this approach particularly in the senior phase of secondary education where high stakes public examinations and accreditation still tend to drive the agenda.

Partnership Working: Policy and Practice

We now move onto discussing two programmes of work that were developed to foster school-to-school and local authority-to-local authority collaboration in the Scottish education system to support the cultural change necessary to shift the system towards more empowered and collaborative ways of working. We indicate how these initiatives map onto wider policy discussions, before providing a discussion of how the authors devised and supported these initiatives.

Partnership working, and the ability of educational professionals to work collaboratively within, between and beyond their own school gates, has been described as key to building capacity of staff, developing their professional autonomy and bringing school improvement discussions down to the local level. Through professional learning communities, teachers are able to collaborate with one another, conduct shared enquiry activities focussing on issues of practice and pedagogy and share collective responsibility for improvements in pupil learning (Hargreves & Fullan, 2012).

In 2013, the then Scottish Cabinet Secretary for Education and Lifelong Learning described partnership working as an important approach to tackle the link between socio-economic deprivation and low educational attainment in Scotland. Partnership working was also referenced in the National Improvement Framework in their discussion that successful professional development is most successful when it is well planned and takes place within, between and beyond school.

The ability of educational professionals to use attainment data in order to implement targeted intervention to raise outcomes for groups of children was described in the 2021 Scottish National Improvement Framework and Improvement Plan (Scottish Government, 2020). The document described that 'almost all schools have planned interventions in place … particularly to provide targeted interventions in literacy, numeracy, and health and wellbeing' (p. 47). These interventions were described as existing both within school and between schools. It also highlighted the importance to ensure schools were able to develop robust procedures to tack and monitor impact and also the impact of working in partnership with other schools.

Robert Owen Centre

The Robert Owen Centre (ROC) at the University of Glasgow has had a key role in developing the research capacity of educational professionals to analyze their own data, implement targeted interventions and tracking and monitoring impact.

There are two key programmes of work which provide examples of how the research team were able to translate policy into practice and, in doing, drive future policy discussions. Both programmes were informed by the burgeoning model of international research linking school-to-school networking and system improvement (Ainscow, 2015; Armstrong et al., 2021; Brown & Poortman, 2019; Hadfield & Jopling, 2011; Madrid Miranda & Chapman, 2021).

Both programmes promote a model of improvement underpinned by collaborative enquiry (Bryk et al., 2011, Cochran-Smith & Lytle, 2009). Central to these programmes is the use of Collaborative Action Research (CAR), whereby schools are encouraged to critically examine their contexts by collecting and analysing data and using the knowledge generated to make changes. Schools are then encouraged to monitor the impact of these changes and adapt practice where appropriate. This forms a cycle of evidence-informed improvement. A number of quantitative and qualitative methods can be used in the CAR process, including surveys, lesson study, instructional rounds, staff visits, focus groups, interviews and pupil engagement activities. Our evidence suggests that by working together on shared issues, the burden of improvement moves from being the responsibility of one teacher to becoming a shared goal of the network. Also, by collectively sharing the roles and responsibilities required in the programme, the practitioners within the network gain confidence in leadership, and learning from this approach is mobilized across the network and ideally the wider system.

In our Scottish examples, the role of the local authority acts as the key broker and facilitator. Another distinct feature of the model underpinning the two programmes is the role of university researchers working closely with teachers, schools and local authority leaders to research the process, facilitate collaboration, develop enquiry skills of practitioners and empower them to use the CAR approach. We begin by briefly detailing the programmes, before exploring the differences at the local authority meso-level and how these differences impacted the running of these programmes.

Reflecting on the School Improvement Partnership Programme (SIPP)

SIPP was designed by the ROC in 2013 and supported by Education Scotland in response to the Scottish government's commitment to investing in leadership, enhancing the use of data and school-to-school collaboration. It created the mechanism to systematically implement an evidence-informed approach that encouraged the use of collaboration and practitioner enquiry to improve learner outcomes and classroom pedagogy (Chapman et al., 2015). The aim of SIPP was to support innovation to tackle educational inequity and reduce the achievement gap across classroom, school and local authority boundaries.

The SIPP approach encouraged staff to take leadership responsibility for embedding these new enquiry activities into their school practices and using CAR to experiment with pedagogy and evaluate the impact it had on learners.

During the period 2013–2016, 75 schools across 14 local authorities engaged in SIPP. These 75 schools did not work alone, but rather in one of eight interconnected partnership projects. Within these projects, the rates of collaboration between schools and across local authority boundaries differed. For example, in three projects, schools collaborated within one local authority; in four projects, schools collaborated across two local authorities; and in one project, schools collaborated across three local authorities. Each project was devised by the schools and was informed by their assessment of local issues. Also, while both primary and secondary schools were invited to participate, the collaborative partnerships mostly focussed on primary or secondary issues, with only two projects spanning the primary/secondary gap.

The collaborative projects were supported by the ROC team, as well as staff from the local authority and Education Scotland. The role of these individuals was to provide advice and guidance on the CAR process and educational improvement, facilitated through regular face-to-face meetings and via email. A series of national events was also held to share knowledge and build the network. The aim of this support was to build capacity and confidence within the school partnerships, particularly with regard to research methodology and evaluation and do so in a way that was sustainable so that the approach would become embedded at school and local authority levels as the university and Education Scotland team withdrew at the end of the pilot programme. *Improving Schools in Scotland: An OECD Perspective* (OECD, 2015) noted the contribution of SIPP:

> the School Improvement Partnership Programme which brings together local authorities and university researchers to address issues of educational inequity … All what GTCS referred to with us as the 'Scottish Way' – to have integrated partnership working at the strategic level which is then reflected in high quality delivery of teaching and learning at the sharp end of the system. (p. 138)

We now move on to consider the evolution of SIPP beyond 2016, into the Network for Social and Educational Equity (NSEE).

NSEE

NSEE was launched in 2017 and built on the work and conceptual framework of the SIPP programme. It used the CAR approach to embed enquiry, collaboration and evidence-based practices in school improvement. While SIPP piloted a nationwide programme of work using the 'CAR approach', NSEE developed this in a way that was more nuanced and focussed on co-developing strategies with local authorities and practitioners.

This programme of work involves the Robert Owen Centre working in partnership with a range of stakeholders including educational psychologists, local development officers, third-sector organizations and local authority leaders, as well as educational practitioners and school leaders.

At the time of writing, NSEE has engaged with 41 schools, 5 secondaries (pupils aged 11–17) and 36 primaries (pupils aged 5–11) across four local authority areas. Unlike SIPP, which was a national pilot funded by Scottish government, NSEE required local authorities and schools to 'buy-in' to the initiative and fund the approach themselves. This shift in programme design also saw a shift in funding, from centrally funded, but locally implemented, to locally funded (albeit through Scottish Attainment Challenge or Pupil Equity Funding). The ability of local authorities or individual schools to fund this programme of work can be seen as a result of the empowerment agenda in Scottish education policy and the devolution of power from national government to local authority. This shift placed local authorities central in making key decisions in school improvement decisions.

Reflecting on the Role of the Local Authority in NSEE

In keeping with the flexibility at the core of the NSEE model, there are substantial variations in the ways that local authorities have adopted and utilized NSEE in their school improvement activity. Therefore, in understanding the role of the policy context in understanding how schools engage in collaborative activity, we must look both at the national and local levels.

Using grid group theory as outlined in Fig. 1, Table 1 maps the cultural engagement of four local authorities with the NSEE programme.

Table 1.   Grid Group Theory and Local Authority Culture.

Local Authority	Culture	Drivers of Programme Adoption in Locality	Other Stakeholders
A	Individualistic	Instigated and driven by schools, little involvement by local authority	Attainment advisor
B	Hierarchical	Instigated by local authority, encouraged schools to participate but with moderate accountability and tight–loose structures/ programmes of work	Attainment advisor, educational psychologist
C	Egalitarian	Instigated by local authority but with high level of autonomy for schools	Attainment advisor, local authority officer, educational psychologist
D	Fatalistic	Instigated by local authority, nominated schools to participate with strong accountability	Attainment advisor, Education Scotland, local authority advisor

Where the local authority had a role in instigating the adoption of the NSEE programme in their school improvement plan, they also offered support in terms of coordination of schools, provided additional professional learning opportunities that supplemented the work of the ROC team, supported event organization, allocated additional resources (either in terms of buying-in resources or ensuring teachers had time out of school to attend training workshops) and ensured the lessons could be embedded in policy and practice in their locality.

In Table 1, local authority B is hierarchical in the sense that it adopted the NSEE approach and had a moderate accountability mechanism built in but invited schools to participate. This is similar to local authority C, who also adopted the NSEE approach but were more egalitarian in their approach due to higher levels of autonomy for any school that self-selected to participate.

In contrast, local authority D nominated schools they felt would benefit from this approach. Therefore, the schools in local authority D experienced a sense of fatalism in their experience of the programme. These contrasting approaches meant the ROC team experienced different levels of initial buy-in from the schools involved. While authority B had initial buy-in from head teachers and therefore had a general enthusiasm for the approach, authority D faced a level of initial scepticism from some schools. In authority D, a number of schools initially felt that, despite the best intentions of the research team, the approach was being done 'to them' rather than being done 'with them'. This created an initial tension, as the ROC team's ethos and the NSEE model stresses a collaborative, co-constructed approach.

In local authority A, where there was low engagement with the local authority, the schools formed their own collaborative network and instigated contact with the ROC team. This guaranteed initial buy-in from schools and an impetus to engage with the CAR approach and develop an enquiry-based focus to their school improvement plan. However, the lack of local authority 'middle-tier' support meant there was additional strain placed on the ROC team and the schools to coordinate and maintain the programme impetus. Ultimately, without local authority support, schools became solely responsible for sustaining the initiative, and this relied heavily on the leadership capacity of individual schools.

However, despite variation in the level of local authority support, across all four authority areas, there were additional stakeholders who supported the development of the programme. For example, an Attainment Advisor[1] in each local authority provided supplementary support to schools, which enabled additional reinforcement for schools. This support may also include additional input to understand datasets (although in the case of areas B and C, this support was offered by Educational Psychologist) as well as advise on curriculum design.

---

[1]Attainment Advisors are members of Education Scotland staff who provide support and challenge to local authorities and focus on issues of educational equity.

Lessons Learned

Both SIPP and NSEE have a strong focus on promoting school-level change with the support of the middle tier. Involving this middle tier as a key partner has maintained the impetus to move from individual-level classroom or school research activity to embedding the learning across and at times between local authority education systems.

This can particularly be seen in the NSEE examples, particularly the differences between areas A (individualist, school led) and B (hierarchical) and C (egalitarian). While the schools in area A were enthusiastic about using the approach to promote school improvement, we found there was little potential for knowledge mobilization across the wider system or to embed the approach further within schools. In areas B and C, the local authorities adopted the approach but offered optional participation to the schools. In having the local authority at the centre of delivery, it allowed for resources to be located, information shared and lessons learned informing wider educational planning and practice. In area D (fatalistic), while the programme was adopted enthusiastically by the local authority, it lacked the local buy-in of schools compared with Areas B and C. Instead, it mandated participation in the schools they felt would benefit from learning about evidence-based enquiry and collaboration. This led to a slower process, with some schools slower to engage as the benefits of participation were unclear. Here the ROC team had to overcome initial reticence among school staff and build relationships.

A key lesson was about the time it takes to build professional networks and the time it takes for these networks to function without support of key intermediaries. SIPP was a three-year programme, with the first year designed to develop professional relationships and the trust between practitioners to allow for open and honest discussions to take place and to build confidence and a baseline capability in terms of understanding and skills. NSEE also operated as a three-year programme of work, with the first year devoted to relationship building and initial testing out of different methods. Teachers are encouraged to start small and focus on their learning rather than of the outcomes of their collaborative work. The ROC team's work is front-loaded, with a great deal of training and support offered in the first year. By the third year, the ROC team have a consultancy role, where the collaborations and enquiry projects are well defined, and can run with minimal input from external voices.

The training of teachers in research methodologies and evaluation was an empowering example of CPD. In an evaluation of SIPP, teachers described their increased confidence in being able to assess school-level data and using this to identify target groups, implement interventions and assess impact. They also suggested that as teachers' knowledge of link between disadvantage and educational outcomes improved, so did their ability to adapt classroom activities and learning approaches to support all learners. In NSEE, teachers described examples of CAR projects developing from a one-classroom exercise to becoming an ethos embedded within the whole school. The sustainability of this approach can also be seen in accounts of teachers training new staff in how to develop enquiry approaches to school improvement, ensuring the learning continues beyond the engagement of the NSEE team.

In addition to positively impacting on teachers' professional learning and skills, the SIPP and NSEE programmes of work have demonstrated a positive impact on learner achievement, aspirations and outcomes, although there have been variations across the different partnerships (Chapman et al., 2016).

Discussion

This chapter detailed some of the more recent developments in Scottish education as they relate to distributed leadership and cross-school collaboration. Compared to other nations within the United Kingdom, this change has been relatively slow, with policymakers keen to lay a path that empowers schools to make decisions that impact their pupil needs but also maintains notions of social justice and equity at its core while rejecting notions of competition seen in other nations. In terms of the grid group theory, we can view Scotland as high cohesion, high regulation system, as a relatively hierarchical culture with bureaucratic educational organizations. In a sense, it is a relatively traditional education system where power and position tend to equate with decision-making power. However, this chapter has illuminated ways in which the role of the local authority blurs or complicates this characterization, especially as there is a considerable level of autonomy at local authority level to interpret national policy.

In doing so, this complication also offers nuance to the question posed by the book: how does wider policy context influence whether, and the extent to which, schools engage in meaningful collaborative activity. What we have seen is that nationally, there are simultaneous agendas towards empowerment and schools working in partnership to support improvement and use of data. On the other hand, we see local authorities working in different ways to interpret these agendas. By providing four examples of NSEE case study sites, we have highlighted the importance striking the balance right between local authorities driving the improvement agenda while involving schools and educational professionals in these conversations. Through these examples, we can see at both ends of the spectrum, there are few opportunities for sustainable collaborative engagement though we have signalled the potential for local authorities supporting an egalitarian culture, which we consider necessary to promote a self-improving educational system.

Systematic and deep-rooted school-to-school collaboration in Scotland is in its infancy and varies across the system. The speed to which schools are able to build their professional networks, even with the scaffolding provided by the ROC team, Education Scotland and attainment advisors, reflects the variations in experience and expertise in this way of working. While the ROC team has been central in developing the professional learning for teachers to begin to work collaboratively with one another, our role is front-loaded. This meant in the beginning stages we provided intensive support, and as the teachers grew in confidence and ability, the team withdrew and became more 'arms-length', allowing them to drive the agenda. Key in the development of the networks was time, particularly time to build relationships and trust between stakeholders. This is particularly the case where individuals see collaboration as threatening their autonomy and where they were asked to invest resources (teacher time and expertise) for uncertain returns. This uncertainty as to the benefit of this approach meant that while the local authorities in all but one of our examples had 'bought in', we also had to ensure that all teachers saw the value and translatability of the approach.

Key to the SIPP and NSEE approaches was the inherent flexibility of the approach. We offer schools frameworks for change and a toolkit of methods they can utilize in creating small interventions focussed on improving aspects of their classroom with the aim to reduce the achievement gap. By offering flexible approach rather than a prescriptive model, we ensure that the participating teachers feel trusted and that their expertise was valued. We do not instruct them how to collaborate to improve practice and outcomes, but rather help to build their capacity to critically appraise data and undertake meaningful changes to their day-to-day practice. In this way, we empower teachers to use evidence and their professional judgement to make decisions about how to improve their classrooms and schools. However, as this chapter illustrates, local authorities (and other stakeholders) have a key role to play in creating the conditions to empower teachers. At best, they can facilitate and accelerate the process, and at worst, they can inhibit the process through power, control, and mandate. The Robert Owen Centre for Educational Change will continue to work to support the system to ensure that the former scenario prevails.

References

Ainscow, M. (2015). *Towards self-improving school systems: Lessons from a city challenge.* Routledge.

Armstrong, P., Brown, C., & Chapman, C. (2021). School-to-school collaboration in England: A configurative review of the empirical evidence. *Review of Education*, 9(1), 319–351. https://doi.org/10.1002/rev3.3248

Arnott, M., & Menter, I. (2007). The same but different? Post-devolution regulation and control in education in Scotland and England. *European Education Research Journal*, 6(3), 250–265.

Brown, C., & Poortman, C. (2019). Professional learning networks: Harnessing collaboration to achieve the scale-up of effective education practices. In M. A. Peters & R. Herauld (Eds.), *Encyclopedia of educational innovation*. Springer. doi: https://doi.org/10.1007/978-981-13-2262-4_6-1

Bryk, A. S., Gomez, L. M., & Grunow, A. (2011). Getting ideas into action: Building networked improvement communities in education. In M. T. Hallinan (Ed.) *Frontiers in sociology of education*. Springer Science and Business Media.

Cairney, P., Russell, S., & St Denny, E. (2016). The 'Scottish approach' to policy and policymaking: What issues are territorial and what are universal? *Policy and Politics*, 44, 333–350.

Chapman, C. (2019). From hierarchies to networks: Possibilities and pitfalls for educational reform of the middle tier. *Journal of Educational Administration*, 57(5), 554–570.

Chapman C., & Ainscow, M. (2021). *Educational equity: Pathways to success.* Routledge.

Chapman, C., Chesnutt, H., Friel, N., Hall, S., & Lowden, K (2016). Professional capital and collaborative inquiry networks for educational equity and improvement *Journal of professional capital and community, 1*(3), 178–197.

Chapman, C., Lowden, K., Chesnutt, H., Hall, S., McKinney, S., Hulme, M., & Friel, N. (2015). *The school improvement partnership programme: Using collaboration and enquiry to tackle educational inequality.* Education Scotland.

Cochran-Smith, M., & Lytle, S. L. (2009). *Inquiry as stance: Practitioner research for the next generation.* Teachers College Press.

Convention of Scottish Local Authorities (COSLA). (2019). *Devolved school management guidelines.* Scottish Government. Retrieved April 21, 2021, from https://www.gov.scot/publications/devolved-school-management-guidelines/

Donaldson, G. (2010). *Teaching Scotland's future*: A Report Of a Review Of Teacher Education in Scotland Edinburgh: Scottish Government.

Douglas, M. (1982). *In the active voice.* Routledge & Kegan Paul.

Educational Institute of Scotland. (2017). *Pupil Equity Funding (PEF) Interim Advice o EIS Local Association Secretaries and School Representatives.* Edinburgh: EIS.

General Teaching Council for Scotland. (2021). *Professional standards for teachers.* Rerieved March 2022, from https://www.gtcs.org.uk/professional-standards/professional-standards-for-teachers/

Hadfield, M., & Jopling, M. (2011). School networks, networked learning and 'Network Theory'. In C. Day (Ed.), *The Routledge international handbook of teacher and school development* (pp. 516–526). Routledge.

Hamilton, G., Forde, C., & McMahon, M. (2018). *Developing a coherent strategy to build leadership capacity in Scottish education. Management in Education, 32*(2), 72–78.

Hargreves, A., Fullan, M. (2012). *Professional Capital: Transforming Teaching in Every School.* New York: Teaching College Press.

Harris, A., Jones, M. (2018). Why context matters: a comparative perspective on education reform and policy implementation *Educational Research for Policy and Practice*, 17, 195–207.

Hartley, D. (1996). Devolved school management: The 'new deal' in Scottish education *Journal of Education Policy, 9*(2), 129–140.

Hood, C. (1998). *The art of the state: Cultural rhetoric and public management.* Clarendon Press.

Madrid Miranda, R., & Chapman, C. (2021). Towards a network learning system: Reflections on a university initial teacher education and school-based collaborative initiative in Chile. *Professional Development in Education.* https://doi.org/10.1080/1 9415257.2021.1902840

Mowat, J., & McMahon, M. (2018). *Interrogating the concept of 'leadership at all levels': A Scottish perspective. Professional Development in Education, 45*(2), 173–189.

Murphy, D., & Raffe, D. (2015). The governance of Scottish comprehensive education. In D. Murphy, L. Croxford, & C. Howieson (Eds.), *Everyone's future: Lessons from fifty years of Scottish comprehensive schooling* (pp. 139–160). Institute of Education Press/Trentham Books.

OECD. (2015). *Improving schools in Scotland: An OECD perspective.* Organisation for Economic Co-operation and Development.

Riddel, S. (2009). Social justice, equality and inclusion in Scottish education. *Discourse: Studies in the Cultural Politics of Education, 30*(3), 283–296.

Riddel, S. (2016). Social justice, equality and inclusion in Scottish education. *Discourse: Studies in the Cultural Politics of Education, 30*(3), 283–296.

Scottish Government. (2016a). Evaluation of the impact of the implementation of teaching Scotland's future. Scottish Government.

Scottish Government. (2016b). *National improvement framework for Scottish education.* Scottish Government.

Scottish Government. (2017). *Pupil attainment: Closing the gap.* Retrieved April 21, 2021, from https://www.gov.scot/policies/schools/pupil-attainment/

Scottish Government. (2020). *Achieving excellence and equity – 2021 national improvement framework and improvement plan.* Scottish Government.

Scottish Government. (2021). *Statistics relating to school inspections: FOI release.* Retrieved April 21, 2021, from https://www.gov.scot/publications/foi-202100140164/

Torrance, D., & Humes, W. (2014). The shifting discourses of educational leadership: International trends and Scotland's response. *Educational Management Administration and Leadership, 43*(5), 792–810.

Torrance, D., & Murphy, D. (2016). Policy fudge and practice realities: Developing teacher leadership in Scotland. *International Studies in Educational Administration, 45*(3), 23–45.

Chapter 3

School Participation in Local and International Collaboration: The Norway–Canada (NORCAN) Programme

Carol Campbell

Abstract

This chapter provides an overview of approaches to collaboration in Ontario and then focuses in particular on the experiences of the Norway–Canada (NORCAN) programme involving nine schools across Alberta and Ontario (Canada) and Norway from 2014 to 2018. NORCAN was established through collaboration by the teachers' unions in Alberta (Alberta Teachers' Association), Norway (Utdanningsforbundet), and Ontario (Ontario Teachers' Federation) and the Ontario Ministry of Education. A central guiding question was co-developed to inform the work of NORCAN: 'How can an international network of schools and educators committed to mindful leadership help to identify obstacles to students' mathematics learning and develop strategies for attaining success?' With funding support, school teams involving school leaders, teachers, and students had opportunities to collaborate at NORCAN-facilitated events, school visits in each jurisdiction, through an online platform, and ongoing communication. The following important features of NORCAN are identified: the development of collaborative structures, processes, relationships, and trust; student voice, agency, and leadership; professional learning and agency; and sharing knowledge and de-privatizing practices. Four lessons for policy and practice are proposed: 1. school-to-school collaboration benefits from adequate resources of time, funding and a support infrastructure; 2. the intentional cultivation of mutually respectful and trusting relationships is essential; 3. bringing together educators and students as co-learners is powerful and beneficial; and 4. mobilizing knowledge and

School-to-School Collaboration: Learning Across International Contexts, 43–60

Copyright © 2022 by Carol Campbell

Published under exclusive licence by Emerald Publishing Limited

doi:10.1108/978-1-80043-668-820221004

de-privatizing practices needs to be central to the purpose and operation of collaboration.

Keywords: International school collaboration; school-to-school collaboration; professional learning; student voice; Canada; Ontario

Introduction

This chapter discusses the Norway–Canada (NORCAN) collaboration involving nine schools across Alberta and Ontario (Canada) and Norway from 2014 to 2018. Generally, school-to-school collaboration is implemented and evaluated within one specific education system and/or locality, whereas NORCAN involved collaboration across three education systems in two countries. International collaborations often primarily involve teachers' professional collaboration to support professional learning; for example, other examples of international collaborations involving Canada include the development of Internationally Networked Professional Learning Communities (ILNPLC) (Huang, 2018) to cultivate comparative understanding and the use of reciprocal learning to co-develop teachers' knowledge and practice for global competence and citizenship teaching (Khoo, 2021). With the rise of online communication, new collaborative possibilities to engage large networks of educators across countries are possible (Velea, 2012). Furthermore, international collaborations can also engage students' global learning (Edge & Khamsi, 2012), and support students' development of intercultural understanding and provide learning to change views on racial and cultural stereotypes (Walton, 2019).

While the findings concerning school-to-school collaboration vary; there is evidence that there is the potential for collaboration to contribute to school improvement, especially when targeted and focussed on teaching, learning, leadership, and supporting vulnerable learners but achieving such outcomes is complex and requires further development (e.g. Ainscow & Howes, 2007; Ainscow et al., 2006; Chapman, 2008; Muijs, 2015). There is also a need for research clarifying the concept and developing theories of school-to-school collaboration, as well as further expanding the evidence about collaboration (Armstrong et al., 2021; Chapman & Hadfield, 2010). This chapter adds to research on school-to-school collaboration with examples from Ontario and specifically findings from the NORCAN programme.

Overview of Ontario Education System

There is not a national school education system in Canada, rather K-12 education is the responsibility of 10 provinces and three territories. The Ontario Ministry of Education is responsible for the governance, funding, regulation, and oversight of Ontario's education system, which involves four publicly funded education systems (English Public, English Catholic, French Public, and French

Catholic) administered through 72 district school boards and 10 school authorities. There were a total of 3,967 elementary and 877 secondary schools in 2019–2020 (Ontario Ministry of Education, 2021) serving over two million students. While there are varying views about Ontario's education system over time; in the most recent study of parental and public attitudes, the majority of respondents were satisfied 'with school system' and 'with job teachers are doing' (Hart & Kempf, 2018, p. 10).

Considering Hood's (1998) social regulation/social cohesion matrix, there is a concern to develop and sustain high social cohesion in Canada including a widespread commitment to the importance of supporting children and young people's learning and development, and also of valuing publicly funded education systems and the work of the education profession (Campbell et al., 2017a). Ontario's education system is hierarchical and bureaucratic in nature (Campbell et al., 2017a) and therefore demonstrates high to moderate levels of social regulation. The teaching profession is highly regulated. All teachers must have completed university-based initial teacher education in Ontario, must register to meet the requirements to become an Ontario Certified Teacher (OCT), and uphold the professional and ethical standards of the OCT throughout their careers. There are provincial curricula which are implemented in schools. Central curricular writing and review can involve teams of education professionals engaged in this work, and teachers do have some autonomy in how they specifically teach the curriculum in their classrooms. There are large-scale provincial standardized assessments, developed and administered by the Education Quality Accountability Office (EQAO) for Reading, Writing, and Math in Grades 3 and 6, Math in Grade 9, and an Ontario Secondary School Literacy Test (OSSLT) as a requirement for high school graduation. While these assessments are not designed to be high stakes, they do exert influence over the work of the education system, schools, education profession, and students (Campbell et al., 2018a). However, there is also an emphasis on assessment as and for learning through teachers' use of classroom-based diagnostic and formative assessments to provide student feedback and inform teaching and learning. Therefore, while overall Ontario could be characterized as having a high degree of social regulation, it is more accurately represented by moving on a continuum from high to moderate as different aspects of the education system, policies, and practices are considered. In particular, approaches to collaboration, partnership working, and networking have attempted to shift Ontario from a purely 'hierarchist way' to involving elements of the 'egalitarian way' (Hood, 1998, p. 9).

Collaboration in the Ontario Education System

In 2003,[1] a new Liberal government inherited an education system where there had been hostile relationships between the education profession and the previous

---

[1]From 2003 to 2018, there were successive Liberal governments in Ontario. In 2018, the Progressive Conservative party formed a majority government.

Conservative government, including substantial strike action. The new government committed to a new way of partnership working with the education profession. One of their first actions was to establish The Partnership Table bringing
together the Minister of Education (politician), Ministry of Education (public
service officials), and all education partners and stakeholders. A series of working
tables and other partnership arrangements were implemented to engage education partners in collaborative working on the co-development of an extensive
series of reforms. While this partnership working was positively viewed and productive, over time education partners raised concerns about diminishing genuine
collaboration with the government and also between formal leaders and staff in
the education system (Campbell, 2021). Subsequently, an Initiatives Table was
formed to co-develop new ways of working and to review any proposed new
initiatives. The concept of Collaborative Professionalism was co-developed by
education partners and government, and enshrined in a Policy and Program
Memorandum which defined Collaborative Professionalism as:

- values all voices and is consistent with our shared responsibility to transform
  culture and provide equitable access to learning for all;
- takes place in and fosters a trusting environment that promotes professional
  learning;
- involves sharing ideas to achieve a common vision of learning, development
  and success for all;
- supports and recognizes formal and informal leadership and learning;
- includes opportunities for collaboration at provincial, district and school levels;
- leverages exemplary practices through the communication and sharing of
  ideas to achieve a common vision. (Ontario Ministry of Education, 2016, p. 2)

Therefore, there was an intentional co-development and – as needed – revising
and updating of approaches to partnership and collaboration as ways of governing, leading, and working in Ontario's education system.

There was also the introduction of a range of forms of collaboration to support school improvement, teaching and learning, student achievement and equity,
professional learning, and leadership development. School districts were encouraged and supported to collaborate with each other provincially and regionally
to discuss, learn about, develop, and share provincial and district improvement
strategies. For example:

> In May 2005, the Ministry of Education allocated $25 million to
> the Council of Ontario Directors of Education (CODE) ... to
> develop and implement a plan to support the recommendations
> in Education for All. The CODE Special Education Project for
> 2005-2006 was designed to assist school boards across Ontario in
> generating lateral capacity-building projects to enhance teacher
> professional practice and to improve academic achievement for
> students with special education needs. (Hargreaves & Braun,
> 2011, p. 5)

An evaluation of this strategy coined the phrase 'leading from the middle' (Hargreaves & Braun, 2011, p. 13) to describe the work of a provincial leadership team charged with supporting this work, plus the work of school district leaders in collaborating both with the government and CODE provincially and with schools to bring about significant transformation in approaches to supporting student learning. The perceived success of this way of working resulted in CODE's decision to continue this work beyond the initially funded project. The second phase embraced 'leading from the middle' as the guiding vision and way of working and resulted in further collaborative work to support student learning, well-being, and identity (Hargreaves & Shirley, 2018).

School collaboration in Ontario has taken many forms: targeted intervention to support lower performing schools, networks of schools for school improvement efforts, or the use of 'families of schools' or other organizational arrangements to support the operational linkages between schools in a geographic region with school district staff and resources. An example of collaboration for school leaders was the Leading Student Achievement (LSA) initiative co-developed by Ontario's three principals' councils, Ministry of Education, and school principals from 2005 to 2019 (OPC, 2021). LSA involved professional learning communities within schools and district-level principal learning teams. There has also been support for teacher networks and collaboration. Of particular relevance to the NORCAN case study was the pre-existing Teacher Learning and Leadership Programme (TLLP):

> The TLLP began in 2007 as a joint initiative between the Ontario Ministry of Education (Ministry) and the Ontario Teachers' Federation (OTF) with shared goals to:

> - support experienced teachers to undertake self-directed advanced professional development;
> - develop teachers' leadership skills for sharing their professional learning and exemplary practices; and
> - facilitate knowledge exchange for spread and sustainability of effective and innovative practices. (Campbell et al., 2018b, pp. 7–8).

In response to an annual call (2007–2018), teachers could submit proposals to lead a TLLP project linked to a provincial education priority and to their own specific contexts and needs, especially connected to their students. Successful teachers/teams received training, support, and a budget to conduct their TLLP over an 18-month period with a culminating *Sharing the Learning Summit* to share their work with all the TLLP teams. An online sharing platform was also developed to support networking and exchange. And building on the work of successful TLLP projects:

> school districts can apply for Provincial Knowledge Exchange (PKE) funding for release time and travel to enable former TLLP

teacher leaders to share their knowledge and practices with other schools and school districts across Ontario (and potentially beyond). (Campbell et al., 2018b, p. 8)

Our longitudinal evaluation of the TLLP identified a range of positive benefits for teacher leadership, teachers' professional learning, knowledge and skills, and improvements in instructional practices, plus benefits for students' engagement, learning, achievement, and leadership (Campbell et al., 2018b). The TLLP is significant also because it was Ontario's experience with this initiative that led to Ontario's involvement in NORCAN.

The NORCAN Collaboration

Drawing on the findings from our case study of NORCAN[2] (Campbell & Alexander, 2019), an evaluation commissioned by the NORCAN partners led by Dennis Shirley (2019), and a final report produced by the NORCAN Ontario Partners (2019), I describe the design features of NORCAN and then discuss the following elements of school-to-school collaboration in the NORCAN case: the development of collaborative structures, processes, relationships, and trust; student voice, agency, and leadership; professional learning and agency; and sharing knowledge and de-privatizing practices.

The Design of NORCAN

From 2014 to 2018, NORCAN was co-led by teachers' unions in Alberta (Alberta Teachers' Association), Norway (Utdanningsforbundet), and Ontario (Ontario Teachers' Federation), plus the Ontario Ministry of Education. A collaborative process with clear criteria and protocols was used to identify the nine schools that became NORCAN partners. Shirley (2019, p. 9) explains:

> [...] not only did the selection of the nine schools require careful consideration by the teacher organizations, but also the school-community characteristics such as different age groups of students, a mix of rural/urban, and representation of the country at large.

---

[2]Our case study of NORCAN (Campbell & Alexander, 2019) focused on the experiences of two Ontario publicly funded schools, Tecumseh Vista Academy (Grade K-12), part of Greater Essex County District School Board (GECDSB), and Monsignor John Pereyma Catholic Secondary School (Grades 9–12), belonging to the Durham Catholic District School Board (DCDSB). Semi-structured interviews with the principal and four teachers at one of the schools and a focus group with the principal and four teachers at the second school were conducted, plus document analysis (websites, blogs, videos created by and shared between NORCAN members) and site observations.

In Ontario, two secondary schools – Monsignor John Pereyma Catholic Secondary School in Oshawa (Durham Catholic District School Board) and Tecumseh Vista Academy in Windsor (Greater Essex County District School Board) – that had previously been involved in the TLLP and PKE were selected to become NORCAN partners.

Although this study explores how Ontario teachers engage in professional learning through the support of NORCAN, the project and its successes cannot be understood without knowledge of how the participating teachers came to be primed for the opportunities that NORCAN afforded. Although all teachers involved demonstrated agency, efficacy, and professional expertise, many teachers attested that it was the learning from their TLLP projects that helped them feel prepared to collaborate and learn through NORCAN (Campbell & Alexander, 2019). A culture and practice of collaborative inquiry, professional reflection, willingness to try out and evaluate new ideas and practices, and collegial support had been generated through the TLLP experiences and were beneficial for expanding and sustaining this work through NORCAN.

A central guiding question was co-developed to inform the work of NORCAN:

How can an international network of schools and educators committed to mindful leadership help to identify obstacles to students' mathematics learning and develop strategies for attaining success?

With funding support, school teams involving school leaders, teachers, and students had opportunities to collaborate at NORCAN-facilitated events, school visits in each jurisdiction, through an online platform, and ongoing communication. An Ontario teacher described the availability of allocated funding and time for collaboration as 'life changing' (Campbell & Alexander, 2019, p. 17).

There were intentional design principles and features of the NORCAN project:

> Important areas of emphasis underpinning the NORCAN programme are: 1) collaboration and trust – programme leaders: believe in the participants' autonomy and capacity to lead their own learning; believe in each partner organisation; build strong relationships. 2) Importance of evidence – the programme relies on a strong research component to enable articulation of success. 3) Formalised support structures – events that bring participants together; technology that serves as central communications and virtual contact mechanism; organisational support at multiple levels. (Campbell & Alexander, 2019, p. 12)

Attention to necessary resources and supporting infrastructure, cultivating a collaborative professional learning culture, and use of evidence were all integral and essential.

Development of Collaborative Structures, Processes, Relationships, and Trust

Each individual school team had to develop collaborative working, including among and between formal school leaders, teachers, and students. Each school team was also supported to engage in collaboration – in-person and online – with the other school teams involved across NORCAN. A further layer of collaboration was the working relationship between the three teachers' unions and the government in Ontario as the overall project team, and the collaboration between the school teams and the overall international project team. All of this required development of structures and processes to support collaboration, for example, joint events, co-development of plans, shared reflection and adaptation of ideas and actions, and continuing communication.

Developing a mutually appropriate and supportive international network involving three different education systems in two countries required careful thought, discussion, negotiation, and flexibility. For example, Shirley (2019) discusses the experience of the inaugural joint NORCAN workshop revealed 'that the language and cultural differences between the Norwegian and Canadian schools would require some careful consideration' (p. 10). Nevertheless, the development of international school-to-school collaboration over time provided powerful learning opportunities and experiences. Ontario participants coined the term the 'overview effect' to describe how the process of visiting other schools within their own province, in Alberta, and in Norway not only opened their eyes and minds to new ideas and practices but also changed how they viewed their local school and own practices too. In the words of one Ontario teacher: 'We went to the moon, and from there we saw the Earth differently'. Shirley (2019, p. 22) explains:

> As the partnership evolved, it became apparent that distance and boundaries were as much psychological as physical. With nine schools involving over 100 students, teachers and school leaders working both within their own jurisdictions and across international boundaries, it became increasingly difficult to distinguish between local and global – in fact, one Norwegian teacher described this experience as 'going global to understand what is local – and even then this is near impossible'. What became clear, in fact, was that the process of going global actually brought about a better understanding of the local.

Ontario participants spoke of the experience of being able to 'bust free, I was sort of like a hamster spinning on a wheel, now I know there's always a better way' (quoted in Campbell & Alexander, 2019, p. 18) and getting out of

> the silo of my own classroom. Because of NORCAN, I am now part of a wide network of educators who are all learning together and supporting each other in implementing new pedagogical practices. (Quoted in NORCAN Ontario Partners, 2019, p. 7)

The collaboration was not simply about visiting different schools and participating in joint activities, it also required developing deep reciprocal relationships and mutual trust. As Shirley (2019) explains:

The often-ignored point is this: educators need to develop trust and 'street credibility' with one another. One kind of trust (bonding social capital) needs to be established amongst educators within schools and another kind of trust (bridging social capital) needs to be developed with educators working outside of schools, in ministries of education and teacher unions, for example. (p. 10)

An Ontario teacher discussed the importance and benefits of developing supportive relationships and a wider professional network:

Closer cooperation with colleagues at school: First and foremost, NORCAN has been working together. We have worked closely with the working group at the school, and there have been meetings and cooperation with students, teachers and management from the other schools in the project … The project has provided me with a large network of committed educators who always stand up as discussion partners, with tips and advice when I need it. (Quoted in Shirley, 2019, p. 19)

As well as an expanded professional network, participants spoke of developing strong interpersonal relationships, collegiality, and friendships. NORCAN also engaged students in developing new relationships with each other and with the educators involved. For example, a Norwegian student reflected:

NORCAN has inspired me for life. It was a sense of belonging and fellowship that became so clear to me. A bridge of trust was built between the teachers and students, which will be absolutely essential for collaboration … On this trip I have developed eternal friendship with students from other cultures. NORCAN has, and will forever, affect my life and view of learning. (Quoted in Shirley, 2019, p. 23)

Therefore, school-to-school collaboration required the design and development of collaborative structures and process *and* mutually trusting and reciprocal relationships over time.

Student Voice, Agency, and Leadership

The involvement of students proved to be extremely valuable learning for the students themselves and for the educators, teacher union leaders, and government officials involved. For example, an Alberta principal commented:

The partnerships succeeded most when initial questions as practitioners were often shown to be the wrong questions. What I mean is thanks to the student involvement they showed us that we already had the answer to our question within the way we thought of the question. (Quoted in Shirley, 2019, p. 13)

Students' different ways of seeing things, their experiences, voices, and leadership were important in changing both professional and student perspectives. As Shirley (2019, p. 5) notes:

> Including students as co-leaders in educational change as a design principle in NORCAN provided assets to all … this is because when students accompany educators on school exchanges to foreign jurisdictions, they notice things that educators overlook … When students are given opportunities to explain what things they like or dislike about a discipline such as mathematics, as has occurred in NORCAN exchanges, they are not only gaining opportunities to learn new ways to solve problems, they are also learning that their educators care about them as part of a united profession.

An Ontario provincial leader commented that through the collaborative team work in NORCAN, senior provincial leaders, educators, and students co-learned together in non-hierarchical ways:

> The nice thing about NORCAN was that people from the Ministry and from the union got to connect with kids around these questions – and the result was that a lot of learning is happening that isn't tied to our roles. (Quoted in Shirley, 2019, p. 13)

School-to-school collaborations directly involving students can be beneficial for supporting educators to learn with and from students in new ways.

Students appreciated when their ideas and suggestions informed changes in the culture and practices in their own schools and raised concerns when this did not happen. For the students, being part of NORCAN enabled them to visit and see new contexts, including for some leaving their home community and/or being on an aeroplane for the first time. One Ontario student spoke of the benefits of these opportunities:

> It was an amazing opportunity to partner with schools across the world to share our ideas and learn from one another. It not only gives us a chance to find out about new ideas, but it helps us to better appreciate our own learning environment when we see that other schools are fascinated about what we do. (Quoted in NORCAN Ontario Partners, 2019, p. 14)

The students learned about the importance of student voice, advocacy and leadership. For example, students collaborated on a video called 'This Is My Voice' discussing what they had learned about student voice and how they could be the change. An Ontario student reflected:

> I learned how important student voice is, and that by speaking up and advocating for what we believe in, we can truly make a

difference. I will continue to use my voice in the future, to advocate for myself, for causes that I believe in, and for others who cannot advocate for themselves. (Quoted in NORCAN Ontario Partners, 2019, p. 14)

For another Ontario student, the experience had re-enforced their career choice to become a teacher and informed their intention to value student voice:

I want to become a teacher and having this experience only amplified that thought ... student voice and involvement is something I will incorporate into my teaching in the future. (Quoted in NORCAN Ontario Partners, 2019, p. 5)

While there can be purposes for exclusively professional collaboration, NORCAN demonstrates that directly involving students in school-to-school collaboration provides opportunities for students' learning, voice, agency, and leadership and also changes (and improves) professional learning.

Professional Learning and Agency

The core of NORCAN is a commitment to professional learning and agency. Importantly, a teacher union from each participating education system led this programme, plus the Ontario Ministry of Education, with dedicated resources and supports for educators' professionalism, learning, and growth. For the educators involved, NORCAN was a powerful learning and development opportunity. For example, as we identified in our evaluation of Ontario's participation in NORCAN:

Having received release time to collaborate with other mathematics teachers across jurisdictions, attend conferences, view presentations by researchers and thought leaders, and leverage their professional expertise to improve practice and share findings, NORCAN teachers now see themselves as lifelong learners who are tasked with the role of continual improvement and sharing. By having their expertise and perspective acknowledged and valued by leaders, they have learned to value their own voices and advocate for the changes they think are necessary. (Campbell & Alexander, 2019, p. 16)

An Ontario provincial leader explained how NORCAN supported the challenging processes of unlearning, new learning, and relearning:

But embracing ambiguity can lead to powerful learning outcomes. Ambiguity is very uncomfortable for educators because you feel all of this sense of responsibility to your students and your school. The ability to wade through that messiness, in the end, leads to great success. It feels very uncomfortable for that moment, but once you get there it's all worth it. (Quoted in Shirley, 2019, p. 19)

One teacher described how these processes had affected them:

For the teachers involved in NORCAN, there was an opportunity to not just learn, but to unlearn and to challenge assumptions about what we know about students and how they learn best. Teachers had the opportunity to think about our context, and what we can do better, to more creatively meet the needs of students. We reflected on our values as a school, and what that meant, felt and looked like at our school. NORCAN was a great opportunity to look, listen, ask questions and just be curious, as we learned from each other. (Quoted in Shirley, 2019, p. 12)

NORCAN provided an important and impactful professional learning opportunity for participants.

While the complex professional learning processes described above were challenging, they were also described as rewarding, affirming, and rejuvenating by NORCAN participants. For example, another Ontario provincial lead partner described

a sense of connectedness and feeling that you are a part of something bigger (a mentoring web) is inspiring for both students and educators – a sense of personal and professional renewal and rejuvenation via reciprocal learning [has] permeated NORCAN. (Quoted in Shirley, 2019, p. 20)

Participants noted their growing professional sense of efficacy and leadership as they contributed to and learned from the NORCAN network. One Ontario teacher described themselves as feeling 'almost unstoppable' as their confidence had grown and they had demonstrated leadership to superiors and colleagues, while another Ontario teacher said they saw 'no barriers in my way' as they committed to continue to develop their agency, leadership, and impact (Campbell & Alexander, 2019, p. 17). A Norwegian teacher discussed how NORCAN had proven to be an affirming experience as they reflected on their work as a teacher:

In a way, I feel that having been a part of NORCAN has helped me to define myself more clearly in the role of teacher. I've received a good response to what I'm doing in the classroom. I have experienced that my ideas are being tried out and have been an inspiration for others. (Quoted in Shirley, 2019, p. 19)

Another Norwegian teacher reflected on how the process of educators visiting their own classroom had made them look afresh at what to them had become taken-for-granted as ordinary:

I have begun to look at my own practices with a more exploratory glance. The times we have had visits from Canada and I've had teachers and students in my classes, I've been so surprised at what they've noticed, what they think is amazing and what they've been amazed by and/or questioned. What I think is simple and trivial, they can find both exciting and interesting. It has led me to reflect more on my method choices and re-visit the reasons for what I do. (Quoted in Shirley, 2019, p. 12)

It should be noted, however, that changes in learning and practice require supports over time. For example, one teacher explained:

Personally, I dare say that I have gained more self-confidence and confidence in the job – the changes have been invisibly slow. But if I look back four years, I know I didn't speak at the math meetings, I do now! (Quoted in Shirley, 2019, p. 19)

This is consistent with evidence that effective professional learning is sustained and cumulative over a period of time (Campbell et al., 2017b). The experiences from NORCAN indicate that when educators are supported to network and learn together collaboratively with adequate resources of funding and time, it can be re-affirming and renewing for their professional practices.

Sharing Knowledge and De-privatizing Practices

NORCAN involved knowledge mobilization – the explicit sharing of knowledge through professional interaction – and de-privatization of practices through opening up classroom doors, engaging in peer observation, and sharing resources online and in-person. An Ontario participant commented:

Knowledge mobilization is an important outcome of this project. It's worth emphasizing this because that is not common and it's not easy to achieve. It may seem very simple, [but] we should speak about it as an accomplishment when great practice spreads quite far. (Quoted in Shirley, 2019, p. 21)

The NORCAN Ontario Partners' (2019, p. 8) final report reflected that:

By making their thinking public – by 'learning out loud' – NORCAN educators simultaneously extended their own practice, while learning how to teach others about their practice. And in so doing, they developed and grew as leaders in their areas of expertise.

NORCAN involved sharing and changing both knowledge and practices. With NORCAN's focus on mathematics, the conversations and observations within teams and across the different education systems contributed to new ways of considering the subject, teaching, learning, and assessing of mathematics. In particular, having students part of the school teams stimulated students' knowledge about their own understanding of mathematics and contributed to educators' (re)thinking about their assumptions and approaches to mathematics. One area where there were major differences in practice between Canada and Norway was in approaches to assessment. In particular, the Canadian school teams were struck by the use of oral assessments in Norway. As an Alberta school principal recalled:

> By pure luck, the Norwegian schools we visited were in the process of preparing for the Norwegian national oral examinations. Amidst apologies from our Norwegian partners that they were 'only preparing for oral exams', our team gained access to the rich history and practice of oral assessments in all Norwegian schools. The time-honoured tradition of every 15-year old student participating in the Norwegian National Oral Assessment program had seemed unimportant to share with NORCAN partners, as the Norwegian teachers claimed that 'oral assessments are just a regular occurrence within the Norwegian education system, so it didn't seem of importance to share! '(Quoted in Shirley, 2019, p. 11)

The Alberta and Ontario school teams were inspired to start an initiative engaging a wider group of schools in their home education systems to develop new approaches to assessment that draw on a wider range of evidence than current standardized testing in Canada. As an example of the 'overview effect' of seeing yourself differently through international collaboration, the Norwegian participants came to realize that they were doing something unique and of wider interest: 'We are actually sitting on a gold mine with oral assessment, and we've never considered it as an asset' (quoted in Shirley, 2019, p. 12).

The NORCAN Ontario Partners (2019, p. 9) summarized the following examples of changes in practices:

- School Math/Learning Councils.
- Students leading learning for teachers.
- Full-day project-based learning, based on real-life situations.
- Innovative assessment practices.

The Math Councils, for example, were widely regarded as a successful improvement:

> The mathematics council, which was the creation of a principal at Tecumseh who was passionate about bringing student voice to the forefront of mathematics teaching, is a cornerstone of the NOR-CAN community of learning. It is a community where students can learn from their peers within and beyond their schools, and

across borders, and where teachers can apply that learning to their approaches in class. Mathematics councils have been founded in all NORCAN schools and have even spread across districts, enabling more teachers and leaders to enhance student voice and choice in their schools. (Campbell & Alexander, 2019, p. 19)

The Math Councils fostered student leadership and voice. One Norwegian student explained how important this experience had been for them:

> NORCAN has ended up being a big thing in my life. It all started when I joined the math council at my school. Already, I pushed myself out of my own little comfort zone and sought after things I was interested in, despite how scary it seemed at the start. I have always wanted to engage and contribute to change where change is needed. The math council was a great opportunity to try it out. When I finally got the opportunity to be one of the leaders in the math council and then a member of the NORCAN group I was very excited. I got into several new situations and learned a lot. (Quoted in Shirley, 2019, p. 28)

This example demonstrates how collaboration resulted in shared practices across all NORCAN schools, which then spread more widely in their education systems.

Conclusions and Key Lessons for Policy and Practice

At the final wrap up summit for the NORCAN participants, they co-developed the following set of conclusions from their NORCAN experiences:

- building meaningful relationships with all students to draw on the profound power of student voice;
- continuing to have opportunities to investigate our sense of wonder;
- the development of nuanced and practical and varied teaching methods;
- an environment where we can learn from our mistakes and are not penalized for them;
- the culture of the school/classroom can allow for students to articulate what they need to be successful;
- realizing that our education needs to reflect the world we live in, which includes the physical environment of our schools; and
- all learn differently so assessment should reflect this: we feel respected when we are provided multiple opportunities in which to learn, assess and teach. (Shirley, 2019, p. 30)

In this chapter, I have discussed the importance of the development of collaborative structures, processes, relationships, and trust; student voice, agency, and leadership; professional learning and agency; and sharing knowledge and changing practices.

In terms of lessons for policy and practice concerning school-to-school collaboration, I propose the following:

1. *School-to-school collaboration benefits from adequate resources of time, funding, and a support infrastructure.*
   The provision of release time and funding to support travel and events was critical to the success of NORCAN. A support infrastructure for collaborative engagement and activities is also necessary, for example, joint meetings, workshops, and visits. The learning in-between in-person events, for example, through an online platform and regular communication was also critical. The fact that NORCAN continued for four years was also beneficial in supporting participants' learning and changes in knowledge and practice over time.

2. *The intentional cultivation of mutually respectful and trusting relationships is essential.*
   Alongside collaborative structures, the essence of the shared learning among participants is relational. This requires the intentional development of supportive professional relationships and networks and continued collaborative engagement to sustain mutually trusting, respectful relationships.

3. *Bringing together educators and students as co-learners is powerful and beneficial.*
   Careful attention to the composition and working of the collaborative teams is required. The teams should operate as genuinely collaborative and non-hierarchical to support co-learning and improvement. Involving students in the school's collaborative team is very important to support and understand students' learning and experiences and to inform educators' learning and future practices. The collaborative working also needs to be informed by evidence of effective professional learning approaches to meaningfully engage adult learners in relevant and beneficial experiences to inform improved knowledge and practices.

4. *Mobilizing knowledge and de-privatizing practices on an agreed priority focus needs to be central to the purpose and operation of collaboration.*
   Mobilizing knowledge and de-privatizing practices do not simply just happen. In designing the purpose and operation of collaborative working, attention needs to be given to a guiding question or specific priority focus for the collaborative work. It is also important to carefully develop ways in which relevant knowledge will be made explicit and shared and how practices will be observed, documented, and adapted by participants. Examples of such approaches include opportunities for interaction and dialogue, classroom observations, online collaboration, and sharing resources/artefacts from professional practice and student learning.

References

Ainscow, M., & Howes, A. (2007). Working together to improve urban secondary schools: A study of practice in one city. *School Leadership & Management*, *27*(3), 285–300.

Ainscow, M., Muijs, D., & West, M. (2006). Collaboration as a strategy for improving schools in challenging circumstances. *Improving Schools*, *9*(3), 192–202.

Armstrong, P. W., Brown, C., & Chapman, C. J. (2021). School-to-school collaboration in England: A configurative review of the empirical evidence. *Review of Education*, *9*(1), 319–351.

Campbell, C. (2021). Improving education systems in changing times: Observations from Ontario, Canada. *Die deutsche Schule*, *1*, 74–84.

Campbell, C., & Alexander, A. (2019). Teacher identity, professional learning and leadership: An Ontario case study. In P. Cordingley, B. Crisp, P. Johns, T. Perry, C. Campbell, M. Bell, & M. Bradbury (Eds.). *Constructing teachers' professional identities: Appendices – Case studies* (pp. 6–21). Education International.

Campbell, C., Clinton, J., Fullan, M., Hargreaves, A., James, C., & Longboat, D. (2018a). *Ontario: A learning province: Findings and recommendations from the independent review of assessment and reporting.* Government of Ontario.

Campbell, C., Lieberman, A., & Yashkina, A. with Alexander, S. & Rodway, J. (2018b). *The teacher learning and leadership program: Final research report.* Ontario Teachers' Federation.

Campbell, C., Zeichner, K., Osmond-Johnson, P., & Lieberman, A. with Hollar, J., Pisani, S., & Sohn, J. (2017a). *Empowered educators in Canada: How high-performing systems shape teaching quality.* Jossey Bass.

Campbell, C., Osmond-Johnson, P., Faubert, B., Zeichner, K., & Hobbs-Johnson, A. with Brown, S., DaCosta, P., Hales, A., Kuehn, L., Sohn, J., & Steffensen, K. (2017b). *The state of educators' professional learning in Canada: Final research report.* Learning Forward.

Chapman, C. (2008). Towards a framework for school-to-school networking in challenging circumstances. *Educational Research (Windsor)*, *50*(4), 403–420.

Chapman, C., & Hadfield, M. (2010). Realising the potential of school-based networks. *Educational Research (Windsor)*, *52*(3), 309–323.

Edge, K., & Khamsi, K. (2012). International school partnerships as a vehicle for global education: Student perspectives. *Asia Pacific Journal of Education*, *32*(4), 455–472.

Hargreaves, A., & Braun, H. (2011). *Leading for all: A research report of the development, design, implementation and impact of Ontario's "Essential for Some, Good for All" initiative.* Council of Ontario Directors of Education.

Hargreaves, A., & Shirley, D. with Wagnia, S., Bacon, C., & D'Angelo, M. (2018). *Leading from the middle: Spreading learning, well-being, and identity across Ontario.* Council of Ontario Directors of Education.

Hart, D., & Kempf, A. (2018). *Public attitudes towards education in Ontario 2018.* Ontario Institute for Studies in Education.

Hood, C. (1998). *The art of the state, culture rhetoric and public management.* Clarendon Press.

Huang, X. (2018). *Teacher education in professional learning communities lessons from the reciprocal learning project* (1st ed.). Springer International Publishing.

Khoo, Y. (2021). Becoming globally competent through inter-school reciprocal learning partnerships: An inquiry into Canadian and Chinese teachers' narratives. *Journal of Teacher Education*, *73*, 1–13.

Muijs, D. (2015). Improving schools through collaboration: A mixed methods study of school-to-school partnerships in the primary sector. *Oxford Review of Education*, *41*(5), 563–586.

NORCAN Ontario Partners. (2019). *NORCAN – Ontario's learning journey*. Ontario Teachers' Federation.

Ontario Ministry of Education. (2016). PPM 159: Collaborative professionalism. Queen's Printer for Ontario.

Ontario Ministry of Education. (2021). Education facts, 2019-2020. Retrieved October 13, 2021, from http://www.edu.gov.on.ca/eng/educationFacts.html

Ontario Principals' Council (OPC). (2021). Leading student achievement. Retrieved October 14, 2021, from https://www.principals.ca/en/professional-learning/leading-student-achievement-lsa-.aspx

Shirley, D. (2019). *The untapped power of international partnerships for educational change: The Norway Canada Project (NORCAN)*. Utdanningsforbundet.

Velea, S. (2012). Transnational school partnerships supported by ICT. Benefits for learning. In *Conference proceedings of "eLearning and Software for Education" (eLSE) 01* (pp. 377–382).

Walton, J. (2019). Korea … it's not really actually an Asian country': Australian children's experiences of an intercultural school partnership programme. *Ethnography and Education, 14*(3), 264–278.

Chapter 4

Education Groups as a Chinese Way of School Collaboration for Education Improvement

Jing Liu

Abstract

Since the early 2000s, China has been actively promoting school collaboration to narrow down educational gaps between schools to achieve inclusive and quality education for all. Among the reforms, building education groups has become one of the most widely adopted approaches for school improvement. This chapter aims at visualizing a hybrid model of school collaboration formulated by both hierarchist and egalitarian approaches in the Chengdu City of China. It starts with policy review on the construction of education groups for education improvement in China to interpret how social cohesion and regulation are constructed at policy level to promote school collaboration. Through data collected from education groups in District A of Chengdu, it then provides an analysis of the practice of improving education quality through promoting education groups among public schools in this province. The study reveals top-down policy initiatives, bottom-up school autonomy, and a shared responsibility for constructing quality education for all are key factors which enabled education groups to contribute to school improvement. The research also reveals how a lack of policy coordination and limited shared value and trust within education groups have become barriers to this reform. It concludes by discussing possible solutions for further promoting a sustainable school collaboration based on experiences of some ongoing practices at school level.

Keywords: Education Group; school collaboration; top-down initiative; bottom-up autonomy; policy coordination; trust

School-to-School Collaboration: Learning Across International Contexts, 61–75
Copyright © 2022 by Jing Liu
Published under exclusive licence by Emerald Publishing Limited
doi:10.1108/978-1-80043-668-820221005

Introduction

Imbalanced development has become one of the biggest challenges of China's education. Besides rural–urban imbalance, there is imbalance between schools in the same area. This has created competition between schools for education resources, human resources, and students. Similarly, gaps between schools have forced parents and students to compete for limited access to high-performing schools (J. Liu, 2015; Liu, 2018a). This competition has facilitated educational exclusion and inequality between families in different socio-economic statuses in China. Since the early 2000s, the Chinese government has been taking initiatives to balance development of education between regions and schools. On the one hand, the government kept raising investment in education to improve school infrastructure and school facilities. On the other hand, they launched innovative reforms to promote balanced development between public schools. One of the key approaches is to share education resource through school collaboration. The central government encouraged local governments to innovate new approaches to promote educational resource sharing through school collaboration for educational improvement. Among many approaches, the construction of the 'education group' has become one of the most widely adopted ways of school collaboration for balancing educational development among schools. 'Education group' in this study refers to a government-initiated school collaboration (The State Council, 2012), in which high-performing schools and low-performing schools form a group to share a common school brand, management structure, leadership, curriculum, teaching resources, and technological infrastructure. The idea is that grouping high-performing schools with other member schools located in the same area will enhance the capacity and improve educational quality among member schools. This chapter begins by reviewing policies on building Education Groups for school improvement to map out the position of these groups, as a Chinese way of school collaboration. Empirical data generated with stakeholders during the construction of education groups in the Chinese province of Chengdu between 2017 and 2019 are then drawn upon to explore stakeholders' engagement in building such groups and their engagement in this reform. This chapter concludes by reflecting on lessons learned for policy and practice.

Education Groups in China

Currently, there are mainly two organizational models of education groups in China. A one-unit model refers to an education group as a school corporation composed of a lead school (high-performing school) and some member schools (low-performing schools). The principal of the lead school becomes the general principal of the whole group. In addition, the principal has the absolute authority to control capital, personnel, and school management in schools of the group. The principal dispatches school managers and high-performing teachers from the lead school to member schools to share the education brand, the concept and culture of school management, and other resources. In contrast, a loosely coupled model refers to a group which constitutes the lead school (high-performing) and member schools (low-performing) that collaborate for improvement through sharing the education brand, school management structure, and other resources (Meng et al., 2016). Besides collaboration between high-performing schools and low-performing schools in the urban context, local education authorities also encourage high-performing schools in the developed areas to collaborate with the newly established schools in the newly developed areas. They also encourage the high-performing schools to collaborate with rural schools for education improvement.

Education groups have generated positive effects for public education. First, they have widened educational provision and provided more students access to quality teaching and learning. Moreover, they have eased the pressure on parents to compete for limited access to quality education in urban China. Second, such collaboration provided teachers, particularly in the low-performing schools, more quality educational resources and training for teaching and research. These enhanced their capacity in teaching and improved educational quality. Also, this process provided opportunities for school leaders and managers to develop professionally (X. Liu, 2015; Liu, 2018b; Yang, 2014). Nevertheless, concerns have been raised about the challenges of the construction of education groups. As a top-down initiative, this reform may not generate motivation in the schools. Also, group-based collaboration may cause disproportionate development and improvement between schools in the same groups or between schools inside and outside of the groups. With the sharing of brand and educational practice, the reform can also risk homogenizing schools in the groups (Yuan, 2012).

Review of Policies on Construction of Education Groups

The following policy review indicates a policy context of building education groups in China formulated by a hierarchist model with both high social cohesion and high social regulation. On the one hand, there is a top-down policy context which formulated a social regulation for constructing education groups to promote school collaboration for educational improvement from the central government to local government in China. This hierachist regulation gives a clear policy direction to guarantee legitimacy of building education groups to boost education resource sharing and to narrow the achievement gap between public schools. On the other hand, a shared culture and social normal of mutual support in the Chinese society develop into a social cohesion which connects institutions, society, and various networks to response to the policies and collaborate for building education groups.

The term *education groups* emerged in Chinese society with a rapid reform of educational marketization in the early 1990s (Gao & Wei, 2011). With the government support for *minban* education (people-run education), individuals and private institutions were allowed to open vocational schools. In order to scale up impact, these schools collaborated to merge into vocational education groups to accommodate the needs from educational market and industry. Then, the model of education groups was widely adopted by other types of *minban* education to complement diversified demands for public education by society. Entering into the twenty-first century, with a shift from 'efficiency first' to 'equity and balance first', the central government took education groups as a major means to promote school collaboration for educational improvement and balanced development of public schools. Under the philosophy of education resource sharing, the government motivated high-performing public schools to collaborate with low-performing public schools, newly established public schools, and rural public schools to establish a group. The high-performing schools are encouraged to share educational resources, human resources, knowledge of school management, curriculum, and other school activities with other schools in the same group in order to enrich educational resources and improve education quality (Yang, 2014).

Since 2005, the government has advocated that public schools with high-quality education resources should take initiative and exemplary role to combine, merge, or share the quality education resources with the low-performing schools for reconstruction (Ministry of Education, 2005; The Central Committee of the Chinese Communist Party, 2006). Under the philosophy of education resource sharing, the central government launched policies which recommended school collaboration by establishing allies and groups. Moreover, they encouraged the high-performing schools and their teachers to work with teachers of other schools within the same group to conduct joint lesson study, teacher training, workshops, and open classes to enhance teachers' professional development (Ministry of Education, Ministry of Finance, & Ministry of Human Resources and Social Security, 2014; The Central Committee of CCP, 2013; The State Council, 2012).

Moreover, policy on constructing school collaboration was further promoted by the government's initiative of integrated rural–urban development. In order to balance educational development between rural and urban areas, the central government highlighted the role of integration of standards of school construction, teacher assignment, and school subsidy. In 2017, the government advocated 'education group'-based schools running to fulfil the balanced development of compulsory education at county (district) level for the urban–rural integration (The Central Committee of CCP & the State Council, 2010; The General Office of the Central Committee of CPC & the General Office of the State Council, 2017, 2019; The State Council, 2012).

By following the central government's initiative, educational administrations at the city level, key players in respect of policymaking for compulsory education at the local level, took action to develop policy for the construction of education groups. In addition to school infrastructure, the city government in Chengdu gave emphasis to establishing regulations for redistribution of human resources for rural schools, promotion of teacher and school leaders' exchange and rotation between schools in rural and urban areas. In 2009, the city government announced *Opinions on Promoting Development of Education Groups* to further promote exchange of human resource and educational resource between schools (Chengdu City Education Bureau, 2009, 2016). The city government set up extra quota of staff for high-performing schools in order to replace the absence of teachers and school managers who were sent to low-performing schools. Moreover, they provided special funds to reward schools which made progress in the construction of education groups from 2012.

In line with the initiatives taken by the city government, the district government took initiatives to create institutional mechanism to further support promotion of constructing education groups. In District A of Chengdu, they launched '*High-performing Schools Go West Project*' to establish new schools or upgrade rural schools to accommodate the needs for quality education from the new residents. Then, the education authority took initiative to promote the collaboration between the high-performing schools and the newly establish schools and rural schools through establishing education groups. In order to promote human resource exchange between schools in the same education groups, in 2007, the district education authority established a District Educational Human Resources Management and Service Center. With a shift of teacher employment from school based to district based, this reform built an institutional pre-condition for the implementation of rotation of teachers and school leaders within the same district (Yuan, 2012). In addition, they set up an annual quota for the exchange of teachers and school managers to push forward the rotation of human resources between schools in the same groups. They also provided a subsidy to motivate teachers who were sent to work in rural areas. By following the city criteria, the district also established the similar evaluation criteria of development of education groups. A fund was also established for supporting group-based activities and rewarding the best performed education groups. The district education bureau also innovated an 'exit system' whereby the most improved schools were encouraged to leave the group and establish their own groups, while the lowest performing schools would also be advised to leave the group for other institutional reform, such as an assignment of new leadership to the school by the district education bureau or integration of the school with high-performing school.

It is important to highlight that this top-down policy context is supported by social cohesion which refers to a widely shared collective social norm on collaboration in the Chinese society. First, there is a policy tradition which promotes the idea that 'the developed help the underdeveloped' whereby public schools in developed areas have got used to supporting schools in developing areas. Since the 1960s, the central government has been actively encouraging the government of economically developed areas to help the underdeveloped areas. Public schools in developed areas dispatched high-performing teachers to schools in the underdeveloped areas. Also, they donated education facilities and provided teacher training for schools in the underdeveloped areas. Entering the twenty-first century, the government took initiatives to promote the one-on-one assistance between schools in the developed and underdeveloped areas to improve education quality. Second, there is a social norm of collaboration between the rich and the poor which is formed by Deng Xiaoping's philosophy of 'let part of people get rich first, lead and help other regions and people, and gradually achieve common prosperity'. Schools which developed first feel their social responsibility to help those which are underdeveloped (Liu, 2019).

From a policy perspective, a hierarchist model with top-down policymaking and implementation appears to most prominent in relation to the development of education groups in this context. The following section will explore the development of these collaborative structures from the perspective of stakeholder involved.

Constructing Education Groups in Chengdu Province

The process of constructing education groups in District A of Chengdu indicates there is an egalitarian way with low social regulation and high social cohesion for school collaboration to improve education. The district education bureau leaves decision-making rights to schools to choose the management structure within the educational groups. Interviews with stakeholders involved in the process of creating and developing education groups in District A reveal that schools have space to lead on the construction and management of these groups. High social cohesion is formulated by an egalitarian culture and mutual support shared among schools within the same groups. This is also enhanced through a shared responsibility among teachers and school leaders in lead schools and member schools.

Despite the top-down policy initiative of constructing education groups, schools were given legitimatized autonomy at district level to build their groups consensually and decide their own group structure. There are two different types of group structure in District A. One is a loosely coupled model, the other is one-unit model. In a loosely coupled model, a lead school and other member schools of one 'education group' shared school brand, education philosophy, school management structure, teacher training and curriculum. Moreover, this group established a responsibility-sharing management mechanism for schools involved in this group to equally share their responsibility and roles. As Fig. 1 indicates, each member school of Education Group A takes a specific responsibility/role related to group management. And each school will take a different responsibility/role once a year. This allows each member to experience different responsibilities/roles for school management. Furthermore, it provides opportunities for member schools to learn from each other. It also motivated each school to present and share their uniqueness and special programmes with other schools in the same group.

In contrast, in the one-unit model, the lead school takes all responsibility for group management. The principal of the lead school in this model becomes the general principal of the group. On the one hand, this structure unifies school management and enhances the efficiency of decision-making and implementation for school management. On the other hand, it can generate an unequal status between lead and member schools discouraging member schools to collaborate. It also creates a burdensome workload for the lead school principal who is responsible for all school management in the member schools. Interviews with school principals showed that many education groups with the one-unit model have already shifted to the loosely coupled model to save more time and energy for the lead school principals to take care of the development of the lead schools. Education Group B transferred from a one-unit model to a loosely coupled model for this reason, as this principal explains:

> [...] there are five member schools of this group. Therefore, as the general principal, I need to spend one day at one member school to handle the reform and make decision on their school management [...] However, it means there is no time for me to take care

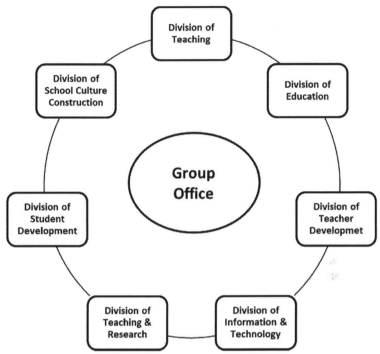

Fig. 1.   Education Group Management Mechanism.

of the lead school [...] sometimes, I even could not have a time to go to my school (lead school) [...] We had concerns that this structure would negatively influence the efficiency and quality of school management in the lead school, from the 4th year, the whole group made a decision to transfer to a loosely coupled model ...

Moreover, the shared management mechanism motivated both lead school and member schools in the same group to take initiatives to fully utilize special education programmes and activities of each school to share and co-create quality education within the same 'education group'. Fieldwork in Education Group A showed schools of this group share responsibility in group management and jointly organize diverse activities for students and teachers in the same group. Every year, each school is in charge of one perspective of the group management, and each school proposes and plans special activities for students and teachers in the same group. This allows each school to share their education resource and experiences and provides opportunities for teachers and school managers to learn from other schools in the same group.

The education groups have served as a platform for the teachers from both lead and member schools to exchange experiences and know-how about teaching and curriculum development. Education Group A organized teachers' competition for teaching skills and curriculum development. Teachers of the same group were encouraged to take part in this annual competition to show their achievement in teaching and exchange experiences in curriculum development. Picture 1 shows a demonstration class from the lead school taking part in this competition held in May 2019. The class fully utilized technology, active learning, and interdisciplinary approach to collaborate with teachers from different subjects to co-teach mathematics.

Opportunities are also provided for students from different schools in the same group to access more education resources and equal opportunities of learning. School B (within of Education Group A) is a newly established school in a newly developed residential area in District A. Before the residential development, this area was populated by internal migrants working in Chengdu, and there were many migrant children who studied in a village school in this area. With the construction of Education Group A, School B merged with the village school and received many migrant children. With the support of the lead school within this group, School B could provide good quality education resources and learning opportunities to migrant children. Moreover, as there was increase in the number of local students in School B, it provided a more inclusive education environment for migrant children. Table 1 indicates how the construction of 'education group' could provide more equal opportunities to migrant children to access to education resource with high quality.

Picture 1.   Education Group Teaching Skills Competition.

Table 1.   Number of Students in School B by Household Registration.

Year	Total	Children With Local Household Registration	Children Without Local Household Registration
2008	636	31	605
2009	859	102	757
2010	921	139	782
2011	976	171	805
2012	1,158	269	889
2013	1,369	440	929
2014	1,614	631	983
2015	1,753	707	1,046
2016	1,762	791	971
2017	1,857	914	943
2018	2,062	1,240	822

Moreover, the exchange of human resources between the lead school and member schools in the same 'education group' creates an institutional norm for promoting educational resources sharing and collaboration for school improvement in the same group. In general, the lead school needs to dispatch a working team (including three to five teachers and school managers) to each member school to support their teaching and school management for three years. The lead schools dispatch teachers and school managers who have expertise which best meet demand from the member schools. The team works with teachers and school managers in the member schools sharing their experiences and educational philosophy. This process is intended to foster a shared norm regarding education which will enhance collaboration among colleagues from both schools. While this process can take time, the dispatched teams from the lead school are seen as the catalyst in this process, as this principal of a lead school elaborates:

> [...] how to construct a consensus between our (the dispatched) team and teachers and school managers in the member schools is one of the key issues which affect the result of this reform (construction of 'education group'). Since the beginning, we emphasized consensus on school values and culture. And the team dispatched to member schools became a catalyst which disseminated our educational concept and philosophy to member schools. Their initiative in explaining these and sharing experience with teachers and school managers in the member schools accelerated this reform ...

In a similar testimony, a teacher at a member school discusses the role of the dispatched team in fostering norms regarding teachers' responsibility to conduct research and develop capacity in this area at the member school:

> [...] before the reform (construction of Education Groups), our school, as a village primary school, did not require teachers to conduct research. I thought my responsibility was to teach my class and keep student safe ... we had no idea of how to conduct research ... with the start of this reform, we learned from the dispatched teachers and school leaders that it is important for teachers to conduct research in order to improve our teaching and education quality ... the collaboration with the dispatched team allowed us to know how to conduct research ... and now teachers in our schools are not satisfied with only completing our class and guaranteeing safety of our students. Rather, we have been motivated to discuss with each other about how to improve our class design and teaching skills. And we have already established a consensus to write research papers on our teaching experiences ...

Aligned to these experiences, Fig. 2 points to the positive influence of joining an education group on teachers' research activities in member school. From 2012, there was an increasing number of research papers published at provincial level by teachers in School B, as a member school of one education group in District A of Chengdu. Teachers in the member schools have been motivated to conduct research on their teaching since their participation in the Education Group in 2009.

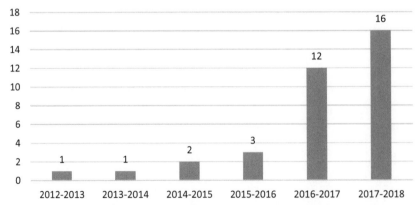

Fig. 2.   Number of Research Papers Published by Teachers at School B.

A shared responsibility within individual schools and between schools within the same education group has facilitated school-to-school collaboration. Interviews with principals of lead schools and member schools reveal a shared reasonability for constructing education groups to improve education quality for all. As a socialist society, adherence to rules and obligations is strongly promoted by the government in China. As most of the principals are Communist Party members, they declared that it is their responsibility for taking part in the reform and taking initiatives in promoting collaboration between schools. Furthermore, as most of the principals of member schools are dispatched from lead schools, they feel it is their duty to disseminate their educational philosophies and experiences to other schools for improving their education and school management.

The experience of building education groups in Chengdu represents a loosely coupled school autonomy among schools in the same groups to engage in building the group for educational improvement. Moreover, a high social cohesion with equal and mutual support initiatives allows teachers and school leaders in the same groups to share knowledge for constructing education groups.

Barriers to Construction of Education Groups

In contrast to the achievements of the reform above, the findings show lack of policy coordination and limited shared value and trust within education groups have become barriers to this reform. For example, the development of education groups cannot be fully realized if there is no policy coordination between the education authority and other related authorities. For example, there is a lack of coordination between policy on subsidy by education authorities and policy on teachers' payment regulation by the finance authority. The district education authority prepared an incentive subsidy for motivating teachers and school leaders to take part in the construction of education groups in 2012. However, with a full implementation of performance-related payment system, schools could not distribute these subsidies to individual teachers as these subsidies were out of category in the payment system. Furthermore, it is necessary to connect incentives related to human resource management of education groups with reform on public servant recruitment. The local authorities provided an extra quota of staff to accommodate the need for extra teachers from the lead schools which need to dispatch their high-performing teachers and school managers to support member schools for three to five years. Nevertheless, the policy was terminated with the reform of public administrative institution by the human resources authority of the central government in 2012. As the reform halted the new recruitment of public servants (including public school teachers and staff), it became impossible for the lead schools to hire extra teachers to fill in their human resource gap. As a result, those local institutional innovations for promoting the construction of education groups became ineffective and the limited policy coordination discouraged school leaders and teachers to engage in the reform.

Interview data also suggest that limited shared values and trust within and between schools in the same education group have created barriers for schools to promote the reform. Mutual respect for shared educational values is central to school collaboration in this context as this member school principal states:

> It is easier for us (member school principals) in this group to work together as all member school principals are dispatched from the lead school. A highly shared value and understanding of educational concept of the lead school allowed us to work closely and efficiently.

Building trust within individual schools is also important for the success of constructing education groups. It is necessary to reach a consensus on educational reality and education concept between team dispatched from lead school to member schools and teachers and school managers in member schools. It takes time and needs communication to foster a mutual understanding between these two groups in order to achieve peer support. It is important for the dispatched team to show their full respect to their colleagues in member schools. One dispatched principal from lead school to member school explains:

> In the beginning, I felt very disappointed as I recognized there was a big gap in understanding of education between myself and teachers in this school (member school) ... I got difficulties in communicating with teachers here regarding how to develop curriculum, how to teach, and how to conduct research ... I could feel that teachers here did not respect me. And there was no mutual trust between us ... It took me five years to fully understand the reality which was very different from my original school. And I told myself that I should not take everything for granted as there are many differences between this school and the lead school ... once I recognized that I could modify my goal for this school step by step. And I tried my best to understand my teachers through talking with them and spending time with them ... gradually, I received increasing support and trust from teachers ...

Reflection and Conclusion

The research presented in this chapter unveils a hybrid model of school collaboration for education improvement in China's context. The construction of education groups as an approach to school collaboration in Chengdu was formulated by both hierarchist and egalitarian approaches (see Fig. 3). On the one hand, there was a top-down policy of building education groups to promote school collaboration for educational improvement from the central government to local government in China. This hierarchist regulation gives a clear policy direction to guarantee legitimacy of building education groups to boost education resource sharing and narrow the gap between public schools. Moreover, the top-down policy initiative of enhancing school infrastructure and promoting human resource

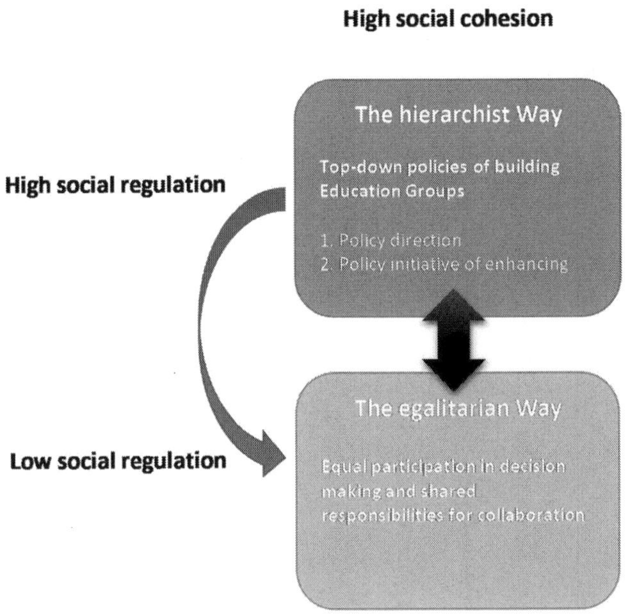

High social cohesion

High social regulation

The hierarchist Way

Top-down policies of building
Education Groups

1. Policy direction
2. Policy initiative of enhancing

Low social regulation

The egalitarian Way

Equal participation in decision
making and shared
responsibilities for collaboration

Fig. 3.   Hood Grid in Chengdu's Context.

exchange between public schools at district level provided a policy context for constructing education groups.

On the other hand, there is an egalitarian approach with low social regulation and high social cohesion for the development of education groups at the school level. Schools received autonomy to construct education groups through their equal participation in decision-making and group management. Moreover, stakeholders involved in this process were encouraged to utilize their specialties and uniqueness to enrich education activities and share know-how of school management. In addition, educational sharing inspired teachers in both lead and member schools to support each other while a shared responsibility between school leaders enhanced school collaboration. Consequently, building education groups in Chengdu enhanced redistribution of education resources, promoted educational resources sharing, guaranteed equal access to quality education for migrant children, and empowered teachers and school managers to improvement education quality for all.

Nevertheless, there are some barriers to this reform. There is a lack of policy coordination between education authorities and other related authorities, such as human resources and finance to work together to coordinate policy consensus for constructing education groups. Moreover, limitation in fostering shared value and trust within individual schools and between schools in the same education groups have become barriers to partnership work.

In summary, there are three key lessons learned from Chengdu's experience of building education groups.

- First, it is necessary to keep balance between top-down policy initiatives and bottom-up autonomy and equal participation between lead schools and member schools. A top-down policy initiative provides high social regulation and policy direction for stakeholders in the development of education groups. At the same time, the bottom-up approach that affords schools some autonomy allows stakeholders to engage in sharing knowledge and resources to build these education groups. How to keep balance between the high and low regulation is a key to the success and sustainability of these collaborative structures.
- Second, how to achieve shared responsibility and build respect and trust among stakeholders is central to formulating high social cohesion that enables stakeholders to be willing to work together to share knowledge and resources.
- Third, it is necessary to ensure policy coordination between education authorities and other related authorities. While this promotes high social regulation, it will also facilitate the development of education groups in this context.

References

Chengdu City Education Bureau. (2009). *Opinions on promoting development of education groups*. Chengdu City Education Bureau.

Chengdu City Education Bureau. (2016). *Opinions on further improvement of development of education groups*. Chengdu City Education Bureau.

Gao, Y., & Wei, Z. (2011). The present situation and developmental trend of educational groups in China (in Chinese). *Journal of Higher Education, 22*(6), 36–42.

Liu, J. (2015). Understanding inequality in public school admission in urban China: Analysis of public discourses on Ze Xiao. *Asian Education and Development Studies, 4*(4), 434–447. https://doi.org/10.1108/AEDS-03-2015-0009

Liu, J. (2018a). *Inequality in public school admission in urban China: Discourses, practices and new solutions*. Springer.

Liu, J. (2018b). Constructing resource sharing collaboration for quality public education in urban China: Case study of school alliance in Beijing. *International Journal of Educational Development, 59*, 9–19. https://doi.org/10.1016/j.ijedudev.2017.09.004

Liu, J. (2019). Development of elite school groups in the context of urban and rural education integration: A case study on Qingyang district in Chengdu (in Chinese). In D. Yang (Ed.), *Annual report on China's education (2019)* (in Chinese) (pp. 204–219). Social Sciences Academic Press.

Liu, X. (2015). A best-know school group: "Chengdu Model" with balanced coverage of high quality education (in Chinese). *Education and Teaching Research, 29*(10), 15–19.

Meng, F., Zhang, L., & She, Y. (2016). Three modes of running schools by group in elementary education in China (in Chinese). *Educational Research, 441*, 40–45.

Ministry of Education. (2005). *Opinions on enhancing the balanced development of compulsory education*. Ministry of Education.

Ministry of Education, Ministry of Finance, & Ministry of Human Resources and Social Security. (2014). *Opinions on rotation of school leaders and teachers in compulsory education schools at county (district) level*. Ministry of Education.

The Central Committee of CCP. (2013). *Decision of the central committee of the communist party of china on some major issues concerning comprehensively deepening the reform*. The 18th Central Committee of the CPC.

The Central Committee of CCP & the State Council. (2010). *Outline of national medium-term and long-term program for education reform and development*. The Central Committee of CCP & the State Council.

The Central Committee of the Chinese Communist Party. (2006). *Resolutions of the CPC central committee on major issues regarding the building of a harmonious socialist society*. Central Committee of the Chinese Communist Party.

The General Office of the Central Committee of CPC & the General Office of the State Council. (2017). *Opinions on deepening reform of education system and mechanism*. The General Office of the Central Committee of CPC & the General Office of the State Council.

The General Office of the Central Committee of CPC & the General Office of the State Council. (2019). *China's educational modernization 2035*. The General Office of the Central Committee of CPC & the General Office of the State Council.

The State Council. (2012). *Opinions on strengthening the balanced development of compulsory education*. The State Council.

Yang, X. (2014). Exploring the new mechanisms of balanced high quality development of regional compulsory education: An example of collective school running (in Chinese). *Research in Educational Development, 24*, 1–9.

Yuan, Z. (Ed.) (2012). *Education quality as the priority for urban-rural integration (in Chinese)*. Educational Science Publishing House.

Section 2

Fatalist Systems

Chapter 5

Barriers for Effective Networking in Competitive Environments: Addressing Distrust and Isolation to Promote Collaboration in the Chilean School System

Mauricio Pino-Yancovic, Álvaro González and Romina Madrid Miranda

Abstract

Evidence suggests that networking can be beneficial to enhance learning in challenging contexts, when there is a shared purpose, trustful relationships, and the development of meaningful collaborative practices. In Chile, the adoption of collaborative network practices has faced some challenges due to the long history of neoliberal policies characterised by hierarchical and market governance that promotes competition over collaboration among schools. Using Hood's (1998) cohesion/regulation matrix, the Chilean education system can be characterized as fatalist, where cooperation among peers is mandated solely to meet external requirements to regulate schools' and practitioners' practice. However, in recent years, collaborative projects have been implemented that are framed and supported in an egalitarian culture, highlighting the importance and value of collaboration and support among peers to develop effective teaching practice. By analysing three experiences of networking in Chile, we identify two barriers for networking, distrust and isolation, and analyze the ways in which these networks attempted to overcome them to sustain effective collaboration. The first experience describes the implementation of the collaborative inquiry networks (CIN) methodology. This programme was designed to facilitate the development of networked leadership capacities of principals and curriculum coordinators to support teachers' practices during COVID-19 in one municipality (Pino-Yancovic &

School-to-School Collaboration: Learning Across International Contexts, 79–90
Copyright © 2022 by Mauricio Pino-Yancovic, Álvaro González and Romina Madrid Miranda
Published under exclusive licence by Emerald Publishing Limited
doi:10.1108/978-1-80043-668-820221006

Ahumada, 2020). In the second, we report on a group of principals who developed focussed interventions in their network of urban primary public schools to enhance the exchange of knowledge and practices among network participants. The third centres on the development of a model to enhance teacher leadership and professional learning in Initial Teacher Education through collaboration in a university–school partnership. Finally, we present some lessons to be considered in similar social and policy environments to successfully introduce a collaborative networked approach.

Keywords: Collaboration; competition; evidence; research; teachers; educational networks

Networking has been advanced as an effective strategy for educational improvement, taking many forms and involving different agents (Ainscow et al., 2006; Brown & Poortman, 2018). Evidence suggests that networking can be beneficial to enhance learning in challenging contexts, when there is a shared purpose, trustful relationships, and horizontal structures that allow the development of meaningful collaborative practices and collective decision-making (Chapman et al., 2016; Rincón-Gallardo & Fullan, 2016).

In several school systems, networking initiatives have been readily adopted and supported by policy arrangements that provide incentives to collaboration (e.g., Armstrong & Ainscow, 2018; Azorín & Muijs, 2017; Brown & Flood, 2019; Chapman et al., 2016; Lee et al., 2012). In Chile, the adoption of networking as an improvement strategy has faced some challenges due to the long history of neoliberal policies characterized by hierarchical and market governance that promotes competition over collaboration among schools (González et al., 2020a). Central to this is the replication of a market logic in education where families are seen as consumers. Based on Hood's (1998) cohesion/regulation matrix, the Chilean education system can be described as a *fatalist*, where social cohesion is low and regulation is high. This fatalist system promotes individual competition over collaboration, and cooperation is mandated solely to meet external requirements to regulate schools' and practitioners' practice, curtailing the possibility of implementing effective networking practices, as there are no tangible incentives for professionals to share their practices and knowledge (Pino-Yancovic & Ahumada, 2020; Pino-Yancovic et al., 2019); on the contrary, individualism seems to be more useful to meet externally the mandated requirements of the high-stakes accountability system in Chile (Falabella, 2020; Munoz-Chereau et al., 2020).

Moreover, because the education system relies so much on competition for parental preference as a driver for improvement, practitioners are not incentivized to engage in the sharing of knowledge and best practices (Pino-Yancovic, 2015; Pino-Yancovic et al, 2019). Nevertheless, and despite the paradoxical circumstances, in recent years, there has been a clear intention in the education policy landscape to keep pursuing the development of school networks for educational improvement (Pino-Yancovic et al., 2019), although they have faced important barriers to initiate and sustain effective collaboration (Montecinos et al., 2021; Pino-Yancovic et al., 2020).

By analysing three cases of networking in Chile, in this chapter, we identify two key barriers for networking, namely distrust and isolation, and the way in which networks attempted to overcome these barriers to sustain effective collaboration. The first experience describes the implementation of the collaborative inquiry networks (CIN) methodology to support collaboration between schools in one municipality, and its results promoting leadership capacities in principals and curriculum coordinators. This example reflects on the challenge faced by leaders using a new methodology that disrupts the hierarchical culture of the municipality, breaking schools' isolation and reframing previous relations to increase trust. The second comes from a professional development (PD) programme for systemic leaders, where a group of principals developed focussed interventions in their network of urban primary public schools to enhance the exchange of knowledge and practices among network participants. This programme required to develop actions to increase interpersonal trust and attempting to break with isolation before being able to mobilize knowledge for collaborative purposes. The third centre on the development of a model to enhance teacher leadership and professional learning in Initial Teacher Education through collaboration in a university–school partnership. The experience illustrated how the network creates a space for building trust relationships among teacher educators, schoolteachers, and pre-service teachers.

Case 1: CIN: A Path for Learning During Critical Challenges

Collaborative inquiry, as presented in this chapter, is participatory action research, focussed on the professional practices of teachers and managers, whose purpose is to understand and improve the teaching and learning processes (Carpenter, 2017; Chapman et al., 2016; Emihovich & Battaglia, 2000; Pino-Yancovic et al., 2019). This methodology is implemented in a cyclical process, where common challenges for schools are identified, joint actions are planned and carried out, and the results of these actions are reflected on (DeLuca et al., 2015; Pino-Yancovic & Ahumada, 2020).

The CIN programme had of 54 participants, 27 principals, and 29 curriculum coordinators. Six network teams have been formed, to build group identity in each one, a fantasy name has been devised, and the teams vary between 3 and 6 schools. Due to the pandemic and its socio-educational effects, this programme was adapted during 2020 to be carried out virtually and with the general objective of supporting leadership processes and school improvement, through collaborative online inquiry, considering priority lines of action in the context of the Coronavirus crisis.

Regarding the first stage of the collaborative inquiry methodology, namely 'identification of common challenges', most of the teams defined a pedagogical focus and some a focus on emotional support. The projects focussed on the following challenges: (A) supporting teachers for the design and implementation of formative assessment strategies with their students; (B) identify indicators that allow the implementation of formative evaluation practices; (C) evaluate the development of cognitive abilities in students to form a recovery plan when returning to face-to-face classes; and (D) adapt distance learning teaching processes to respond appropriately to the socio-educational context of students and their families. Regarding the focus of emotional, the challenges are the following: (A) identify and promote safety and a socio-emotional accompaniment to the educational community in the face-to-face return to classes; and (B) encourage collaboration to develop professional trust among teachers. For each challenge, the participants have proposed an inquiry question in order to specify their collaborative inquiry projects.

Regarding the second stage of the collaborative inquiry methodology, corresponding to 'inquiry and action', the network teams have established an action plan and executed it as network teams. In these network projects, the number of educational actors and actions varies according to their emphasis, where management teams, teachers from kindergarten to eighth grade and exceptionally psychosocial pairs have been involved. This allowed them to work collaboratively to share knowledge and develop skills among the professionals of the schools. Many of the teams promote collaboration, holding workshops for teachers and socio-emotional support staff to share strategies that promote collaboration in their schools, to distribute these practices and promote these practices, and some teams designed and applied questionnaire to identify the development of cognitive skills in students.

In the monitoring and reflection phase, the results of the actions that the network teams have implemented to respond to their challenges were analyzed. Throughout the project, participants answered reflection questions that aimed to learn about their contributions to the work of the network and what learning took place in it were members highlighted how this project allowed them to collaborate with other, creating meaningful professional relationship of solidarity and mutual support. Among the results of project, it stands out that the exercise of collecting information and implementing actions collectively entails a validation of the teaching work, since they are actively involved in the prioritization of educational challenges. In this sense, the recognition of teaching work is considered as a source of motivation for them, generating a positive effect on the organizational climate from the empowerment of leadership and a participatory and democratic focus. In addition, it has made it possible to identify and build new initiatives for pedagogical work, carrying out actions that are of interest to them, especially from the remote modality that has characterized this year.

Responses from participating principals, curriculum coordinators, and teachers indicate that the collaborative work tool and prior knowledge of the diversity of practices and experiences of other schools are the most valuable elements for them. They also highlight the creativity, innovation, and adaptability of other teachers to address the challenges that arise in schools. This example reflects on the challenge faced by leaders using a new methodology that disrupts the hierarchical culture of the municipality, breaking schools' isolation and reframing previous relations to increase trust.

Case 2: Enhancing Trust in a School Improvement Network

In 2015, the Chilean Ministry of Education (MINEDUC) developed and launched the school improvement networks (SIN) strategy to support public-municipal schools. These networks grouped between 5 and 10 schools, each represented by their principal and curriculum coordinator, in addition to a ministry supervisor and a representative of the municipal department of education. SIN seeks to create a space for leaders to obtain information about relevant policies, address shared problems they face in their schools, share successful experiences, develop joint practices, and learn collectively from their peers (Mellado Hernández et al., 2020; Pino-Yancovic et al., 2019).

During the 2019 school year, a group of principals, curriculum coordinators, ministry supervisors, and professionals from municipal departments of education took part in a system leadership PD programme. This programme was designed and implemented by a university-based educational leadership centre, and it entailed applying the programme's key contents to develop a focussed intervention in their SINs, aimed at strengthening the conditions for collaboration and enhance the exchange of knowledge and practices among network participants (see Ahumada-Figueroa et al., 2016; González et al., 2018). Among the participants of this programme was a group of four principals who had been participating in an SIN with other four schools from the same urban municipality for two years. Their network met once a month in four-hour sessions, with schools alternating as hosts. The time of each session was devoted to delivering information about educational policies promoted by the ministry and presenting successful experiences of the host school. All network meetings were led by the ministry supervisor based on the official guidelines for the SIN strategy.

As part of the PD programme, this group of principals developed a diagnosis of their network to analyze its internal organization and impact on participant leaders and their school practices. This diagnosis served as a self-evaluation experience that helped stimulate collaboration and peer learning within the network. To do this, they applied a survey provided by the PD facilitators (Pino-Yancovic et al., 2019), conducted interviews with the ministry supervisor and municipality representative, and led a workshop to explore relationships among network members. They found that there was demotivation of the participants regarding the work of the network because the methodologies were not participatory, and the topics addressed were not in accordance with their needs. In addition, they found evidence of unidirectional relationships between the network members and the ministry supervisor who defined the topics to be addressed in each network meeting, while the concerns of the participating school leaders took a backseat and were only encouraged to present successful experiences to their peers.

The principals who conducted the diagnosis presented their results and discussed them with their peers from the SIN. This process of collective analysis led them to conclude that there was little clarity about the purpose of their SIN and a low level of trust among the members of the network. This represented a barrier to sustain an effective collaboration where different members of the network felt safe to expose their needs for improvement, identify common challenges, implement solutions collectively, and promote distributed leadership.

To address these challenges and produce effective collaboration, school principals who participated in the PD programme proposed to the ministry supervisor to reorganize the way they plan and lead network sessions. First, they set up a small coordination team that would meet prior to each monthly session to plan activities that would stimulate bidirectional communication and relationships. Second, they reduced the time spent relaying information about ministry policies and spent more time on activities aimed at improvement needs from schools and fostering distributed leadership within the network. Third, they established two specific methodologies to strengthen the technical (use of data) and social (trust) aspects of collaboration between school leaders.

To address the technical challenge, the directors who participated in the PD programme used an instrument called 'Diagnosticography', which consists of a data dashboard that represents elements of context, actions or strategies, results, and perceptions. It was highly valuable that school leaders were able to share their data and information and reflect upon the reality of each school. Participants were also able to leave aside concerns about exposing perceived 'weaknesses' to their competitors that might hamper meaningful exchange and collaboration. To address the social challenge, the directors used an instrument they called 'Moodmeter' which took the form of a thermometer and helped to know and share the mood of each participant at the beginning and end of the monthly meetings. With this, they observed how a person's mood and emotions evolve during the session and become a positive practice to get to know each other and generate a higher level of trust. Giving importance to emotions was essential to be able to carry out a more adequate intervention in the SIN, to create deeper ties between the participants of the network.

The intervention led by the principals in their SIN delivered some satisfactory results. Among the effects reported in the network, it was possible to establish a common purpose, focussed on strengthening support for the most disadvantaged students, which is worked and reflected through collaborative work activities. In addition, all school leaders were able to present their schools' achievements and challenges through confidence-building work and collectively analyze their data and information. As a result, the members of the network validated this workspace as valuable and began to participate more frequently, contributing ideas and solutions. They were interested in communicating and taking responsibility for fulfilling the tasks defined by the network. These results are reflected in two quotes taken from the evaluation carried out by the group of principals who participated in the PD programme.

> I believe we have established a baseline for collaboration, as we have given relevance to build associations based on common interests and motivations, which makes sense with the network structure, and its methodology is close and motivating. This allows to relax the atmosphere, generate trust and promote the participation of all. (Principal)

The SIN was without a clear goal; it was only to meet external requirements. In each network meeting a new topic was addressed, there was no continuity and there was no visible result. Currently the network is active, there is a common thread between meetings. There are results that can be visualized. In summary, between last year's meetings (2018) and the current ones, a substantial change has been produced. Now it makes me want to go to network meetings! (Curriculum coordinator)

Case 3: 'Research Teams': Towards the Development of a Networked Learning System

The Research Teams are part of a university-led initiative, organized into two cohorts (each lasting one year) over a three-year period, supported by the Chilean government. The aim is to strengthen Initial Teacher Education by developing professional capacity through the link between the university and the school system for the benefit of joint teaching and school-based research. The initiative seeks to be a catalyst for the development of a network learning system (NLS), which has been defined as an educational system that:

> is connected through networks across different types of boundaries. These may be physical (e.g. classroom, organisational, geographical) and/or professional (e.g. phase, sector, curricula) and is driven by design-based research and collaborative enquiry to innovate, test and refine practice and to build leadership capacity through practice-based professional learning. (Madrid Miranda & Chapman, 2021, p. 5)

A key purpose of the Research Teams is to build an inter-professional learning community that is based on mutual trust and respect. The initiative is underpinned by the following core principles:

- Professional and relational trust
- Capacity building
- Learning community
- Research-informed professional learning

The initiative involves Initial Teacher Education (ITE) staff, schoolteachers, and pre-service teachers forming *Research Teams* that design, implement, and conduct collaborative research on school-based problems of practice. As a result of this work, it is expected that each Research Team sends an academic article for publication.

The first cohort of participants started in March 2020 and involved six Research Teams of a total of 24 participants. The teams undertook biweekly meetings during the first six months and monthly meetings during the final six months of the initiative. These meetings reunited Research Teams with the coordinator team and the external adviser, who acted as 'critical friends' focussing on the development of collaborative research and the NLS and drew out the learning and lessons from the process. Additionally, each Research Team met regularly as a group to work in their research project.

The Research Teams initiative seeks to enhance teacher leadership and professional learning in Initial Teacher Education through collaboration in a university–school partnership. Findings from the first cohort of participants illustrated how the network creates a space for exploring more horizontal and less isolated professional relationships among teacher educators, schoolteachers, and pre-service teachers, which disrupts the artificial historical divide between education research and practice.

One of the main characteristics of this school–university collaboration is that it integrated, in the process of developing a school-based research project, people with different roles, levels, and areas of expertise. These three diverse roles (schoolteachers, ITE staff, and pre-service teachers) are part of two institutional cultures that have a long tradition of hierarchical relationships, which the collaborative model of the initiative aims to disrupt by establishing a horizontal structure and values in place. In the process, participants learned about each other's professional context, and a deeper sense of respect and empathy for each other's world was developed: 'I feel I have gained a better understanding of teacher's day to day work and because of that I have a bigger respect for their professionalism' (ITE staff 1).

By interrupting the hierarchical structure between school and university, the initiative allowed participants to gain a new perspective around the need and use of research in a new way, where theory both emerged from and in turn fed onto practice. Some talked about how the initiative met the need to complement theory and practice, and particularly articulating clinical experiences with research. For ITE staff who were part of the cohort, this was important as they were expected to dedicate most of their time to direct teaching. For schoolteachers' participants, this meant losing the 'fear' of conducting research 'I began this project feeling a lot of fear because I did not have any previous experience doing research nor collaborating with ITE staff' (Schoolteacher 4) and then felt it as part of their teaching work 'I never understood as now the value of research and how it can informed my daily work as teacher' (Schoolteacher 3).

Teacher isolation has been recognized as one of the main challenges that constitutes teachers' work, and it has become a source of concern especially for first-year teachers not only in Chile but worldwide (Schlichte et al., 2005). ITE educators also experience isolation, and these experiences have become worse in the current context of pandemic (González et al., 2020b; Socolovsky, 2020). In the sessions, participants reflected on how the initiative offered a space to engage in collaborative learning 'I felt in the session we were able to learn together' (ITE staff 2). ITE staff highlighted specific learning they gained from sessions that were led by colleagues around doing collaborative academic writing and qualitative analysis. 'I remember the session led by Theresa when she taught us how to structure the article' (ITE staff 5).

Concluding Remarks

The analysis of the three experiences points towards distrust and isolation among network partners as significant barriers for successful networking and effective collaboration. We argue that both barriers emerge from the marketization and hierarchical organization of the Chilean education system, as previously explained as a fatalist society based on Hood's (1998, cited by Chapman, 2019). The logic of individual rewards and sanctions from accountability policies maintains a logic of competition that fosters distrust and drives people and schools to isolate. Nevertheless, all three cases show ways in which network arrangements and the values that underpinned them can address and overcome these barriers.

The CIN case reflects on the challenge faced by leaders using a new methodology that disrupts the hierarchical culture of the municipality, breaking schools' isolation and reframing previous relations to increase trust. In the system leadership PD programme, developing actions to increase interpersonal trust and attempting to break with isolation was key for the four principals to create the necessary conditions to mobilize knowledge for collaborative purposes among their peers. The experience of the ITE network of Research Teams illustrated how the network creates a space for building trust relationships among teacher educators, schoolteachers, and pre-service teachers, enhancing teacher leadership and professional learning.

In the context of the COVID-19 pandemic, issues of distrust and isolation might become more disruptive if the policy environment does not introduce incentives and structures suitable for collaborative work. Also, collaboration has emerged in some cases intuitively as the way to overcome difficulties in education systems (Honigsfeld & Nordmeyer, 2020). During this unprecedented time, principals, teachers, students, and parents have been faced with addressing new and emerging problems with creativity and flexibility. The three examples presented here show how, despite the fatalist culture of the Chilean school system, the provision of adequate conditions for the implementation of networking initiatives can enhance social cohesion, collective professional learning, and joint practice development, which can become vital to respond to the changing circumstances.

Summarizing, the three cases offer key lessons that could be considered by other school systems attempting to introduce a networked approach in similar policy environments:

- First, it is crucial to attend the social aspect of networked collaboration, investing time and effort for people to get to know each other and find common ground about the issues that they wish to address; there is no point in devising collaborative arrangements if we do not pay attention to the ties that bind them together.
- Second, networks need to translate their common goals into concrete outcomes that are relevant for participants; thus, people who participate in the network will be able to see how the time and effort invested in the collaborative work with others translates in new and better practices in their own schools.

- Third, the well-being of everyone is a central aspect of any social group, and networks can be a good vehicle to offer social and emotional support to people by encouraging self- and group-care practices. Fourth and final, networking and collaboration is strengthened when it is developed based on an inquiry mindset based on horizontal professional relationships, allowing the meaningful transformation of practices.

Acknowledgement

Support from ANID/PIA/Basal Funds for Centers of Excellence FB0003 is gratefully acknowledged.

References

Ahumada-Figueroa, L., Pino-Yancovic, M., González, Á., & Galdames, S. (2016). *Liderazgo Sistémico: 7 Lecciones para la Formación de Líderes Educativos que Aprenden en Red*. Nota Técnica No. 5. LIDERES EDUCATIVOS, Centro de Liderazgo para la Mejora Escolar. http://www.lidereseducativos.cl/recursos/liderazgo-sistemico-7-lecciones-para-la-formacion-de-lideres-educativos-que-aprenden-en-red/

Ainscow, M., Muijs, D., & West, M. (2006). Collaboration as a strategy for improving schools in challenging circumstances. *Improving Schools*, 9(3), 192–202. https://doi.org/10.1177/1365480206069014

Armstrong, P. W., & Ainscow, M. (2018). School-to-school support within a competitive education system: Views from the inside. *School Effectiveness and School Improvement* 29(4), 614–633. https://doi.org/10.1080/09243453.2018.1499534

Azorín, C. M., & Muijs, D. (2017). Networks and collaboration in Spanish education policy. *Educational Research*, 59(3), 273–296. https://doi.org/10.1080/00131881.2017.1341817

Brown, C., & Flood, J. (2019). *Formalise, prioritise and mobilise: How school leaders secure the benefits of professional learning networks*. Emerald Professional Learning Network Series.

Brown, C., & Poortman, C. (2018). *Networks for Learning: Effective collaboration for teacher, school and system improvement*. Routledge.

Carpenter, D. (2017). Collaborative inquiry and the shared workspace of professional learning communities. *International Journal of Educational Management, 21*(1), 17–28.

Chapman, C. (2019). From hierarchies to networks: Possibilities and pitfalls for educational reform of the middle tier. *Journal of Educational Administration, 57* (5), 554–570. https://doi.org/10.1108/JEA-12-2018-0222

Chapman, C., Chestnutt, H., Friel, N., Hall, S., & Lowden, K. (2016). Professional capital and collaborative inquiry networks for educational equity and improvement? *Journal of Professional Capital and Community*, 1(3), 178–197. https://doi.org/10.1108/JPCC-03-2016-0007

DeLuca, C., Shulha, J., Luhanga, U., Shulha, L. M., Christou, T. M., & Klinger, D. A. (2015). Collaborative inquiry as a professional learning structure for educators: A scoping review. *Professional Development in Education, 41*(4), 640–670.

Emihovich, C., & Battaglia, C. (2000). Creating cultures for collaborative inquiry: New challenges for school leaders. *International Journal of Leadership in Education, 3*(3), 225–238. 225–238.

Falabella, A. (2020). The ethics of competition: accountability policy enactment in Chilean schools' everyday life. *Journal of Education Policy, 35*(1), 23–45. https://doi.org/10.1 080/02680939.2019.1635272

González, Á., Améstica, J. M., & Allendes, P. (2018). *Seguimiento a egresados del Diplomado en Liderazgo Sistémico y Aprendizaje en Red, cohorte 2017: Lecciones y desafíos para promover colaboración y aprendizaje en redes escolares.* Nota técnica N°10. LIDERES EDUCATIVOS, Centro de Liderazgo para la Mejora Escolar. https://www.lidere seducativos.cl/wp-content/uploads/2018/12/NT10.pdf

González, Á., Ehren, M. C. M., & Montecinos, C. (2020a). Leading mandated network formation in Chile's new public education system. *School Leadership & Management, 40*(5), 425–443. https://doi.org/10.1080/13632434.2020.1783649

González, Á., Fernández, M. B., Pino-Yancovic, M., & Madrid, R. (2020b). Teaching in the pandemic: Reconceptualizing Chilean educators' professionalism now and for the future. *Journal of Professional Capital and Community, 5*(3/4), 265–272.

Honigsfeld, A., & Nordmeyer, J. (2020). Teacher collaboration during a global pandemic. *Educational Leadership, 77*(10), 47–50.

Hood, C. (1998). The Art of the State, Culture Rhetoric and Public Management. Oxford: Clarendon Press.

Lee, M., Seashore Louis, K., & Anderson, S. (2012). Local education authorities and student learning: The effects of policies and practices. *School Effectiveness and School Improvement, 23*(2), 133–158.

Madrid Miranda, R., & Chapman, C. (2021). Towards a network learning system: Reflections on a university initial teacher education and school-based collaborative initiative in Chile. *Professional Development in Education,* 1–15. https://doi.org/ 10.1080/19415257.2021.1902840

Mellado Hernández, M. E., Rincón-Gallardo, S., Aravena Kenigs, O. A., & Villagra Bravo, C. P. (2020). Acompañamiento a redes de líderes escolares para su transformación en comunidades profesionales de aprendizaje. *Perfiles Educativos, 42*(169), 52–69. https://doi.org/10.22201/iisue.24486167e.2020.169.59363

Montecinos, C., González, Á., & Ehren, M. (2021). From hierarchy and market to hierarchy and network governance in Chile: Enhancing accountability, capacity and trust in public education. In M. Ehren & J. Baxter (Eds.), *Trust, Accountability and Capacity in Education System Reform* (pp. 201–221). Routledge: Global Perspectives in Comparative Education. https://doi.org/10.4324/9780429344855-10

Munoz-Chereau, B., González, Á., & Meyers, C. V. (2020). How are the 'losers' of the school accountability system constructed in Chile, the USA and England? *Compare: A Journal of Comparative and International Education,* 1–20. https://doi.org/10.108 0/03057925.2020.1851593

Pino-Yancovic, M., & Ahumada, L. (2020). Collaborative inquiry networks: The challenge to promote network leadership capacities in Chile. *School Leadership and Management, 40*(2–3), 221–241. https://doi.org/10.1080/13632434.2020.1716325

Pino-Yancovic, M., González, Á., Ahumada, L., & Chapman, C. (2020). *School improvement networks and collaborative inquiry: Fostering systemic change in challenging contexts.* Emerald Publishing.

Pino-Yancovic, M. (2015). Parents' defense of their children's right to education: Resistance experiences against public school closings in Chile. *Education, Citizenship and Social Justice. 10*(3), 254–265.

Pino-Yancovic, M., Gonzalez Parrao, C., Ahumada, L., & Gonzalez, A. (2019). Promoting collaboration in a competitive context: School improvement networks in Chile. *Journal of Educational Administration, 58*(2), 208–226. https://doi.org/10.1108/ JEA-11-2018-0213

Rincón-Gallardo, S., & Fullan, M. (2016). Essential features of effective networks in education. *Journal of Professional Capital and Community, 1*(1), 5–22. https://doi.org/10.1108/JPCC-09-2015-0007

Schlichte, J., Yssel, N., & Merbler, J. (2005). Pathways to burnout: Case studies in teacher isolation and alienation. *Preventing School Failure: Alternative Education for Children and Youth, 50*(1), 35–40.

Socolovsky, Y. (2020). Preguntas a la coyuntura. Reflexiones, problemas y preocupaciones acerca del trabajo docente, el uso de las tecnologías y las desigualdades ante la pandemia. *Trayectorias Universitarias, 6*(10), 1–8.

Chapter 6

Interprofessional Collaboration Between Childcare Services and Primary Schools in the Netherlands

Trynke Keuning, Rachel Verheijen-Tiemstra, Wenckje Jongstra and René Peeters

Abstract

In the Netherlands, childcare and primary schools are governed by two different systems of two ministries, and although these institutes are usually located nearby, there always have been low levels of cohesion with respect to institute-to-institute collaboration. However currently, there is a national trend in enhancing interprofessional collaboration (IPC) with the aim of inclusion and equity. This study focuses on getting insight into the differences in intensity of collaboration and how IPC is organized. A two-dimensional Child Centre Integration Model which accounts for the variations in the degree of IPC in child centres and gives insight into IPC at different levels and into conditions for intensifying IPC is presented. That Dutch education and childcare systems do not connect with each other is seen to be an important cause of the failure or complication of IPC. Because the systems do not connect at the macro level, we see struggles in the necessary normative dimension due to status differences (i.e., inequality between employees) and differences in funding and autonomy. Differences between public (education) and private (childcare) institutions also lead to difficulties when it comes to fostering closer collaboration. This chapter ends with key lessons for practice and policy, including the suggestion that one strong ministry for child affairs, including education and childcare, which stimulates an unambitious course at national level, is required. This course can then be translated at regional and local levels.

Keywords: Interprofessional collaboration; childcare; early childhood education; primary education; child centre; Child Centre Integration Model

School-to-School Collaboration: Learning Across International Contexts, 91–126
Copyright © 2022 by Trynke Keuning, Rachel Verheijen-Tiemstra,
Wenckje Jongstra and René Peeters
Published under exclusive licence by Emerald Publishing Limited
doi:10.1108/978-1-80043-668-820221007

Introduction

Unlike in most European countries, there is a separation in the Netherlands between childcare services and primary schools (van der Werf et al., 2021). Childcare services include day care for children from 0 to 4 years old, early childhood education (ECE) at playgroups for children from 2½ to 4 years old and out-of-school care (OSC) (before and after school) for children from 4 to 12 years old. The separated system of childcare services and primary school includes different settings, authorities, staff qualifications and educational guidelines. The Netherlands is the only country in Europe that relies on a market-driven system for childcare services for children under four, and the monthly fees are relatively high in comparison with other European countries. Yet, there are subsidies for targeted ECE programmes aiming to reach children from a disadvantaged background (around 45,000 children). Regarding OSC, the situation appears to be similar: with recent research (Fukkink & Boogaard, 2020; Verheijen-Tiemstra et al., 2020) concluding that there are few links between OSC and primary schools. However, in the past decade, we have seen a trend towards more collaboration between professionals in childcare organizations and primary schools (van der Grinten et al., 2019). We define this interprofessional collaboration (IPC) as the process in which organizations interact with each other to share information, resources, activities and expertise with the aim of achieving a common result (Bryson et al., 2015; Page et al., 2015; Thomson & Perry, 2006; Willumsen, 2006).

In this chapter, we focus on the IPC between childcare services and primary schools, aimed at the creation of continuous learning paths from childcare services through primary school, inclusion of all children and promotion of equal opportunities for children (Fukkink & van Verseveld, 2020). In particular, we focus on what are known as community-based centres or child centres, where various professionals with different types of expertise are situated in the same building working together to optimize children's opportunities for development.

First, we describe the Dutch childcare and educational systems and relate them to Hood's (1998) social cohesion matrix. Second, we describe the trend towards more IPC in this context. We present the Child Centre Integration Model (CCIM) to study this IPC occurring in child centres and illustrate with two cases how IPC varies between institutions. Enablers and barriers to IPC in this setting are discussed. This chapter ends with concluding thoughts and key lessons for practice and policy.

Dutch Educational and Childcare System: Two Fragmented Systems

In the Netherlands, support for younger children (0–6 years old) is regulated at the macro level by different ministries, as depicted in Fig. 1, with different funding and quality frameworks.

The Ministry of Social Affairs and Employment is responsible for childcare services, including day care (for children ages 0–4) and out-of-school childcare facilities – covering the time before and after school (ages 4–12). From the moment

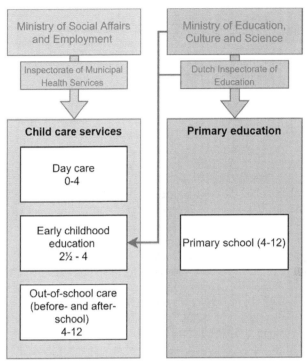

Fig. 1.   The Dutch Childcare Services and Primary Education Systems.

a child is six weeks old until the moment they leave primary school at the age of 12, parents can make use of childcare for their children. Childcare costs are paid partly by the government and partly by parents (income-related) (OECD, 2016). The quality of childcare is monitored at the level of the municipality, by the Municipal Health Services. Among other things, the Municipal Health Service inspectorate looks at group size and the number of children per childcare worker; training of employees; safety, hygiene and health of children; housing and furnishings; pedagogical policy and pedagogical quality; and parental involvement and participation (NJI, n.d.). The inspectorate produces an annual inspection report that is intended for both the institution and the parents.

Childcare services also include ECE. From 2½ to 4 years old, children can attend ECE. This ECE is primarily aimed at children at risk of educational disadvantage. Such risk is calculated based, for example, on the educational level of both parents, the mother's country of origin, the mother's length of stay in the Netherlands and whether the parents are in debt. The precise conditions are determined at the municipal level: with municipalities receiving a budget for ECE for targeted children who are aged 2½–4 years old (OECD, 2016). In addition to targeted children, other children may also attend ECE. This ECE is offered by childcare organizations. As with day care and OSC, the Municipal Health Services assesses the basic quality of ECE. In addition, the quality of ECE is assessed by the Dutch Inspectorate of Education. The quality framework consists of (1) informing parents and parental involvement; (2) quality of the education; (3) development, care and supervision of children; and (4) quality assurance.

The Ministry of Education, Culture and Science is responsible for general education policy and funding. In the Netherlands, full-time education is mandatory for children from 5 to 16 years old. Between the ages of 4 and 12, Dutch children receive primary education. Besides mainstream primary schools, which are attended by nearly all children (95.4%), there are also special schools for primary education for children with more serious learning difficulties (2.4%) and schools for special education for children with specific types of needs (e.g., children who are visually impaired or blind; children with communication problems; children with cognitive or physical abilities; or children with psychiatric or serious behavioural issues) (2.2%) (Onderwijs in cijfers, 2020a).

The Dutch national level Inspectorate of Education monitors the quality of primary schools, in relation to five defined quality areas: 1) educational processes, 2) school climate, 3) learning outcomes, 4) quality assurance and ambition and 5) financial management. The assessment by the inspectorate involves an annual analysis of students' achievement, and an inspection every four years, of governing bodies and schools (Inspectorate of Education, n.d.). The Inspectorate of Education is part of the national government.

Taking this all together, the 'walls' between ministries are also reflected in practice. Traditionally, there is little cooperation between the different child-related organizations. A separation between childcare services (including day care, ECE and OSC) and education is typically apparent in all areas, for example: separate settings, different ministries responsible and different funding (van der Werf et al., 2021). Until recently, there was little cooperation. Schools and childcare providers were very internally oriented. Based on this information, the Dutch education and childcare systems can be characterized as having 'low social cohesion' and 'high social regulation'. In the social cohesion/regulation matrix (Hood, 1998; Malin et al., 2020), these systems can be categorized as following 'the *fatalistic way*'.

Trend Towards IPC in the Netherlands

Recent developments, both nationally and internationally, have caused a shift towards more collaboration between professionals working around children, in practice and policy (Carlson et al., 2017). There are several causes for this shift towards more IPC.

Increased Numbers of Children at Risk in Complex Societies

Large-scale European research on families in societies has shown that more diverse societies are emerging and that there should be a joined up approach: one comprehensive policy to meet the needs of vulnerable children, in which measures from different services are integral, embedded and complementary (Carlson et al., 2017). In the Netherlands, the group of 'vulnerable' children has seemed to increase in recent years: there is a large group of children in intensive youth care (CBS, 2020), increasingly complex problems in regular education (Ledoux & Waslander, 2020) and the number of early school leavers is large (Ministerie van Onderwijs, Cultuur en Wetenschap, 2020). In addition, the number of students in special education has increased in recent years (Onderwijs in cijfers, 2020b). It is precisely this group of children at risk who could benefit greatly if professionals with different areas of expertise joined forces. First, effective IPC could, for example, ensure that potential challenges are identified earlier and can therefore be tackled more quickly or even prevented (Dumčius, 2014; Garvis et al., 2016). In addition, professionals with different areas of expertise have a larger joint repertoire of expertise. Thus, more options can be weighed to guide children's development as optimally as possible.

The Dutch government has expressed the ambition to offer more inclusive education. The education council (Onderwijsraad, 2019) recommends gradually working towards more inclusive education: in other words, a situation where all children can attend a regular school close to home and receive the support and equipment they need. This development requires school leaders and administrators to organize what is necessary to provide this support: 'The preconditions concern people, resources, time, space and expertise' (education council, 2020, p. 8).

Changes in Children's (School) Day

An increasing number of children are experiencing the combination of some form of childcare or out-of-school childcare with their school and home environments. While in 2005 only 345,000 children attended day care or OSC, in 2019 this number more than doubled to 824,000 (Rijksoverheid, 2019; van Oploo et al., 2008). Connecting these different environments has added pedagogical value for children (Doornenbal & Fukkink, 2014). Children can profit from continuous learning paths, for example, from ECE to primary school. And on a more daily basis, good coordination between professionals working around the child can ensure a better connection between the different life worlds in which children grow up, such as the family, school, day care, ECE and after-school care, street and neighbourhood (Doornenbal & de Leve, 2014). In collaboration, complex and less complex issues concerning education, development and instruction can be tackled integrally, instead of being isolated (Doornenbal & de Leve, 2014). In that context, further IPC can also promote broader development of children. By working with partners outside the school and childcare context – such as the music school, sports club or drama club, the broader development of students can be promoted (Vesterinen et al., 2017).

Scarcity of Professionals and Shrinking Rural Regions

Another reason driving a greater need to collaborate is the increasing shortage of professionals in education, childcare, youth care and social work, which requires a different organization of child-related services (CAOP, 2017; ROA, 2019, p. 13).

Also, we see in more shrinking rural areas (i.e., places with fewer and fewer inhabitants, and where the number of children is shrinking) a trend towards having more integrated child centres to keep child facilities up to standard (i.e., by working together and placing various facilities in the same building).

Because of these above-mentioned developments, both practitioners and policymakers feel the need to enhance IPC and break down the walls between education and childcare. IPC between the fields of primary education (4–12) and childcare services (day care, ECE and out-of-school facilities) is more and more held to be essential in order to create alignment in children's pedagogical and learning pathways (Doornenbal & Fukkink, 2014; Onderwijsraad, 2019). In this respect, intensive and structural collaboration between primary schools and childcare centres is essential (SER, 2016; Taskforce Samenwerking Onderwijs en Kinderopvang, 2017). Recent research has shown that currently 9 out of 10 primary schools acknowledge some form of collaboration with one or more childcare organizations and, vice-versa, two-thirds of all childcare organizations indicate collaboration with a primary school (van der Grinten et al., 2019). About a quarter of primary schools and childcare organizations present themselves as (integrative) child centres, which can be compared with community schools or Ganztagschulen. This increased collaboration is reflected in the increasing number of child centres. In other words, there seems to be a trend from low social cohesion towards high social cohesion: the willingness to collaborate increases.

At the same time, the national educational and childcare systems, with multiple ministries responsible for the different professionals, the laws and regulations, still apply. There are various initiatives (Peeters, 2018 & PACT voor kindcentra, 2018) that have forced changes at the level of policy, until now this has not reflected in actual policy changes at the national level. As a lack of standardization, we do see differences in the way things are organized at the municipal level and (school) administrative level. Note that in the Netherlands, most primary schools are part of a *school board* with multiple schools, and most childcare services within child centres are part of an overarching childcare organization. Schools and childcare organizations are (partly) free to determine whether and how they will collaborate in an interprofessional manner. Moreover, analysis of the research by van der Grinten et al. (2019) and Kieft et al. (2016) shows that an increase in the intensity of the collaboration over the last five years is not present in all circumstances; the highest intensity of collaboration is just as much of an exception. Similarly, the Dutch Education council has observed that the desired substantive and organizational integration between education and childcare has not been sufficiently realized (Onderwijsraad, 2019). In the following examples, this differences in intensity of collaboration and how IPC is organized in the first place is illustrated in the two instances of child centres below:

Child Centre A

Child centre A is located in the 'West' district, built in the 1950s in a municipality of 100,000+ inhabitants. This municipality has a longstanding policy to develop child centres for children from 0 to

13 years of age, based on the idea that such centres enable children to develop optimally. The school board and childcare organization involved in child centre A have been working together for several years, 'for the benefit of a good transition between day care, ECE playgroups, primary school and out-of-school care (OSC)'. The motto of this child centre is 'together and sometimes apart'. The number of pupils in the primary school is stable, at around 350 children, divided over 14 heterogeneous groups. The capacity of the childcare section is 150 children per day, divided between two baby groups (babies up to 18 months) and three toddler day care groups, two ECE playgroups (2½-4 years old) and three OSC-groups. Interprofessional cooperation is especially focussed on the ECE playgroups and ECE at school during the first two grades of primary school: there are regular consultations, including coordination on content-related themes. A lot of attention is paid to early warning concerning possible special (educational) needs (SEN), for example in joint consultations every 8 weeks, in which besides ECE staff from both playgroups and primary school, also youth care experts and the internal SEN officer are involved.

Despite the size of the OSC (60 children), there is little involvement between OSC staff and teachers from the upper grades. The disparity in facilitation of transition moments between staff members of a day care or ECE playgroup and primary school teachers is salient. Child centre A pays a lot of attention to shared pedagogical vision, for instance, by organizing common study evenings. Still, an 'us and them culture' is found between educational staff and childcare staff. Operational management is largely centralized: the management team consists of the school leader, the school's middle management and the childcare manager. In addition, the school leader and childcare manager have structural bilateral consultations.

Child Centre B

Child centre B is a small village school with 96 students. Since 2019, the school has been expanded with a childcare section (for children 0-4 years old) and after-school care (for children 4-12 years old). In addition, in October 2020, a toddler group (early childhood education) was started (for children 2½-4 years old) two mornings a week. What is unique is that this childcare service was not organized by an external party but was set up by the school board: the school leader is also the formal leader of the childcare facility. In addition to the formal leader, the team at child centre B consists of three childcare employees, 8 teachers (all part-timers, 4 groups), a physical education teacher and trainer in the school, an internal supervisor and a teaching assistant. In addition, the speech therapist is present every week for speech therapy and the youth nurse is regularly at the school.

Interprofessional collaboration between the childcare employees and the teacher team is hardly regulated at all. Everyone knows each other because it is a small team. The conversations that take place are often at the coffee table. The collaboration is expressed in working on the same themes (e.g., 'spring' or 'the Middle Ages'). In addition, when children from childcare and the toddler group turn four, teachers from the first-grade consult with their colleagues from childcare about these children. In fact, the teachers in the lower grades and the childcare section notice something of this collaboration, but little has changed for the upper and middle grade teachers since the addition of the childcare section.

In the following section, we present the CCIM that is helpful to better understand variations in the degree of IPC in child centres.

Understanding Differences in IPC: The CCIM

Despite the focus – in policy and practice as well as politics – on this topical issue, IPC between childcare providers and primary schools is still a very young field of research, and scientific knowledge of collaboration between the specified sectors is still highly limited. Moreover, earlier models for detailed mapping of IPC between the two sectors were found not be adequate (van der Grinten et al., 2019). Therefore, building on the Rainbow Model for Integrated Care (Valentijn, Boesveld, et al., 2015; Valentijn, Schepman, et al., 2013), Verheijen-Tiemstra et al. (2020) developed an IPC model addressing IPC between primary schools and childcare providers, the CCIM, which is explained in more detail here. As can be seen in Fig. 2, apart from a systemic dimension on the macro level, the model distinguishes five areas of possible collaboration: the child-centred, professional, organizational, functional and normative dimensions. The *child-centred* dimension aims at smooth development of the primary educational and pedagogical process, as evident from a uniform pedagogical approach and alignment of pedagogical and learning pathways. The *professional* dimension refers to shared service delivery by professionals and the *organizational* dimension centres on the formalization of collaboration mechanisms and shared ambitions. Both the *functional* and *normative* dimensions are enablers in order to reach intensification of IPC on the meso level. (Valentijn, Boesveld, et al., 2015; Valentijn, Schepman, et al., 2013). The functional dimension centres on elements of business operations such as Information and communication technology (ICT) or housing, and the normative dimension is about 'social enablers' such as shared values and an organizational culture based on mutual respect and valuing diversity.

In addition to these IPC dimensions, IPC intensity is a relevant aspect. There is consensus in the literature that there is an IPC continuum ranging from full

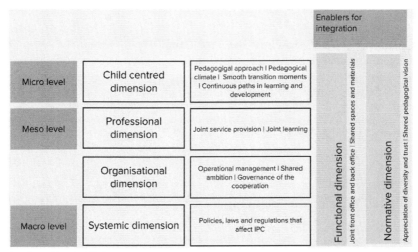

Fig. 2.   The CCIM.

segregation, through what is called a middle range to full integration (Ahgren & Axelsson, 2005; Boon et al., 2004; Gaboury et al., 2010; Keast et al., 2007; Maslin-Prothero & Bennion, 2010; Willumsen, 2008). The 3C typology (cooperation–coordination–collaboration) by Keast et al. (2007) has proven to be useful to describe that middle range (Mandell et al., 2017). In their typology, *cooperation* is regarded as the low-intensity starting point of IPC: this form of interaction focuses exclusively on informally sharing basic information, frequently small-scale and short-term oriented. *Coordination* is an instrumental form of partnership with moderate intensity. In this form, not only exchange of information takes place but also harmonization focussed on the realization of one's own goals. However, organizations still predominantly act in accordance with their own procedures and practices (Mandell et al., 2017). *Collaboration* is the form of IPC that is characterized by high intensity, aimed at achieving new and common goals. Participating organizations are aware that they are interdependent in achieving these goals. This form of partnership requires a considerable time investment as well as a high degree of trust. A full elaboration of the model can be found in Appendix.

Based on the CCIM, Verheijen-Tiemstra et al. (2020) conducted a multiple case study at 16 child centres, in order to research dimensions and intensity of IPC on the micro and meso levels. Their research showed that IPC is a multidimensional construct: IPC simultaneously takes place with different levels of intensity for different dimensions. At the child centres participating in this study, the IPC intensity was at the level of cooperation for seven sub-dimensions, which indicates a low IPC intensity, characterized by informality. At this level, the IPC was also strongly focussed on collaboration about ECE, while OSC was less involved. The lowest IPC intensity was found for the 'softer characteristics' of IPC, such as the two sub-dimensions of the normative dimension and the child-centred dimension (uniform pedagogical approach). Here the level of cooperation had not yet been achieved, and there was still a clear 'us and them culture'. It seems that the dimensions and levels of intensity can be connected to both the degree of regulation and involvement within the microsystem and the degree of regulation and involvement within the child centre and the regional system (mesosystem), and the microsystem and mesosystem influence each other. Besides the systemic dimension, both functional and normative dimensions appear to play an important role that leads to relatively low IPC intensities in the child centres studied. A possible explanation for this, in spite of the high ambitions of the management teams involved, was offered by issues that arose in the interviews that will be elaborated on in the next section.

Perceived Barriers to Engaging in IPC

As mentioned earlier in this chapter, the degree of system and policy integration in childcare services and schools is very low in the Netherlands (European Commission/EACEA/Eurydice, 2019). Although there appears to be a recent trend towards more intensive IPC (van der Grinten et al., 2019), we also see major differences between the ways in which organizations implement IPC, as illustrated by the examples of two child centres. The CCIM model helps us to gain greater insight into factors that may be hindering further intensification of IPC. Despite the sometimes-high ambitions of directors and management regarding IPC, the lack of system integration may be the biggest obstacle to improving IPC between childcare services and primary schools. Van der Grinten et al. (2019) found that board directors of both primary schools and childcare organizations experienced the separate laws and regulations as the most hindering factor, followed by separate – and limited – financial circuits, and issues with shared spaces within a child centre. It is noteworthy that childcare managers and school leaders (the formal leaders in a child centre) seemed to perceive these factors as less critical. When respondents were asked if they encountered barriers to IPC, 91% of the childcare board directors replied that they did, versus 66% of the school board directors. At the child centre level, 46% of the childcare managers encountered barriers, versus 41% of the school leaders (van der Grinten et al., 2019).

The CCIM is used to get additional insights into issues perceived by staff members, childcare managers and school leaders in relation to IPC (Verheijen-Tiemstra et al., 2020). In Table 1, the issues per dimension (as mentioned earlier) are shown. In total, 619 issues were coded, and the range of bottlenecks varied between 12 and 92 per child centre. In 4 of the 16 child centres, bottlenecks seemed hardly an issue (<25); in 9 of the child centres, the number of identified issues ranged from 25 to 50; and in 3 of the child centres, the number of issues exceeded 50.

Issues within the *child-centred dimension* often related to finding moments for information exchange during the day; a lack of time often played an important role. Moreover, not all teachers considered passing on of information as part of their job, as reflected by this schoolteacher's comment:

I don't think the passing on should be ours. Recently [child's name] had to take two puffs during the day, so the parents let us know. But then I would have to pass that on to the OSC-staff member. I'm not comfortable with that.

Table 1.   Number of Issues per Dimension.

Issues per Dimension	*n*	% of Total	Min–Max Per Child Centre
Child-centred dimension	86	13.89	0–19
Professional dimension	144	23.26	0–19
Organizational dimension	122	19.71	1–16
Functional dimension	63	10.18	0–14
Normative dimension	204	32.96	2–43
Total number of issues	*619*	*100*	*12–87*

Within the *professional dimension*, the lack of equality that people experience as far as time for professional development was the biggest issue. Childcare staff members, in particular, have small budgets for collaborative learning. For OSC staff members, there was also the practical issue that professional development events often take place during OSC hours. Within the *organizational dimension*, issues had to do with lack of equality in competences, budgets and prioritization. One childcare manager commented:

Traditionally schools have always had a lot of autonomy. Compared to us, they can make their own choices much more often. For instance, they can choose certain teaching materials or educational methods.

And although observation is the key method for assessing children in ECE in order to offer a child-centred approach, in the Netherlands, there are no guidelines on assessment methods, which gives schools autonomy in this area.

Regarding the *functional dimension*, both staff members and managers indicated that lack of space is sometimes a problem. If so, in practice, this means that OSC groups are not assigned their own room, as illustrated by this quote: 'We are now in a nursery classroom, but the oldest children are eight and their knees hit that there [points]. And I sit there as well, don't I?'. Issues within the *normative dimension* were frequently related to status differences based on educational attainment or expertise and dissimilar values and job perceptions. Respondents from 10 of the 16 child centres identified differences in expertise. 'Didactics is often seen as something you really had to study for, while pedagogical is seen as "something we all can do", that is more or less the conviction', according to a childcare manager. Perceived status differences due to differences in educational level were specifically mentioned by respondents from 11 of the 16 child centres. Issues concerning differences in values and job perceptions were mentioned by respondents from 15 of the 16 child centres. These could be more practical differences, such as greater flexibility within the childcare sector compared with the education sector, for example:

> *Schools plan very meticulously: they make a yearly calendar and then everything is set. And then in April I got the question if I already knew the meeting dates for the whole of the next school year. It took a while to get used to that.* (Childcare manager)

Respondents from primary schools, on the other hand, must get used to the fact that the childcare sector is a market sector and thus more frequently subject to change: 'If parents get fired, they will take their children out of day care, but not out of school' (school leader). This conception was reflected in, for example, the way in which 'collaboration with parents' – considered important by both parties – is covered. In primary schools, this means that teachers clearly indicate to parents what they stand for:

> *If you notice that a child is lagging behind or shows some particular behaviours, you mustn't be afraid to raise the issue. But in childcare the vision is 'parents pay for us' so it's hard for them to report. (Teacher)*

A childcare worker from another child centre actually confirmed this interpretation:

> *Parents are our customers: they bring their children to us, allowing them to go to work themselves. So if we were to close the place down because of a seminar, we would actually go against our own core business.*

In conclusion, this analysis of issues per dimension demonstrates a rather high degree of inequality between education and childcare on both the board director level and management level. Whereas at the board director level, issues follow from the lack of system integration, childcare managers and school leaders are – in varying degrees – affected by issues that arise from the dimensions at the meso level (in particular, the professional and organizational dimension) and the normative dimension. This is relevant since the normative dimension is necessary in order to reach intensification of IPC on a micro, professional or organizational level (Valentijn, Boesveld, et al., 2015; Valentijn, Schepman, et al., 2013).

Concluding Thoughts

We started this chapter by outlining the Dutch context, which is characterized by a separation between childcare services and primary education, reflected by different responsible ministries, different laws and regulations and different quality frameworks. The high social regulation on the macro level seems to hinder IPC. As a result of the increased number of children at risk in our complex society, changes in children's school day, scarcity of professionals in all sectors and shrinking of rural regions, organizations feel more and more the urge to work together (high social cohesion). In a growing number of child centres, schools and childcare providers are jointly trying to implement this collaboration to achieve optimal development opportunities for children (van der Grinten et al., 2019). There are major differences between the way these child centres give shape to this collaboration, which was illustrated by the two cases presented in this chapter. The CCIM seems to be an appropriate model for understanding such differences between child centres and provided insights into the enablers of and barriers to IPC. In recent years, a lot has been invested in the functional dimension (that is, a shared building, joint front office and back office). Many differences in the degree of collaboration were found for the other dimensions (normative, child focussed, professional and organizational) at the micro and meso levels, so that the intensity level of 'integration' is hardly achieved. One of the most obvious explanations is that there is still *segregation* in the systemic dimension.

The Dutch education and childcare system, or rather, the different systems that do not connect with each other seem to be an important cause of the failure or complication of IPC. Because the systems do not connect with each other at the macro level, we see struggles in the necessary normative dimension due to status differences (i.e., inequality between employees) and differences in funding and autonomy. The difference between public (education) and private (childcare) institutions also leads to difficulties in getting closer together.

If we translate this into the social cohesion regulation matrix, we see that high social regulation in this context stands in the way of collaboration. There is a strong willingness to collaborate, but due to laws and regulations, professionals still feel little freedom of movement to actually collaborate.

It is important to mention that along dimensions such as the functional and child-centred dimensions, many child centres have achieved valuable progress towards collaboration. Moreover, despite the difficulties, we see pioneers throughout the country where there is indeed collaboration within the various dimensions. For these pioneers as well, to reach *integration* on all levels, changes are needed at the macro level, but it is possible to achieve smaller steps at the meso and micro levels. In that sense, school and childcare managers have a crucial role. Managers who can think outside of the box, who know how to bridge across the rules and who show that they themselves can cross the boundaries of their own profession and sector are essential for strong IPC.

This chapter focussed on collaboration between childcare and education. However, the insights presented here would benefit better understanding of collaboration between all professionals around the child as is illustrated in this quote by a school leader:

> *Suppose, for example, that a language development disorder is suspected. This may already be identified at the ECE playgroup. Then*

> *in general, a 'special educational needs' consultation takes place, together with the Special Educational Needs (SEN) officer and the youth nurse of the consultation bureau. The SEN officer will then start to observe the child. Thus, early identification and interventions may take place before the child starts at the first grade of primary school. This works well between school and ECE playgroup, but this method does not apply to the children in day care.*

There is a group of children who see more professionals with different expertise than the 'average' child: professionals from youth care, social work, a physiotherapist or speech therapist. Also, in these cases, high quality of IPC is crucial for the child, and in the Dutch system, we see similar issues for collaboration with these professionals (e.g., different ministries responsible, hindering laws and regulations).

Key Lessons for Practice and Policy

This chapter shows how policies, laws and regulations affect IPC. If one wants to strengthen IPC in order to optimize the development of children, then the buttons must be pushed at a national level. There are various initiatives that are currently working on this (Coalitie Aanpak met Andere Ogen, PACT). In our view to enhance IPC, a shared vision is the starting point for achieving structural IPC. Without a common vision that is recognized by all professionals from different expertise involved, collaboration depends on coincidental circumstances and as a consequence temporary and unstable. This joint vision must be both horizontally and vertically congruent. Vertically, meaning one strong ministry for child affairs, including education and childcare, who stimulates an unambitious course at national level. This course can then be translated at regional and local levels. For IPC for young children (0–6 years), directions from municipalities is a condition for reaching long-term binding agreements. The municipality is taking the initiative to arrive at a joint vision and have it translated by the partners into long-term substantive agreements and agreements related to funding. A hierarchical organizational structure does not suit collaboration between professionals who are very different from each other. A network structure seems more appropriate.

More specific, for collaboration between childcare services and primary education in a child centre, it is necessary to know each other's expertise well. Maximum transparency towards each other in content, operations and objectives is conditional (the normative dimension of the CCIM). Valuing each other's expertise and responsibilities is crucial to be able to take further steps towards more IPC.

References

Ahgren, B., & Axelsson, R. (2005). Evaluating integrated health care: A model for measurement. *International Journal of Integrated Care, 5*(3). https://doi.org/10.5334/ijic.134

Boon, H., O'Hara, D., Findlay, B., & Verhoef, M. (2004). From parallel practice to integrative health care: A conceptual framework. *BMC Health Services Research, 4*(1), 1–5. https://doi.org/10.1186/1472-6963-4-15

Bryson, J. M., Crosby, B. C., & Stone, M. M. (2015). Designing and Implementing Cross-Sector Collaborations: Needed and Challenging. *Public Administration Review, 75*(5), 647–663. https://doi.org/10.1111/puar.12432

CAOP. (2017). *Anders organiseren, minder tekort. Verkenning naar het anders organiseren van onderwijs en de mogelijkheden om het voorspelde lerarentekort in het primair onderwijs (deels) op te vangen.* CAOP.

Carlson, L., Oláh, L. S., & Hobson, B. (2017). *Policy recommendations changing families and sustainable societies: Policy contexts and diversity over the life course and across generations.* http://www.familiesandsocieties.eu/wp-content/uploads/2017/06/WorkingPaper78.pdf

CBS. (2020). *Jeugdhulp 2019.* Centraal Bureau voor Statistiek. https://www.cbs.nl/nl-nl/publicatie/2020/18/jeugdhulp-2019

Coalitie Onderwijs-Zorg-Jeugd. (2019). *Programma Verbeteren aansluiting onderwijs-zorg-jeugd; implementatieplan van de coalitie onderwijs-zorg-jeugd.* http://www.onderwijsjeugd.nl/wp-content/uploads/2019/06/Implementatieplan-Coalitie-Onderwijs-zorg-jeugd-publieksversie.pdf

Doornenbal, J., & De Leve, C. (2014). *De pedagogische professional van de toekomst 21st. Century Skills Professionals 0- tot 6-jarigen.* Retrieved from https://www.pedagogischpact.nl/sites/default/files/files/21stcentury-skills-13-6-HR(1).pdf.

Doornenbal, J., & Fukkink, R. (2014). Samenwerking aan de randen van het onderwijs. In R. Oostdam & P. De Vries (Eds.), *Samenwerken aan leren en opvoeden: Basisboek over ouders en school* (pp. 227–236). Coutinho.

Dumčius, R., Peeters, J., Hayes, N., Van Landeghem, G., Siarova, H., Peciukonyte, L., ... & Hulpia, H. (2014). Study on the effective use of early childhood education and care in preventing early school leaving. European commission. https://op.europa.eu/en/publication-detail/-/publication/7548dd37-c626-4e2d-bd70-625edf707adc

European Commission/EACEA/Eurydice. (2019). *Key data on early childhood education and care in Europe – 2019 edition.* Publications Office of the European Union.

Fukkink, R., & Boogaard, M. (2020). Pedagogical quality of after-school care: Relaxation and/or enrichment? *Children and Youth Services Review, 112,* 104903. https://doi.org/10.1016/j.childyouth.2020.104903

Fukkink, R. G., & van Verseveld, M. (2020). Inclusive early childhood education and care: A longitudinal study into the growth of interprofessional collaboration. *Journal of Interprofessional Care, 34*(3), 362–372. https://doi.org/10.1080/13561820.2019.1650731

Gaboury, I., Boon, H., Verhoef, M., Bujold, M., Lapierre, L. M., & Moher, D. (2010). Practitioners' validation of framework of team-oriented practice models in integrative health care: A mixed methods study. *BMC Health Services Research, 10*(1). https://doi.org/10.1186/1472-6963-10-289

Garvis, S., Kirkby, J., McMahon, K., & Meyer, C. (2016). Collaboration is key: The actual experience of disciplines working together in child care. *Nursing & Health Sciences, 18*(1), 44– 51. doi: 10.1111/nhs.12226.

Hood, C. (1998). *The art of the state: Culture, rhetoric, and public management.* Clarendon Press. http://bvbr.bib-bvb.de:8991/F?func=service&doc_library=BVB01&doc_number=008296736&line_number=0001&func_code=DB_RECORDS&service_type=MEDIA

Inspectorate of Education. (n.d.). *The Inspectorate's approach.* Retrieved February 1, 2021, from https://english.onderwijsinspectie.nl/inspection/inspection-of-schools-by-the-dutch-inspectorate-of-education/the-inspectorate's-approach

Keast, R., Brown, K., & Mandell, M. (2007). Getting the right mix: Unpacking integration meanings and strategies. *International Public Management Journal, 10*(1), 9–33. https://doi.org/10.1080/10967490601185716

Kieft, M., Van der Grinten, M., & De Geus, W. (2016). *Samenwerking in beeld.* Oberon.

Ledoux, G., & Waslander, S. (2020). *Stand van zaken Evaluatie Passend Onderwijs. Deel 4: Governance in de samenwerkingsverbanden.* Kohnstamm Instituut.

Malin, J. R., Brown, C., Ion, G., van Ackeren, I., Bremm, N., Luzmore, R., Flood, J., & Rind, G. M. (2020). World-wide barriers and enablers to achieving evidence-informed practice in education: What can be learnt from Spain, England, the United States, and Germany? *Humanities and Social Sciences Communications, 7*(1), 99. https://doi.org/10.1057/s41599-020-00587-8

Mandell, M., Keast, R., & Chamberlain, D. (2017). Collaborative networks and the need for a new management language. *Public Management Review, 19*(3), 326–341. https://doi.org/10.1080/14719037.2016.1209232

Maslin-Prothero, S. E., & Bennion, A. E. (2010). Integrated team working: A literature review. *International Journal of Integrated Care, 10*(2), 1–11. https://doi.org/10.5334/ijic.529

Ministerie van Onderwijs, Cultuur en Wetenschap. (2020). *Brief van de minister aan de Tweede Kamer 30 januari 2020 betreffende 'Thuiszitters in het funderend onderwijs'.* Ministerie van OCW.

NJI. (n.d.). *Toezicht en handhaving kwaliteitseisen.* Retrieved February 1, 2021, from https://www.nji.nl/nl/Kennis/Dossier/Kinderopvang-en-peuterspeelzalen/Toezicht-en-handhaving-kwaliteitseisen

OECD. (2016). Starting strong IV: Early childhood education and care data country note: Netherlands. https://www.oecd.org/education/school/ECECDCN-Netherlands.pdf

Onderwijs in cijfers. (2020a). Ontwikkeling van het aantal leerlingen in het primair onderwijs. https://www.onderwijsincijfers.nl/kengetallen/po/leerlingen-po/aantallen-ontwikkeling-aantal-leerlingen

Onderwijs in cijfers. (2020b). Omvang van scholen in het primair onderwijs. https://www.onderwijsincijfers.nl/kengetallen/po/instellingen/omvang-instellingen-po

Onderwijsraad. (2019). *Doorgeschoten differentiatie in het onderwijsstelsel. Stand van educatief Nederland 2019* (Vol. 20190019/1107). Onderwijsraad

PACT voor kindcentra. (2018). *Ontwikkel de toekomst: programma 2018-2021 & activiteiten 2018.* Retrieved from 180702_Programma-PACT-Kindcentra-2018-2021-b.pdf (pactvoorkindcentra.nl)

Page, S. B., Stone, M. M., Bryson, J. M., & Crosby, B. C. (2015). Public value creation by cross-sector collaborations; a framework and challenges of assessment. *Public Administration, 93*(3), 715–732.

Peeters, R. (2018). Met andere ogen; advies voor versnelling en bestendiging van de samenwerking onderwijs-zorg-jeugd. De Coalitie Onderwijs-Zorg-Jeugd. https://www.tweedekamer.nl/kamerstukken/brieven_regering/

Rijksoverheid. (2019). *Kwartaalrapportage kinderopvang: eerste kwartaal 2019.* Retrieved from https://www.rijksoverheid.nl/binaries/rijksoverheid/documenten/publicaties/2019/06/07/kwartaalrapportage-kinderopvang-eerstekwartaal-2019/1e+Kwartaalrapportage+2019+def.pdf

ROA. (2019). *Arbeidsmarkt naar opleiding en beroep tot 2024.* Maastricht University.

SER. (2016). *Gelijk goed van start. Visie op het toekomstige stelsel van voorzieningen voor jonge kinderen* (Vol. Advies 16/01). Sociaal Economische Raad. Retrieved from https://www.ser.nl/-/media/ser/downloads/adviezen/2016/gelijk-goed-van-start.pdf

Taskforce samenwerking onderwijs en kinderopvang. (2017). *Tijd om door te pakken in de samenwerking tussen onderwijs en kinderopvang.* Rijksoverheid.

Thomson, A. M., & Perry, J. L. (2006). Collaboration Processes: Inside the Black Box. *Public Administration Review, 66*, 20–32.

Valentijn, P. P., Boesveld, I. C., van der Klauw, D. M., Ruwaard, D., Struijs, J. N., Molema, J. J. W., ... Vrijhoef, H. J. M. (2015). Towards a taxonomy for integrated care: A mixed-methods study. *International Journal of Integrated Care, 15*(1), 1–18. https://doi.org/10.5334/ijic.1513

Valentijn, P. P., Schepman, S. M., Opheij, W., & Bruijnzeels, M. A. (2013). Understanding integrated care: A comprehensive conceptual framework based on the integrative functions of primary care. *International Journal of Integrated Care, 13*(1), 1–12. https://doi.org/10.5334/ijic.886

Van der Grinten, M., Kiefst, M., Kooij, D., Bomhof, M., & Van den Berg, E. (2019). *Samenwerking in beeld 2: Basisscholen, kinderopvang en kindcentra: De stand van het land 2019.* Oberon. https://www.pactvoorkindcentra.nl/images/pdf/190327-Oberon-rapport-Samenwerking-in-Beeld-2019.pdf

Van der Werf, W. M., Slot, P. L., Kenis, P. N., & Leseman, P. P. M. (2021). Inclusive practice and quality of education and care in the Dutch hybrid early childhood education and care system. *International Journal of Child CareChildcare and Education Policy, 15*(1), 2. https://doi.org/10.1186/s40723-020-00079-x

Van Oploo, M., Van Velzen, A., Van der Werf, C., & Engelen, M. (2008). *Groei van kinderopvang. Een onderzoek naar Oorzaken.* https://www.eerstekamer.nl/id/vi5fh1zl41np/document_extern/bijlage_bij_brief_kinderopvang/f=/vi5fh2z1atny.pdf

Verheijen-Tiemstra, M. R. E., Ros, A. A., & Vermeulen, M. J. M. (2020). Werelden van verschil: Aard en intensiteit van interprofessionele samenwerking tussen basisonderwijs en kinderopvang. *Pedagogische Studiën, 97*(1), 59–75.

Vesterinen, O., Kangas, M., Krokfors, L., Kopisto, K., & Salo, L. (2017). Inter-professional pedagogical collaboration between teachers and their out-of-school-partners. *Educational Studies, 43*(2), 231–242.

Willumsen, E. (2006). Leadership in interprofessional collaboration – the case of childcare in Norway. *Journal of interprofessional care, 20*(4), 403–413.

Willumsen, E. (2008). Interprofessional collaboration - a matter of differentiation and integration? Theoretical reflections based in the context of Norwegian childcare. *Journal of interprofessional care, 22*(4), 352–363.

Child Centre Integration Model (CCIM) version 2.0 (2019)

This model is measuring the intensity of interprofessional collaboration (IPC) within the identified dimensions and sub dimensions of IPC between two sectors: childcare providers and primary schools in the Netherlands. The sector childcare consists of three sections and includes day care for children from 0-4 years old, early childhood education (ECE) at playgroups for children from 2 ½ to 4 years old and out-of-school-care (before- and after school) for children from 4-12 years old. Thus, within a child centre four sections can be found: the school section and day care, ECE playgroups and out-of-school care. For each sub-dimension and intensity of IPC one or more brief characteristic descriptions are given.

	SEGREGATION *separate*	COOPERATION *non-committal*	COORDINATION *aligned*	COLLABORATION *collective goals*	INTEGRATION *demonstrably integrated*
CHILD-CENTRED DIMENSION Unambiguous pedagogical approach	1.1 Professionals act in accordance with the practices, procedures and protocols of their own organisation. 1.2 Professionals do not know how colleagues from the other sector establish a pedagogical relationship - such as guiding interactions between children and interactions between children and professionals - or make their own choices in this respect.	2.1 Professionals generally act in accordance with the practices, procedures and protocols of their own organisation. 2.2 There are a few colleagues who, on their own initiative, are concerned with how colleagues from the other sector establish a pedagogical relationship such as guidance of interactions between children and interactions between children and professionals. These colleagues often work in ECE at playgroups or ECE at primary schools.	3.1 Education and childcare staff generally learn from each other how to act and approach the guidance of interactions between children and interactions between children and professionals. 3.2 Professionals act in accordance with the practices, procedures and protocols of their own organisation. However, attempts are sometimes made to co-ordinate matters in certain areas, often in relation to ECE at playgroups or ECE at primary schools. .	4.1 Education and childcare staff have - or are working on - joint agreements in order to realise an unambiguous pedagogical climate with regard to guiding interactions between children and between children and professionals. 4.2 Education and childcare staff work within a joint working group on common goals regarding the pedagogical approach. 4.3 These agreements apply to all four sections of the child centre.	5.1 There are demonstrable child centre-wide agreements on an unambiguous pedagogical approach and what this means for the pedagogical behaviour of all employees. 5.2 Periodic reviews show that children experience interactions between children and between children and professionals in a similar way throughout the day.

	SEGREGATION *separate*	COOPERATION *non-committal*	COORDINATION *aligned*	COLLABORATION *collective goals*	INTEGRATION *demonstrably integrated*
CHILD-CENTRED DIMENSION Unequivocal pedagogical climate: atmosphere and rules of conduct	1.1 Education and childcare staff do not know how colleagues from the other sector deal with (social) rules, and structure or make their own choices in this respect. 1.2 Professionals do not know whether children experience the same safe and welcoming environment throughout the day. This is made more difficult by the fact that a child sees many faces during the day and there is a lack of coordination.	2.1 Generally speaking, education and childcare staff do not know each other's rules or make their own choices in line with their own organisation's practices, procedures and protocols. 2.2 A number of colleagues are investigating on their own initiative whether children experience the same safe and welcoming environment throughout the day and how they can contribute to this. These colleagues often work in ECE at playgroups or ECE at primary schools.	3.1 Education and childcare staff are generally aware of the way in which colleagues from the other sector deal with rules (of conduct) and structure. 3.2 Education and childcare staff act in line with their own organisation's practices, procedures and protocols.	4.1 Professionals from the education and childcare sectors have goal-oriented agreements in order to realise an unambiguous pedagogical climate with regard to rules (of conduct) and a safe environment for all four sections within the child centre. 4.2 This is evidenced, for example, by a child centre-wide working group working on shared goals that relate to all parts of the child centre.	5.1 There are demonstrable child centre-wide agreements on rules (of conduct) and how to realise a safe environment for all children. 5.2 Periodic evaluations show that children experience the same safe environment throughout the day, with childcare and education staff using the same standards.

1.3 Professionals in education and childcare see the school atmosphere and out-of-school atmosphere as two different environments that co-exist alongside each other.

3.3 Sometimes attempts are made to co-ordinate rules (of conduct) in certain areas. This can take place around ECE at playgroups or ECE at primary schools. or apply to a specific area, such as common playground rules.

(Continued)

	SEGREGATION separate	COOPERATION non-committal	COORDINATION aligned	COLLABORATION collective goals	INTEGRATION demonstrably integrated
CHILD-CENTRED DIMENSION Smooth transition	1.1 There is no organised transfer of individual child data between professionals in childcare services and education: this applies to both horizontal (school to out-of-school care) and vertical (playground or day care to primary school) transition moments.	2.1 At the transition from playgroup or day care to the first grade of primary school, a paper transfer of child data between school and childcare staff takes place. On an ad hoc basis - if one of the professionals involved takes the initiative - this can be expanded upon, but it is not given support in terms of time or space.	3.1 There is agreement on a face to face transfer of child data from the playgroup to first grade of primary school, supported by a transfer form. 3.2 When a specific situation arises, this form is usually expanded upon orally (ad hoc). 3.3 With regard to horizontal transition moments, it depends on the individual whether incidents that occur during the day (e.g., accidents, bullying, fights) are passed on to each other by the education and out-of-school care colleagues involved.	4.1 There is a purposeful and structured handover with respect to the transition from pre-school to primary school, in which time and space are provided for professionals from both sectors. In these consultations, the transfer form is discussed, as well as other matters relevant to the child's functioning.	5.1 Childcare and education staff work in a fully integrated way and therefore transition moments are the same for all age groups. There is no specific transfer of childrens'data when attending the first grade of primary school because this is not a special transition moment. Transition moments - both horizontal and vertical - during which information is transferred are self-evident and transparent.

1.2 Children enter school from different childcare providers, or children did not attend day care or ECE playgroup. There are more OSC-providers connected with the school.

2.2 Information transfer at horizontal transition moments between education and out-of-school care (ages 4-13) is barely an issue, if at all; the timing and/or lack of support makes this virtually impossible.

4.2 With regard to horizontal transition moments, it is customary for the educational and out-of-school care colleagues involved to report incidents throughout the day (e.g., accidents, bullying, fights) to each other.

5.2 Periodic evaluations show that there is an integrated approach to the transfer of information at horizontal and vertical transition points.

	SEGREGATION *separate*	COOPERATION *non-committal*	COORDINATION *aligned*	COLLABORATION *collective goals*	INTEGRATION *demonstrably integrated*
CHILD-CENTRED DIMENSION, Continuous path in learning and development	1.1 There is no continuous path in learning and development. 1.2 Childcare and education staff act according to their own methodologies, practices and methods for their own target groups (ages 0-4, 2,5-4 and 4-13).	2.1 There are a few colleagues who contact colleagues from the partner organisation on their own initiative to see if there is an occasional opportunity to connect on a theme or activity related to this theme. 2.2 Occasional initiatives to connect with a theme or approach of the co-operation partner mainly concern ECE at playgroups and ECE at primary schools. 2.3 Childcare staff is invited to join an school activity with their group occasionally, but timing makes this virtually impossible.	3.1 There is regular coordination between professionals from childcare and education, especially between staff from ECE at playgroups or ECE at primary schools. 3.2 The curricula of the domains of language and mathematics and socio-emotional developmental areas are - in part - co-ordinated with each other, for example, by choosing themes that match.	4.1 Education and childcare staff work on a single, continuous programme for 0- to 13-year-olds for the curricula of the domains of language and mathematics and social-emotional developmental areas, or there are clear agreements that work on the basis of shared goals and themes. 4.2 Within this programme, there is a specific role for out-of-school care, with a focus on stimulating the broad development of children, including the targeted stimulation of social development.	5.1 Education and childcare staff demonstrably work together using the same methodologies and practices for 0- to 13-year-olds, thus ensuring the continuity of the content. 5.2 Children's development is continuous through formal and informal learning. E.g. what happens at out-of-school care, is linked to what happens at school and vice versa. 5.3 This integration leads to more opportunities for development of the child than in the separate systems.

PROFESSIONAL DIMENSION Joint service provision					
1.1 There is no joint service provision: childcare and education staff members operate strictly separately from each other. 1.2 Education and childcare have their own, separate care structures.	2.1 There is no joint service provision: apart from one exception, childcare and education staff operate separately from each other. 2.2 Education and childcare have their own care structure. Sometimes a colleague will make (informal) contact on their own initiative regarding a specific child about whom there are concerns e.g. when special (educational) needs are suspected.	3.1 It may occasionally happen that a childcare staff member joins the education side or vice versa: for example, co-ordination may take place on the joint provision of lessons or activities. 3.2 There is a form of coordination between ECE staff of playgroups and schools concerning early warning, e.g. when special (educational) needs are suspected, especially when children turn 4 and start to attend school. The school's special needs officer may have an active role in this. 3.3 Coordination around early signalling when special (educational) needs are suspected, is not self-evident for children from out-of-school care or day care services.	4.1 Education and childcare staff work together on collective goals for education, development, care and recreation for a group of children. 4.2 To this end, the personnel policy is co-ordinated to the greatest possible extent within the legal possibilities. This leads to the use of combined functions as much as possible so that children see the same faces as much as possible. 4.3 There is structural and purposeful coordination when special (educational) needs are suspected which is generally aimed at early warning and interventions within all four sections of the child centre.	5.1 There is a single inter-professional team with shared responsibility for education, development, care and recreation for a group of children. 5.2 There is an integrated care structure throughout the child centre, in which all sections are involved.	

(Continued)

PROFESSIONAL DIMENSION Joint learning	SEGREGATION *separate*	COOPERATION *non-committal*	COORDINATION *aligned*	COLLABORATION *collective goals*	INTEGRATION *demonstrably integrated*
	1.1 There are no joint courses, learning teams or study days for education and childcare staff.	2.1 Occasionally there are small-scale initiatives for joint learning: for example, a single childcare worker is invited (possibly on their own time) to participate as a representative in a study session or a learning team on a specific subject. Or education and childcare staff visit each other to learn about each other's work; often these colleagues work in ECE at playgroups or ECE at primary schools.	3.1 Coordination takes place on training and education for child centre-wide tasks, such as a joint first aid training. 3.2 Participation in joint study days and learning teams is coordinated, whereby the choice of time and/or giving support makes it possible for pedagogical staff members to participate. 3.3 There is agreement on initiatives whereby staff from childcare and education visit each other on a more regular basis to familiarise themselves with each other's work.	4.1 Joint learning for education and childcare staff is structurally embedded in shared goals. A large number of employees from all sections are involved. 4.2 Every year, joint study days and learning teams take place around the continuous path in learning and development, from within domains or development areas. 4.3 Child centre-wide study days and learning teams are planned and/ or given support to ensure the participation of all sections (day care, playgroups, out-of-school care and school).	5.1 There is a demonstrable single programme of joint learning through peer review, child centre-wide study days, training courses, workshops and external meetings for education and childcare staff.

ORGANISA-TIONAL DIMENSION Operational management				
1.1 The operational management is organised separately. 1.2 Managers from both sectors hardly or never speak to each other.	2.1 The operational management is organised separately, but managers from both sectors consult with each other on a regular basis. 2.2 Consultation between managers from both partners mainly relates to facility or practical issues within the child centre.	3.1 Operational management is organised separately, but there is structured consultation between both sets of managers. 3.2 In this structured consultation, not only practical and facility matters are discussed, but also substantive or organisational aspects within the child centre.	4.1 There is a (child centre) Management Team in which education and childcare managers have a seat and in which joint decision making takes place. MT members are accountable to their own sector. 4.2 The education manager has no formal powers over care staff and vice versa. 4.3 Operational management is organised centrally, but legal and formal matters are dealt with separately.	5.1 There is a single child centre management that is integrally responsible for both education and childcare.

	SEGREGATION *separate*	COOPERATION *non-committal*	COORDINATION *aligned*	COLLABORATION *collective goals*	INTEGRATION *demonstrably integrated*
ORGANISA-TIONAL DIMENSION Shared ambition	1.1 There is no shared ambition at the child centre level. 1.2 Staff from childcare and education are not familiar with each other's mission and/or strategy and what goals they wish to achieve, or they make their own choices in this respect.	2.1 At the management level, discussions take place about goals that can be achieved through cooperation; these discussions are mainly exploratory and/or non-committal. For example, education and childcare managers do not give the same priority to the child-centre structure. 2.2 Employees are not familiar with these future plans: they mention very different subjects or refer to the management for this.	3.1 A small group of stakeholders – usually managers from both sectors – discuss what they would like to achieve together in the child centre in the long term and the contours of a shared ambition are clear. 3.2 Staff can name some elements of these contours.	4.1 There is a shared ambition and managers of both sectors are convinced that cooperation helps to realise these goals. 4.2 Employees are able to interpret this shared ambition in broad terms.	5.1 There is a shared ambition at the child centre that is attractive and meaningful to both childcare and education staff. 5.2 Staff members feel that education and childcare want to achieve the same things with the child centre.

ORGANISA-TIONAL DIMENSION Governance of the cooperation				
1.1 There is no cooperative relationship at the management level.	2.1 There is occasional contact at the management level, also concerning cooperation, but these contacts do not necessarily specifically concern the intensification of the current cooperative relationship between the sectors.	3.1 There is regular contact at the management level during which organisational coordination takes place. 3.2 There is a desire to formalise the cooperative relationship: for example, a steering committee and possibilities for a declaration of intent are being explored.	4.1 There is a cooperation agreement in which partners from education and childcare have relinquished part of their autonomy on a number of specific aspects and have established agreements on objectives, tasks, competences and decision-making within a specific child centre or several child centres, but acting from within their own organisation.	5.1 A new organisational structure has been created in the form of a new legal entity (umbrella legal person or personal union).

(Continued)

FUNCTIONAL DIMENSION Joint front office, back office	SEGREGATION separate	COOPERATION non-committal	COORDINATION aligned	COLLABORATION collective goals	INTEGRATION demonstrably integrated
	1.1 No joint front office or back office functions are apparent. There is no need for this because education and childcare are separate systems. 1.2 Parents maintain separate contact with staff from both sectors. 1.3 Education and childcare each have their own image and accessibility information (e-mail addresses, telephone numbers).	2.1 The childcare provider and primary school do not manifest themselves as a single organisation to the outside world: parents maintain separate contact with both sectors. 2.2 On a small scale, some education or childcare staff share information from external parties (e.g., parents) on their own initiative (e.g., absence reports).	3.1 Coordination takes place on specific components of a joint front or back office. For example, coordination can take place regarding specific facility matters, use of the same formats or ICT applications. 3.2 The adoption of certain communication messages in one's own communication resources is agreed upon. 3.3 For specific joint activities, it may be decided to set up a communication resource with a shared face (for example, a joint newsletter or Facebook page).	4.1 There are structural agreements on the use of and support for certain front office and back office functions within the child centre (e.g., facilities, ICT support). 4.2 Joint goals are reflected in the implementation of a joint information system and an overarching image in communications.	5.1 There are joint front office and back office functions. A joint information system is used in a demonstrable and unambiguous manner for all sections (day-care, ECE playgroups, primary school and out-of-school care) of the child centre. 5.2 There is a common front office with unambiguous accessibility data (e-mail addresses, telephone and website) provided to parents.

2.3 ICT systems and forms are not compatible. This is seen by some employees as a hindrance because it is difficult to share information between the two sections.

3.4 In addition to these joint communication resources, each section has its own communication resources and channels with its own face and tone of voice.

4.3 Parents experience a shared (digital) entrance area, through which they can make contact (mail, telephone, face-to-face) in an unambiguous way about registration and enrolment, absence notifications, etc.

5.3 The child centre has a single shared house style in all communications and manifests as a single organisation to the outside world.

	SEGREGATION *separate*	COOPERATION *non-committal*	COORDINATION *aligned*	COLLABORATION *collective goals*	INTEGRATION *demonstrably integrated*
FUNCTIONAL DIMENSION Shared spaces and materials	1.1 All facilities are housed in one building (or within safe walking distance of each other), but both sectors operate alongside each other. 1.2 No spaces are shared between education and childcare. 1.3 Each organisation purchases its own sports and games equipment for its own use. 1.4 No materials (e.g., printers, equipment) are shared.	2.1 All facilities are housed in one building (or within safe walking distance of each other), but sectors generally operate alongside each other. 2.2 Childcare sector rents space in the building, but the lease or use ends when the school needs these spaces for its own use. This sometimes leads to sub-optimal accommodation for childcare services, in particular in out-of-school care.	3.1 All facilities are housed in one building. 3.2 Some non-teaching-specific areas are shared, such as a copy room and/or a team room. 3.3 There is agreement on long-term rental/use of spaces for education, development and recreation, such as a playroom, workshop, computer room or kitchen. 3.4 Education-specific rooms are sometimes also used as out-of-school care rooms.	4.1 There is a policy plan that states which spaces can be used multifunctionally and for what purpose in the longer term. For example, a classroom may be made available for out-of-school care for young children in combination with another room in which out-of-school care for older children is organised. 4.2 Out-of-school care spaces focus on development and recreation, not education.	5.1 Housing is organised integrally, with agreements on the use of space having a sustainable character. 5.2 Support spaces - e.g., outdoor space, team room, kitchen, meeting room(s), management and staff work rooms - are used by staff from both sectors. 5.3 The design of multifunctional rooms with an educational/childcare function is in line with the various functions of the room and appropriate to the age group(s) using it.

2.3 There is little or no sharing of sports and games equipment for educational, developmental and recreational purposes. Each organisation uses its own materials.

3.4. There is agreement on the sports and games materials that may be used by both education and childcare.

4.3 Non-education-specific multifunctional areas - such as outdoor space, kitchen, manager(s) room and team room - are shared, with education and childcare acting as joint tenants.

4.4 There are multi-year agreements on the purchase, use and responsibility for certain sports and games materials.

5.4 There are sustainable agreements on investment in and sharing of materials by both education and childcare.

	SEGREGATION *separate*	COOPERATION *non-committal*	COORDINATION *aligned*	COLLABORATION *collective goals*	INTEGRATION *demonstrably integrated*
NORMATIVE DIMENSION Appreciation of diversity and mutual trust	1.1 Education and childcare staff do not form a single unit: solidarity relates to one's own colleagues.	2.1 Education and childcare staff mainly experience solidarity with their own colleagues.	3.1 There is some mutual solidarity or loyalty between colleagues involved in the collaboration. Among these employees, a few dare to stand up for employees with a different background (e.g., expertise or role).	4.1 Childcare and education staff from all sections work based on shared goals and seek to understand each other's practices.	5.1 Education and childcare staff form a single unit and - regardless of expertise or level of training - feel appreciated for their contribution to the child centre.
	1.2 Status and cultural differences are an issue: there is an 'us' and 'them' mentality.	2.2 Status and cultural differences are discussed to a limited extent: as an observation but also as a source of mutual irritation in which us/them thinking occurs.	3.2 Any Irritations are expressed by these colleagues directly to the person(s) concerned.	4.2 Status and cultural differences are barely an issue.	5.2 Mutual loyalty is self-evident; within this, there is sufficient confidence to maintain one's own position, even if this deviates from the prevailing norm.
	1.3 Lack of appreciation for diversity regularly leads to irritation about other colleagues, but these situations are rarely expressed to the people involved.	2.3 People feel insecure about expressing themselves directly to the person(s) involved: a few, however, discuss these things with their own manager.	3.3 During informal moments (break time and/or team outings), these colleagues seek each other out spontaneously.	4.3 Education and childcare staff dare to express misunderstandings or sources of conflict directly to each other	
				4.4 Education and childcare staff dare to take a different stance from each other.	

1.4 Pressure may be felt to conform to one's own group norm.

1.5 Education and childcare staff generally do not know each other and show no interest in getting to know each other. Greeting each other is not a matter of course.

1.6 On both sides, there is hardly any trust in specific capacities, such as offering good quality or sticking to agreements.

1.7 Willingness to place things in the hands of the other sector is low.

2.4 During informal moments, childcare and education staff members do not seek each other out (they sit separately).

2.5 There is limited confidence in the other sector's specific capacities, such as offering good quality or sticking to agreements.

2.6 Willingness to place matters in the hands of this other sector is limited, with the exception of a few colleagues in whom staff do have this confidence (e.g., ECE staff both at playgroups and schools.

3.4 Because a (limited) group of education and childcare staff understand each other's working methods and backgrounds, they have mutual trust in their specific qualities. This often occurs between ECE staff in ECE in both playgroups and school.

3.5 Willingness to place matters in the hands of this other sector is present.

4.5 Because more employees from all sections understand each other's working methods and backgrounds and have had successful experiences while co-operating, trust exists in the other sector's specific qualities.

4.6 There is a willingness to place matters in the hands of the other sector.

5.3 Education and childcare staff generally trust each other's specific capabilities, for example, in sticking to agreements or providing good quality care/ quality education. This applies to all four sections of the child centre.

5.4 Willingness to place matters in the hands of the other sector is high and this leads to demonstrable added value for the child centre.

	SEGREGATION *separate*	COOPERATION *non-committal*	COORDINATION *aligned*	COLLABORATION *collective goals*	INTEGRATION *demonstrably integrated*
NORMATIVE DIMENSION Shared pedagogical vision	1.1 Education and childcare staff apply the pedagogical beliefs or vision of their own organisation. 1.2 Educational and care workers are generally not familiar with each other's pedagogical vision or values, or they make their own choices in this respect.	2.1 Generally speaking, childcare and education staff members are not familiar with each other's pedagogical vision or beliefs and act on their own accord. 2.2 There are a few colleagues (especially in the pre-school and early primary school years) who take the initiative to look into the pedagogical vision/beliefs of the partner organisation.	3.1 Incidental initiatives or activities concerning the exploration of each other's pedagogical beliefs are given a more structured character 3.2 Exploratory meetings are held with a number of employees to determine what elements must be included in a shared vision and for what elements their own pedagogical vision should take the lead.	4.1 One pedagogical vision is (soon to be) implemented for the entire child centre and, in addition to the management of the child centre, many employees from all sections (day care, pre-school, out-of-school care, primary education) were involved in the development of the vision. 4.2 The vision is known to a significant proportion of staff in all sections.	5.1 Child centre-wide vision development is a process that demonstrably takes place on an ongoing basis and involves all stakeholders affected by this vision. 5.2 The vision is widely supported and shared pedagogical values and beliefs are recognisable in the daily actions of staff in all sections within the child centre.

Chapter 7

School-to-School Collaboration in Poland: Mapping (Untapped) Potential

Marta Kowalczuk-Walędziak, Hanna Kędzierska and Alicja Korzeniecka-Bondar

Abstract

This chapter aims to explore Polish experiences of school-to-school collaboration (SSC): a mosaic of dynamic interplay between history, culture, politics, economics, and education. Starting with a diagnosis of Poland's education system as 'fatalist' via the lens of the cohesion/regulation matrix, this chapter reveals the complex nature of SSC in this country, which is underpinned by conflicting logics: the decentralized education system, the state's desire for control over that system's key mechanisms, and the heavily capitalistic influence of neoliberal pressures. Then, drawing on data from available policy reports and legal acts, as well as the authors' own research experiences, this chapter offers some insights on promising policy developments and examples of good practices in SSC at national and international levels. Furthermore, this chapter identifies possible barriers that block the full utilization of the potential inherent in collaboration between schools. These include formal/legal barriers (e.g. lack of policies regulating the collaboration between schools, unstable education policy after 1989, and competition between schools) and normative/cultural barriers (e.g. lack of long-standing tradition and experience of cooperation between schools, the bureaucratic school management model, and lack of cooperation skills among the main stakeholders). This chapter concludes with a discussion of some key lessons for policy and practice in tangibly harnessing the potential of SSC as a means of addressing current education challenges in Poland.

Keywords: school-to-school collaboration; Poland; post-socialist transformations; decentralization; education policy; international school partnerships

School-to-School Collaboration: Learning Across International Contexts, 127–141
Copyright © 2022 by Marta Kowalczuk-Walędziak, Hanna Kędzierska and
Alicja Korzeniecka-Bondar
Published under exclusive licence by Emerald Publishing Limited
doi:10.1108/978-1-80043-668-820221008

Introduction

In recent years, the value of school-to-school collaboration (SSC) has been increasingly recognized in Western countries (e.g. the UK, Australia, Germany, and Spain), considering it as one of the significant drivers for improving student learning outcomes (e.g. Armstrong et al., 2021; West, 2010). Yet, there is a paucity of knowledge in understanding the nature and effects of school-to-school in other contexts and societies, which – as some research shows – may crucially shape the dynamics of such collaborations across those potential new sites (Armstrong & Ainscow, 2018; Gallagher, 2016; Roulston et al., 2021; West, 2010). This chapter therefore expands this body of knowledge by focussing on Poland: a post-socialist country in central Europe.

Polish experiences of SSC are a mosaic of dynamic interplay between history, culture, politics, economics, and education. In 1989, with the fall of the communist regime, like many other Central and Eastern European countries, Poland began its journey towards Western models of democracy, decentralization, building civic society, privatization, and market economy. This was also a time of profound structural and curricular reforms in education, developed not only in line with the general national transformations summarized above but also in line with the programmes and values of governing parties (promoting slogans such as school 'autonomy', 'collaboration', 'partnerships', and 'self-improvement'), as well as global neoliberal projects (e.g. standardized testing, league tables, and rankings) (e.g. Wiśniewski & Zahorska, 2020). From this snapshot of post-1989 education transformations in Poland (which will be explored more later in this chapter), it can perhaps be inferred – at first glance – that this new social and political order created a conducive climate for supporting SSC. However, at the same time, a keen observer will quickly spot the heavily capitalistic influence of neoliberal pressures on the budding, post-regime education system, demanding and normalizing competition within and between schools (Cervinkova & Rudnicki, 2019; Potulicka & Rutkowiak, 2013). As previous research has shown, this call for competition may be problematic in terms of establishing meaningful collaborative relationships (Armstrong et al., 2021).

Poland's long-standing, rich, and well-documented tradition of collaboration and professional dialogue with the local community has its roots in the early twentieth century, where schools cooperated with families, churches, and societal institutions, such as the justice system and police, in order to support students and their needs (e.g. Mendel, 2000; Theiss, 1996; Wołczyk & Winiarski, 1978). However, in this history (and present), any national experience of SSC is often unheard and undocumented in a comprehensive and wide-reaching way.

Against this backdrop of both new opportunities and new challenges post-1989, important questions arise as to what the nature of SSC *is* in contemporary Poland. What (if any) are the forms of SSC in Poland? Does Poland's recent investment in decentralized schooling allow for the building of effective school networks? What are Poland's enablers and barriers to engaging in SSC? How does SSC hold the potential to solve Poland's education challenges? This chapter aims to address these questions by referring to the extant data and other information derived from available policy reports and legal acts, as well as to our own experiences and research work – indeed, SSC has not been given the attention it deserves in the literature to date; thus, our work is significant in that it maps the terrain of this untapped potential and offers a basis for further explorations.

This chapter begins by giving an overall description of the Polish education system through the lens of the cohesion/regulation matrix. Then, we outline some recent promising policy developments and practices for setting, implementing, and sustaining SSC at national and international levels. Reflecting on these local and international experiences allows us, then, to offer some insights on barriers to engaging in SSC. This chapter ends with discussing some key lessons for policy and practice in terms of using the rich potential of SSC to solve current Poland's education challenges.

Poland's Education System: The 'Fatalist' Approach

In Hood's social/cohesion matrix (1998), the 'fatalist' approach (top right quadrant) is characterized by rule-bound approaches to organization carried out with little cooperation to achieve outcomes, thus is perhaps the most relevant for describing Poland's education system. In the following section, we describe the key features of this education system which predispose it to be located within this approach. These features were shaped by the profound socio-political and educational changes taking place in Poland after 1989, which – under the pretence of democratic values, in fact, have created and are still creating conditions 'where co-operation is rejected, distrust widespread, and apathy reigns' (Hood, 1998, p. 9).

Fatalistic systems – according to Hood (1998) – are characterized by high social regulation and low social cohesion. Applying this understanding to the education context, it may be implied that these types of education systems and schools operate under strong centralist regulations, which limit their autonomy and capacity for self-improvement, as well as their potential for self-governed cooperation. This is exactly the case with the Polish education system, which can be, generally speaking, characterized as based on 'centralized decentralization': a phenomenon present in many post-communist countries (Menter et al., forthcoming). This means that, on the one hand, governments have officially decentralized control over the introduction of changes in the field of education, while, on the other hand, they want to retain a tight grip over dominant aspects of the teaching process and corresponding policy. Indeed, in Poland, since 1991, the responsibility for running schools has been gradually delegated to local government authorities, resulting in municipalities (*gminy*) becoming responsible for kindergartens and primary schools, and districts (*powiaty*) becoming responsible for secondary schools, special education schools, and other education institutions (e.g. lifelong learning centres). The scope of these responsibilities covers two main tasks: firstly, school administration and, secondly, financing (e.g. maintenance of buildings; provision of didactical equipment for learning and conducting exams; payment of teacher salaries; and decisions regarding the creation, merging, transformation, and closure of schools). However, the actual quality of teaching and learning processes in schools, as well as corresponding education policies, have remained under the control of the minister of national education and school superintendents. The minister's tasks include, for example, specifying the list of demands on schools, defining and approving core curricula for each subject, as well as setting the list of textbooks for each educational level. Monitoring and evaluation of schoolwork (i.e., pedagogical supervision) were responsibilities given to the superintendent's inspectorates (*kuratoria*), although acting partially under the minister's control. This strong control of central government, via pedagogical supervision mechanisms, means that teacher communities lose (or abandon) their autonomy and try to meet (or even exceed) the expectations of the authorities: for example, in a bid to satisfy the conservative authorities, in some Polish schools girls are not allowed to exercise wearing shorts during physical education lessons, despite the fundamental appropriateness of the attire for the activity. Such a situation – as indicated by Brzezińska and Czup (2013, p. 37) – deepens the mistrust which

> results in teachers adopting non-constructive attitudes, such as excessive caution, withdrawal, resignation and avoidance, unjustified anticipation of failures, lack of hope for a good future or extreme individualism and focus only on achieving their own goals, with limited ability to respect the interests of others and respect for socially established norms and rules.

Core to the decentralization strategy was a change in the mechanism of education financing: the introduction of a complicated algorithm for educational subsidy distributions, which increase or decrease the amount of money allocated to local governments based on individual schools' characteristics (e.g. the size of the school, the number of pupils with various special educational needs, or the number of pupils belonging to minoritized ethnicities, and the level of teachers' qualifications) (Herbst et al., 2009). Although not directly responsible for the quality of the teaching process in schools, local governments, concerned about the educational subsidy as well as their own positions in local elections,

> are trying to shape the quality of their schools and motivate head-teachers by using a variety of tools – from soft tools, consisting of interviews and feedback on the work of the school, to hard tools, making the level of funding dependent on the results achieved, or using the results as a criterion for evaluation and selection of the head teacher. (Herbst & Levitas, 2012, p. 148)

While these efforts have led to the improvement of students' learning achievements (including in the international arena, e.g., as measured by Programme for International Student Assessment (PISA) testing), they have also stimulated competition both between local governments and between schools, which, in a time of demographic decline, has turned into a fight for the survival of schools and teachers' jobs (Klus-Stańska, 2017).

This competition was further exacerbated by implementing key standardized elements to the decentralized education system, in order to ensure its overall coherence – but, in the process, forcing students, teachers, and schools into direct, ongoing comparison with one another. The most important of these elements are *Teacher's Charter* (i.e., a law regulating, in detail, the functioning of teachers and the teaching profession); centrally defined core curriculum content; the compulsory, external student examination system implemented at the end of each stage of compulsory education; as well as the external evaluation of schools. Moreover, data on average student achievements and on schools' 'educational value-added' indicators were made publicly available, thus showcasing the comparative effectiveness of schools in elevating pupils' exam results.

In view of such strong powers given to local authorities, as well as the influences of centrally planned education policy, the autonomy of schools and teachers is obviously limited. Indeed, as Herbst and Wojciuk (2014, p. 15) argue, what clearly distinguishes the Polish model of education management from those adopted in other post-communist, Visegrad Group countries is the significantly lower percentage of decisions granted to the school level. As such, the situation of head teachers and teachers can be understood as a fundamental paradox: autonomous but controlled. Two simple examples illustrate this paradox clearly. Firstly, although head teachers technically have autonomy with regard to decisions on hiring and evaluating school staff, especially teachers, they can only employ them within the framework dictated by the local authority. Secondly, teachers officially have the right to choose curricula and textbooks by themselves, but only from the list stipulated by the ministry (Krzychała & Zamorska, 2012).

These above-described features of the Polish education system have been successively reinforced since 2015 by education reforms introduced by a right-wing conservative government whose main goal is to centralize – and thus control – this system even further. Currently, the ministry of science and national education is working on new regulations aimed at expanding the responsibilities of school superintendents, in order to tighten central control over schools and head teachers. Under the proposed legislation, firstly, superintendents will be able to immediately dismiss head teachers who fail to implement their recommendations. Secondly, school superintendents will decide which non-governmental organizations (NGOs) will be allowed to organize extracurricular classes in Polish schools. Thirdly, the new education regulations also foresee prison sentences for head teachers for exceeding their state-allocated powers or failing to fulfil their state-mandated duties in the care or supervision of pupils.

In sum, the national strategies reforming education in Poland after the collapse of communism – whatever their tangible benefits in terms of decentralization – have tended, in fact, to maintain the state's position overseeing the accessibility and quality of education. This has been architected via strengthening the position of school superintendents, depriving local communities' right to co-decide on the education system, deciding on the amount of funds allocated to local governments, controlling the content of curricula, and strengthening the mechanisms of accountability and standardization of teachers' work. These contemporary realities position Poland's education system firmly within the realm of the fatalist approach. Such a situation creates a climate of mistrust towards teachers and the education system and enforces competition between schools which then become insular microcosms, each focussed on the battle for their own survival in national and international rankings. These tensions in Poland's education reforms would seem to confirm West's (2010, p. 94) suggestion, albeit made in a different context, that 'policy-makers believe competition to be an essential ingredient, if the much needed "transformation" of the education system is to be realised'.

SSC in Poland: Mapping Promising Policies and Practices

The above discussion on key features of Poland's education system leads us to take a more detailed look at the potential for SSC that exists (if at all) in the face of conflicting logics: i.e., the decentralized education system, the state's desire for control over that system's key mechanisms, and the heavily capitalistic influence of neoliberal pressures. Therefore, in this section, we will outline what we believe have been the most promising policies and practices over the past 30 years in terms of developing, directly or indirectly, the project of SSC in Poland.

One of the most encouraging and promising policy initiatives in this field was the introduction of a new law on in-service teacher training institutions (MEN, 2012). According to this law, the main task of these institutions should be providing 'tailor-made' support to schools, kindergartens, or other education institutions via building partnerships between them, thus enriching teachers' and head teachers' professional learning. The main reasons behind these partnerships were, firstly, that belonging to a network gives teachers and schools the opportunity to establish close contacts with other schools and organizations facing similar challenges – thus, to exchange knowledge and experiences in solving shared problems; and secondly, to transform the existing ad hoc and non-institutionalized cooperation between schools into institutionalized cooperation and learning networks led by a network coordinator (Stronkowski et al., 2014). Between 2010 and 2015, the Centre for Education Development (CED) (*Ośrodek Rozwoju Edukacji*) – the national teacher training centre run by the ministry of national education – implemented a pilot programme for the creation of such networks within the framework of the *Human Capital Operational Programme* co-financed by the European Union. The project was targeted primarily at 'high achieving' and 'low achieving' district-run schools and yielded diverse learning outcomes, i.e., at least 10% of the schools participating in the programme scored below the district average in the test taken at the end of a given education stage and at least 10% of the schools scored above the average. Each participating district was obliged to establish four thematically different networks (e.g. on the theme of how to strengthen students' mathematics competencies) – including at least two where the premises had been developed under the CED framework, meaning that these themes were set by policy-makers rather than by the teaching community.

Looking at the results of this pilot, but relatively large-scale, project – as documented by Stronkowski et al. (2014) – it can be concluded that the network-creating programme yielded many benefits for schools as it enabled them, for example, to exchange knowledge and best practices, as well as to improve the professional competences of their staff. However, this project also had weaker points, hindering the full capitalization and potential of the networks created within its framework.

Firstly, teachers' participation in these networks was not voluntary, but in most cases imposed by head teachers – indeed, as Stronkowski et al. (2014) show, only one third of teachers declared that they applied to these networks by themselves. This coercion led to situations whereby – as observed by our second author, who served as an expert for this project – teachers sometimes did not even know what the cooperation they were participating in was about, for example, they expected certificates for their participation as per short-term workshops or courses. Secondly, at this time (2010–2015), Polish schools were in fierce competition with each other not only for positions in rankings, pupil exam results, and subsidies, but for pupils themselves (as the allocation of funding was contingent on enrolment numbers), thus had no interest in sharing their strategies for success within newly created, compulsory attendance networks, halting the very operation of these networks. Thirdly, both participating teachers and coordinators complained about inadequate planning of the corresponding work they were expected to carry out, as well as a lack of inspirational themes offered as guidance.

Despite these weaknesses, this initiative, although no longer as strongly formalized and far-reaching, is still in existence. For example, schools and teachers can further use the online 'improvement in the network' platform to maintain and develop the interpersonal networks established via the project, and the school partnerships established have given rise to further school networks managed by the CED, such as the *Talent Discoverers* schools network and the *Health Promotion* schools network.

Another stimulus for Poland to develop school-to-school cooperation came in the form of the *Regulation of the Minister of National Education on the list of requirements for schools and other education institutions* (first announced in 2009 as an annexe to the regulation on pedagogical supervision, then published in 2017 as a separate regulation). The regulation specified the obligatory tasks for schools to carry out in order to ensure optimal conditions for teaching and learning processes, as well as other statutory school activities (MEN, 2017). One of the key responsibilities that Poland's schools have under this framework is the authentic and intentional cooperation of schools with institutions and organizations operating in the local area and – in the case of vocational schools – with employers. In characterising this requirement, the ministry specifies that, firstly, the school's use of resources in its local area serves to improve the quality of its work and, consequently, the development of pupils; and, secondly, this cooperation may take various forms – from the exchange of information to the co-organization of educational events – and may involve a different number of entities depending on the objectives, needs, and resources of the local community (MEN, 2017).

Although this document does not directly mention cooperation between schools, it could be considered as a starting point for principals to view other schools as possible partners in fulfilling this policy requirement. Indeed, Hernik et al.'s (2012) research on the cooperation of schools with other entities in their local areas shows that other schools (coming only after businesses and NGOs) were regarded as the most vital partners for cooperation. The report also details the scope of SSC mainly as including activities such as (Hernik et al., 2012, pp. 34–36):

- co-organizing or joining events with or on the premises of other schools (e.g. joint celebrations, exhibitions, and performances);
- promoting schools to pupils from lower stages of education;
- informally exchanging information about pupils who need support;
- writing joint applications for funding; and
- exchanging staff and equipment or jointly purchasing resources that all schools in the municipality need.

On the whole, this report indicates an apparent readiness on the part of schools to bundle their capacities and resources, in order to support each other in the implementation of different educational tasks or ideas. This readiness to cooperate seems to be further confirmed by other well-known, although not officially documented, forms of partnerships established more recently between schools, such as the cooperation of schools focussed around developing: broader ideas (e.g. promoting health values via the *Health Promotion Schools' Network*, and the dissemination of UNESCO's aims and activities via the *UNESCO Associated Schools' Network*), educational programmes (e.g. the *Spring of Education: National Programme of Cooperation between Schools and Teachers* and the *Network of Learning Schools*), and teachers' professional needs and interests (e.g. the *Network of Kindergarten Headteachers, Digital Dialogue*, and *Active Blackboard*). Other types of educational partnerships include NGOs running schools (e.g. *Białystok Education Association*) or Polish-run community schools abroad (e.g. *School 6.0*).

In addition to these examples of SSC developed at the national level, Polish schools also have relatively rich experiences in networking with schools from other countries. Indeed, since 2004 when Poland joined the European Union, a rich repertoire of new international possibilities for cooperation has been offered to teachers and schools: ranging from *Erasmus+* mobility-based programmes, through national and local government and NGO programmes, to online networks. Over the last five years, of these, *eTwinning* – the community for schools in Europe (and beyond) to collaborate across borders via a purpose-built online platform – has attracted the greatest number of Polish teachers and schools, growing to 79,556 teachers and 19,358 schools by October 2021 (FRSE, 2021), placing Poland in a leadership position in these endeavours Europe-wide. The discrepancy between this dynamic development of international school partnerships and the slowness in terms of building partnerships between schools across local municipalities or districts has led us to reflect on the possible reasons for this need for a new onward trajectory.

Some interesting explanations for this phenomenon could be derived from the small-scale, interview-based study carried out by the first author of this chapter, into teachers' perceptions and experiences of working with teachers from other nations, and the impact that these experiences have on their professional practice and identity (Kowalczuk-Walędziak & Underwood, 2021). The participants for this study were 13 teachers who had long-standing and broad experience in engaging with teachers on an international basis via the *eTwinning* programme or other international initiatives, such as the *Erasmus+* programme, as well as projects funded by governmental and non-governmental foundations. Two key messages found via this study are relevant for the focus of this chapter.

Firstly, the interviewed teachers highlighted some of the key, unique characteristics and factors that make international networking an inherently interesting and inspiring space for their professional development (beyond their local teacher professional development networks), including the voluntary nature of their participation, i.e., not dictated by management or local authorities; the opportunity to flexibly, autonomously, and collectively build activities in project teams; the interesting, encouraging, and inspiring content of their international projects; the space to create an open and stimulating work environment; and the opportunity to build on professional symmetry leadership structures and relationships between members (Kowalczuk-Walędziak & Underwood, 2021). The juxtaposition of these enriching characteristics of international networks with teachers' experiences from participating in the networks created by the CED project suggests that the former are a significant contrast to what teachers experience in national school networks. However, on the other hand, teachers involved in Kowalczuk-Walędziak and Underwood's study (2021) also indicated that being in an international network offered – for both them and for their schools – a kind of prestige and an additional advantage in the fight with other schools for student enrolment.

Secondly, these international programmes organized out with local regions can also be understood as a product of the top-down, neoliberal drive to 'internationalize' and 'standardize' education across the European continent and beyond (Engel et al., 2020), despite the great and nuanced diversity definitively present across Europe's many communities. As such, this means that a wealth of local resources are ignored in favour of homogenized methodologies – which, while perhaps seeming more spectacular than locally organized initiatives, are ultimately less tailored to contemporary Poland's immediate socio-political contexts and needs. Indeed, some of the interviewed teachers clearly indicated that not all education policies, trends, and approaches originating in Western countries could be fully implemented in Poland.

Barriers

Despite the positive initiatives and experiences of cooperation between schools described above, we believe that there is still much that needs to be developed in this area; therefore, in this section, we reflect on some of the possible barriers currently blocking Poland's full utilization of the potential inherent in SSC. These barriers can be divided into two groups: formal/legal and normative/cultural (Dorczak, 2012).

As for the formal/legal barriers, firstly, there are no clear regulations governing the forms and principles of SSC in Poland. Although the *Regulation of the Ministry of National Education on requirements for schools* (MEN, 2017) highlights the importance of school cooperation with institutions and organizations operating on a local level, there are no specific regulations defining the nature and forms of relationships between schools; there is no clear means of financing such cooperations; and there is a lack of solutions regarding the problem of how to bring the outcomes and influences of teacher network efforts into schools themselves.

Secondly, such cooperation is certainly not facilitated through the priorities of Poland's post-1989 education policy, which, instead, has forced the country's schools into direct competition with each other via decentralizing the education system (i.e., transferring the responsibility for schools onto local governments, while affording a low degree of autonomy to schools and head teachers); changing the mechanisms of school financing (i.e., introducing a new, complicated algorithm for distributing educational subsidies); and adopting uniform evaluation standards for students' and schools' work (i.e., pressuring students into striving for high results in external examinations, and pressuring schools into focussing on winning or ranking highly in contests, league tables, and rankings). These pressures, combined with the current demographic decline in Poland, mean that schools have to compete with each other for students, resources, funds, and ranking positions.

Thirdly, inconsistent and unstable policy moves post-1989 act as a significant barrier to the development of SSC in contemporary Poland by enacting permanent, often extremely contradictory, changes in the education system via the powers of successive governments who do not share any coherent, student-centred vision for the country's education system, thus failing to provide a sense of stability or confidence in the profession, as well as discouraging partnerships between schools by creating an insular, distrustful culture in the teaching community (Śliwerski, 2012).

Regarding normative/cultural barriers, firstly, it should be noted contemporary Poland has not had the opportunity to develop a well-connected or long-standing tradition of cooperation between schools. Under the communist system imposed by the Soviet Union from the late 1930s onwards, following its invasion of Poland, the ideological principle of uniformity was not conducive to building cooperation between schools due to the nationwide obligation to follow strict, identical rules. Later, after regaining independence, the 'decentralization' of Poland's education system from 1991 onwards was based not on principles of bottom-up collaboration but on capitalistic mechanisms – such as calculating education provision in terms of profit margins and viewing students as future workers and taxpayers (Cervinkova & Rudnicki, 2019). Rooted in inter-school competition, this neoliberal reform also failed to contribute to the perception of cooperation between schools as being a valuable means for improving the quality of education on offer for Poland's students. Furthermore, the ever-deepening entrenchment of the bureaucratic school management model in subsequent years largely reduced teachers' roles to executing centrally devised instructions (Stronkowski et al., 2014; Żebrok, 2017).

Against this capitalistic backdrop, teachers' and head teachers' workloads should also be understood as a significant challenge in developing successful SSC networks and projects. For example, as evidenced in numerous studies (e.g. Nowakowska, 2013; Stronkowski et al., 2014; Tołwińska, 2019), teachers and head teachers working in school-to-school networks find that excessive demands on their time (e.g. being obligated to attend large numbers of training courses), as well as rigid, overloaded timetables, make it impossible for them to allocate time or energy to investing in SSC.

Thirdly, moving from a systemic level to a more interpersonal level, another barrier to SSC in Poland today is teacher-to-teacher relationships, especially in terms of initiating, maintaining, and carrying out cooperative activities (Korzeniecka-Bondar, 2015). Concrete examples of these fraught relationships can be seen in difficulties in setting common goals and a resistance to team activities, as well as poor quality relationships between school leaders in terms of taking responsibility for shared tasks. Indeed, in Elčurj's (2013, p. 201) study on barriers to collaborative learning in school networks, one fifth of the respondents said that they felt great resistance to collaborative learning, with their initial feelings being described as reservation, apprehension, and embarrassment. In explaining this, they further reported that they did not want to reveal their views, ideas, and problems to the group, because they doubted their value. Additionally, several of the interviewed teachers pointed out that they simply are not used to working together. As such, perhaps the idea of a 'network' was too distanced from and incompatible with their community: one where the very idea of communication and interaction with unknown peers was an unfamiliar or unappealing one, and one where it cannot be forgotten that the long process of recovering from the violent influence of the Soviet regime is still very much ongoing (Korzeniecka-Bondar, 2015; Kamińska, 2019).

Key Lessons for Practice and Policy: How Does SSC Hold the Potential to Solve Contemporary Poland's Education Challenges?

This chapter has shown that although there have been some promising school-to-school collaborative initiatives to date, taken together they are not far-reaching or well-documented and do not amount to a coherent or vibrant national culture of SSC – signalling the need for both greater collaboration and more extensive research in the future. That said, the picture of Poland's existing SSC depicted in this paper is most definitely limited, thus not wholly representative, given that it drew mainly on reports and data generated under politically driven agendas, or our own experiences. As such, there is much to be done in this field, on both policy and practice levels.

However, anyone seeking to make policy recommendations for SSCs must be mindful of a core paradox: on the one hand, an absence of recommendations from policy-makers on the concept of SSC can make it difficult to identify clear routes forwards; on the other hand, it is our belief that meaningful and sustainable SSC should not be an issue reserved for government policy, but driven from the grassroots, by school communities themselves on an autonomous basis (Armstrong et al., 2021). Going forwards, in this section, rather than offer concrete recommendations, we would like to draw attention to specific sites where we believe that the practice of SSC could be key in bringing about positive changes and transformations in Poland's education system: ranging from increasing students' learning outcomes to preventing the closure of rural schools.

Firstly, perhaps most generally, the teaching processes running Poland's schools are often criticized by various stakeholders (e.g. parents and students themselves) for being uninteresting, unengaging, and not offering extracurricular activities (e.g. NIK, 2021; Stańczyk, 2012). These weaknesses could be greatly alleviated through the frameworks of SSC. For example, sharing personnel between schools is not yet standard practice in Poland but may allow each and every school to have access to the teaching staff and specialist staff that they need, especially where there are particular shortages (e.g. speech therapists and psychological counsellors; NIK, 2017). Additionally, this method of sharing could be applied to great effect in terms of courses (both curricular and extracurricular) and learning materials (e.g. mutually open access to specialist sports equipment, art materials, and technological resources). This movement and sharing of personnel and resources would ultimately offer students more fruitful, supportive, and well-resourced environments in which to grow, both in terms of formal learning outcomes and their personal development.

Secondly, following the government's decision to abolish Poland's gymnasium school system (i.e., lower secondary schools) in 2017, many teachers working at these levels found themselves without jobs (Kędzierska, 2019). Without employment contracts, they were forced to create patchwork careers across multiple schools, in order to obtain work totalling the required hours for their profession (e.g. 10 hours in one school, 4 in another, and 4 in another making the necessary 18). In practice, these enforced patchwork careers mean that such teachers are subjected to multiple work contracts, multiple head teachers, and multiple school frameworks simultaneously (Kędzierska, 2012). These combined sets of pressures often overlap and clash, e.g., in terms of lengthy commutes in the middle of the day. We believe that if schools set up formal regional networks, this would create a singular, unified platform for agreements and partnerships between member schools, thus simplifying and smoothing out the day-to-day demands on teachers with patchwork careers.

Thirdly, closer SSC would allow Poland's teachers to share good practices, thus providing access to a spectrum of new professional development opportunities and new perspectives, all while embedded in professional contexts already similar and relatable to their own. Such efforts to share good practices may also increase teachers' longer term potential of working together, in a way that they deem to be trustworthy, which is critical given Poland's current individualistic culture of professionalism in teaching communities (Kamińska, 2019).

Fourthly, as was mentioned before, funding for individual schools comes from the government via local councils, meaning that the increasing cuts to the education budget made by the current government are perhaps most acutely felt by rural schools, where their small size is used as the reason for their closure. However, being part of a regional school-to-school network would protect smaller schools by putting them into partnerships with other schools in their area, sharing resources, and reducing their running costs (e.g. sharing one school bus between three small neighbouring schools is cheaper than running three) (Uryga, 2018).

While SSC is not the single solution to these (and other) problems faced by Poland's contemporary education system, we whole-heartedly believe that building on these emerging and existing connections between schools will only improve access to this great, but as yet untapped, potential for students, teachers, and their communities.

References

Armstrong, P. W., & Ainscow, M. (2018). School-to-school support within a competitive education system: Views from the inside. *School Effectiveness and School Improvement, 29*(4), 614–633.

Armstrong, P. W., Brown, C., & Chapman, C. J. (2021). School-to-school collaboration in England: A configurative review of the empirical evidence. *Review of Education, 9*(1), 319–351.

Brzezińska, A. I., & Czub, T. (2013). Zaufanie społeczne jako wyzwanie i ratunek dla polskiego systemu edukacji [Social trust as a challenge and a rescue for the Polish education system]. *Nauka, 1*, 31–44.

Cervinkova, H., & Rudnicki, P. (2019). Neoliberalism, neoconservatism, authoritarianism. The politics of public education in Poland. *Journal for Critical Education Policy Studies, 17*(2), 1–23.

Dorczak, R. (2012). Modele współpracy szkoły z organizacjami w środowisku lokalnym [Models of school cooperation with organisations in the local environment]. In G. Mazurkiewicz (Ed.), *Jakość edukacji: Różnorodne perspektywy* [Quality of education: Multiple perspectives] (pp. 311–335). Wydawnictwo Uniwersytetu Jagiellońskiego.

Elčurj, J. (2013). Sieci uczących się szkół [Networks of learning schools]. In D. Elsner (Ed.), *Sieci współpracy i samokształcenia. Teoria i praktyka* [Cooperation and self-development networks. Theory and practice] (pp. 194–214). Wolters Kluwer.

Engel, L. C., Maxwell, C., & Yemini, M. (Eds.). (2020). *The machinery of school internationalisation in action: Beyond the established boundaries.* Routledge.

Foundation for the Development of the Education System (FRSE). (2021). *Krajowe Statystyki Rejestracji w Programie eTwinning* [National Statistics for eTwinning Programme]. https://etwinning.pl/statystyki-2/

Gallagher, T. (2016). Shared education in Northern Ireland: School collaboration in divided societies. *Oxford Review of Education, 42*(3), 362–375.

Herbst, M., Herczyński, J., & Levitas, A. (2009). *Finansowanie oświaty w Polsce – Diagnoza, dylematy, możliwości* [Financing education in Poland - diagnosis, dilemmas, opportunities]. SCHOLAR.

Herbst, M., & Levitas, A. (2012). Decentralizacja oświaty w Polsce 2000-2010: Czas stabilizacji i nowe wyzwania [Decentralisation of education in Poland 2000-2010: Time of stabilisation and new challenges]. In M. Herbst (Ed.), *Decentralizacja oświaty* [Decentralisation of education] (pp. 118–153). Wydawnictwo ICM Uniwersytetu Warszawskiego.

Herbst, M., & Wojciuk, A. (2014). *Common origin, different paths. Transformation of education systems in the Czech Republic, Slovakia, Hungary and Poland.* Instytut Badań Edukacyjnych.

Hernik, K., Solon-Lipiński, M., & Stasiowski, J. (2012). *Współpraca szkół z podmiotami zewnętrznymi. Raport z badania otoczenia instytucjonalnego przedszkoli, szkół podstawowych i gimnazjów* [Cooperation of schools with external entities. Report on the study of the institutional environment of kindergartens, primary and lower secondary schools]. Ośrodek Rozwoju Edukacji.

Hood, C. (1998). *The art of the state, culture rhetoric and public management.* Clarendon Press.

Kamińska, M. (2019). *Współpraca i uczenie się nauczycieli w kulturze organizacyjnej szkoły. Studium teoretyczno-empiryczne* [Teacher collaboration and learning in the organizational culture of school]. Impuls.

Kędzierska, H. (2012). *Kariery zawodowe nauczycieli. Konteksty – Wzory – Pola dyskursu* [Teachers' careers. Contexts – Patterns – Fields of discourse]. Wydawnictwo Adam Marszałek.

Kędzierska, H. (2019). Nauczyciele gimnazjum – W poszukiwaniu nowej, profesjonalnej tożsamości [Middle school teachers – Looking for a new professional identity]. *Przegląd Pedagogiczny, 2,* 66–78.

Klus-Stańska, D. (2017). Walka o testo-maniakalne przetrwanie, czyli po co i czego uczą się przyszli polscy nauczyciele? [The struggle for testo-maniacal survival, or what are future Polish teachers learning for and what?] *Rocznik Pedagogiczny, 40,* 71–87.

Korzeniecka-Bondar, A. (2015). The dark sides of individualism in the work of junior high school teachers: Implications for education. In L. Daniela & L. Rutka (Eds.), *Selected papers of the association for teacher education in Europe.* Cambridge Scholars Publishing.

Kowalczuk-Walędziak, M., & Underwood, J. (2021). International communities of practice: What makes them successful vehicles for teachers' professional development? *Educational Studies.* Advanced online publication.

Krzychała, S., & Zamorska, B. (2012). Zamknięte i otwarte zmiany kultury szkoły [Closed and open changes in school culture]. In B. D. Gołębniak & H. Kwiatkowska (Eds.), *Nauczyciele. Programowe (nie)przygotowanie* [Teachers. Curricular (un)preparedness] (pp. 57–76). Wydawnictwo Naukowe DSW.

Mendel, M. (2000). *Partnerstwo rodziny, szkoły i gminy* [Partnership of family, school, and municipality]. Wydawnictwo Adam Marszałek.

Menter, I., Kowalczuk-Walędziak, M., Sablić, M., & Valeeva, R. A. (forthcoming). Teacher education in Central and Eastern Europe: Emerging themes and potential future directions. In M. Kowalczuk-Walędziak, R. A. Valeeva, M. Sablić, & I. Menter (Eds.), *The Palgrave handbook of teacher education in Central and Eastern Europe.* Palgrave Macmillan.

Ministry of National Education (MEN). (2012). *Rozporządzenie Ministra Edukacji Narodowej z dnia 26 października 2012 r. zmieniające rozporządzenie w sprawie placówek doskonalenia nauczycieli* (Dz.U. 2012 poz. 1196) [Regulation of the Minister of National Education of October 26, 2012 amending the Regulation on teacher training centres (*Journal of Laws* of 2012, item 1196)].

Ministry of National Education (MEN). (2017). *Rozporządzenie Ministra Edukacji Narodowej z dnia 11 sierpnia 2017 r. w sprawie wymagań wobec szkół i placówek* (Dz. U. 2020.2198 t.j.) [Regulation of the Minister of National Education of August 11, 2017 on requirements for schools and other education institutions (*Journal of Laws* of 2020, item 2198)].

Naczelna Izba Kontroli (NIK). (2017). Przeciwdziałanie zaburzeniom psychicznym u dzieci i młodzieży [The prevention of mental disorders in children and adolescents]. https://www.nik.gov.pl/plik/id,15392,vp,17874.pdf.

Naczelna Izba Kontroli (NIK). (2021). *Organizacja pracy nauczycieli w szkołach publicznych* [The organisation of teachers' work in public schools]. https://www.nik.gov.pl/aktualnosci/nik-o-organizacji-pracy-nauczycieli-w-szkolach-publicznych-czesc-i.html.

Nowakowska, K. B. (2013). Sieć 'Kujawy' [Schools' network 'Kujawy']. In D. Elsner (Ed.), *Sieci współpracy i samokształcenia. Teoria i praktyka* [Cooperation and self-development networks. Theory and practice] (pp. 183–193). Wolters Kluwer.

Potulicka, E., & Rutkowiak, J. (2013). *Neoliberalne uwikłania edukacji* [Neoliberalism and Education]. Impuls.

Roulston, S., McGuinness, S., Bates, J., & O'Connor-Bones, U. (2021). School partnerships in a post-conflict society: Addressing challenges of collaboration and competition. *Irish Educational Studies*. Advanced online publication.

Śliwerski, B. (2012). Dokąd zmierza polska edukacja? [Where does the Polish education go?]. *Neodidagmata, 33/34*, 65–74.

Stańczyk, P. (2012). Nuda w szkole – Między alienacją a emancypacją [Boredom at school – Between alienation and emancipation]. *Teraźniejszość - Człowiek - Edukacja, 3*(59), 35–56.

Stronkowski, P., A. Szczurek, M. Leszczyńska, & A. Matejczuk. (2014). *Ewaluacja modernizowanego systemu doskonalenia nauczycieli – Projekt 'System doskonalenia nauczycieli oparty na ogólnodostępnym kompleksowym wspomaganiu szkół', Poddziałanie 3.3.1 PO Kapitał Ludzki* [Evaluation of the modernised teacher in-service training system – The project 'Teacher in-service training system based on generally available comprehensive support for schools']. Ośrodek Rozwoju Edukacji.

Theiss, W. (1996). Edukacja środowiskowa. Zarys problematyki. *Problemy Opiekuńczo-Wychowawcze, 10*(1–2), 3–9.

Tołwińska, B. (2019). Teachers team learning in the context of creating learning schools: Implications for teacher education. In M. Kowalczuk-Walędziak, A. Korzeniecka-Bondar, W. Danilewicz, & G. Lauwers (Eds.), *Rethinking teacher education for the 21st century. Trends, challenges, and new directions* (pp. 269–282). Barbara Budrich Publishers.

Uryga, D. (2018). 'Association Schools' – A step towards the revitalization of the idea of community school in Poland. In D. Keller, K. O'Neil, H. Nicolaisen, D. Schugurensky, & K. Villaseñor (Eds.), *Social pedagogy and social education: Bridging traditions and innovations* (pp. 191–204). Wydawnictwo Akademii Pedagogiki Specjalnej.

West, M. (2010). School-to-school cooperation as a strategy for improving student outcomes in challenging contexts. *School Effectiveness and School Improvement, 21*(1), 93–112.

Wiśniewski, J., & Zahorska, M. (2020). Reforming education in Poland. In F. Reimers (Ed.), *Audacious education purposes* (pp. 181–208). Springer.

Wołczyk, J., & Winiarski, M. (1978). Rzeczywistość a założenia modelowe szkoły środowiskowej [Reality versus ideal assumptions of the community school]. In S. Frycie (Ed.), *Szkoła środowiskowa. Pierwsze doświadczenia. Zbiór artykułów i reportaży o pracy szkół środowiskowych* [Community school. First experiences. A collection of articles and reports on the work of community schools]. Wydawnictwa Szkolne i Pedagogiczne.

Żebrok, P. (2017). Szkoła wobec wyzwań współczesności. Sieci współpracy i samokształcenia [School in the face of contemporary challenges. Networks of cooperation and self-education]. *EduAkcja. Magazyn Edukacji Elektronicznej, 1*(13), 95–103.

Chapter 8

School-to-School Collaboration – Kenyan Context

Andrew Kitavi Wambua

Abstract

Collaborative teaching and learning in Kenya is at relatively immature phase. There is dearth of empirical research undertaken on school-to-school collaboration and its impact and influence on the students' learning outcomes. The 8:4:4 system of education, which begun in 1985, and which was short of insights into the impact of collaborative, is coming to an end to pave way for 2-6-3-3-3 education curriculum framework which is largely seen as progressive. As such, collaborative teaching and learning across the whole-school system is slowly beginning to evolve – with the learners being expected to learn, un-learn and re-learn collaboratively. The Kenyan education system is highly marketized and when coupled with lack of clear national policy guidelines on inter-school collaboration, it falls short of obligating teachers to initiate or even deepen the few existing collaborative designs within and beyond their schools' boarders. Given that the challenges facing learning appear to increase exponentially, it appears to be timely to have students and teachers from different schools come together to network and share ideas, knowledge, expertise, resources and best practices – bearing in mind that cultures that work together hold the prospect of long-term impact that is not dependent on a few individuals but the whole team (Hargreaves & O'Connor, 2017).

Keywords: Collaboration; competence-based curriculum; symposium; Accelerated Learning Programme; competition; education policy

School-to-School Collaboration: Learning Across International Contexts, 143–153
Copyright © 2022 by Andrew Kitavi Wambua
Published under exclusive licence by Emerald Publishing Limited
doi:10.1108/978-1-80043-668-820221009

Introduction

The Kenyan education system is highly centralized but still leaves room for school-to-school collaboration. In the decades since Kenya became a republic in 1963, policy-makers have called for school reforms that improve teacher practices and student outcomes. Under the Kenya Basic Education Act (Republic of Kenya, 2013), access to basic education is a fundamental human right, and as such, the government of Kenya recognizes the role of partnerships in enhancing access, equity, quality and relevant education (Ministry of Education, 2018). It appreciates the importance of creating linkages, promoting collaborations and networking with other key stakeholders to ease the current heavy household financial burden in education – though falls short of formulating clear policy guidelines on school-to-school collaboration.

The Cohesion/Regulation Matrix in the Kenyan School System

The Kenyan school governance model can be classified in the quadrant of the *fatalistic way* – a mix of high social regulation and low social cohesion as argued by Hood (1998). There is a dominant hierarchical culture with associated bureaucratic management of schools – which highly advocates for accountability and strict compliance to policy guidelines. The Executive Order No. 2/2013 on the Organization of the Government of the Republic of Kenya made it clear that the Ministry of Education is responsible for management of education in Kenya (Republic of Kenya, 2013). The ministry oversees key functions such as school administration and programmes, teacher education and management, curriculum development and education policy management, among others. Further to the Executive Order, the National Government – through the Ministry of Education – as contained in schedule 4 of the Kenyan Constitution (Republic of Kenya, 2010) formulates education policies, sets education standards in both primary and secondary schools, reviews curriculum, manages higher education and promotes sport education. The Ministry of Education in so many ways determines control and how accountability should function in school system.

High social regulation and low social cohesion have achieved prominence courtesy of top-down system of management. On the side of low social cohesion, teachers hardly participate in key decision-making. Theirs is majorly to implement what comes from the 'above'. Their craving for attention from the system leaders has been promoting competition – with collaborative learning being seen as just like another fad. There is little cooperation by schools to achieve outcomes and little is known about educational policies that promote collaborative learning across schools. Even after devolving a few functions such as pre-primary education, village polytechnics, home-craft centres, farmers training centres and childcare facilities, the government has retained a firm grip on education management – with low social cohesion.

The following three initiatives have been crucial in collaborative learning within and between schools:

a) Competence-based curriculum

Competence-based curriculum was first piloted in 2017 before the official rollout was done in 2019–spelling out collaboration as one of the key competencies to be achieved by every learner (Republic of Kenya, 2017). The framework defines collaboration as a process where two or more people or schools are guided by a common vision to achieve shared goals/objectives. Through collaborative learning experiences, students are expected to develop the social aspect of well-being at an early age. Equally, teachers are expected to prepare, teach and evaluate lessons together. Though school-to-school collaboration in primary school grades is yet to take shape, there is already light 'within' the tunnel as educators are motivated to undergo professional development on collaborative teaching practices. System leaders are beginning to provide the focus through training initiatives to help teachers cross the bridge to new pedagogies as argued by Fullan and Langworthy (2014).

The more the teachers learn and candidly discuss the competence-based curriculum, learning and assessment, the better placed they are to guide their students and respect the knowledge and experience everyone bring into the classroom. Though in its early stages of implementation, the competence-based curriculum is designed around a set of key competences that are cross-curricular and subject bound. Teachers are beginning to understand that when they work together, they extend their own professional learning and through continued efforts, they find ways of improving the quality of education they provide for their students (Ainscow et al., 2006). Collective learning stimulates new thinking, experimentation and better practice. This is echoed by Conner and Sliwka (2014) when they note that working together regularly on long-term projects enable teachers to be reflective practitioners. It highly regards teacher empowerment, continuous learning and student-centred learning as key pillars in building deep collaborative cultures. Culture includes vision, values, beliefs, language, assumptions, systems, symbols as well as norms (Needle, 2004) and shaping it must be given more importance over structural change (Chapman, 2019).

b) Symposiums

At the secondary school level, one of the collaborative designs is symposiums – which are mainly schools' initiatives. A school academic year is divided into three terms – with most of the symposiums being held in first and second. Symposiums act as a platform through which students develop competences. They take place through informal discussions and learning procedures in the school halls and in contrast to many regular classrooms where majority of the students are docile and passive, with the teacher and textbooks being seen as the final authority of knowledge.

Symposiums in part shift the greater part of the responsibility in the learning process from the teacher to the student. They alleviate the general charge that secondary schools have been largely dominated by the teacher and that they have provided too little opportunity for students other than those deemed to think creatively and critically and assume a greater responsibility in the learning process (Maaske, 1949). Topics of discussion range from science projects to humanities, to environmental conservations. Symposiums take place under the patronage of subject teachers from the participating schools and they may include a single-year level, mixed-year level or even a whole-school depending on the subject and the school population. The participating schools are informed of the topics of discussion prior to the date of symposium for adequate preparation. Though they lack a formal structure, most of the symposiums take the following format:

- Welcome remarks delivered by the host school.
- Introduction of a moderator for the symposium who will in turn introduce the panellists from the participating schools.
- The keynote speaker who will deliver remarks of overall theme of the symposium. The keynote speech is usually short and mostly touch on the topics of discussion.
- Depending with the subject of discussion, the moderator introduces each presenter/panelist and the school he or she comes from. He/she then guides the discussion among the panelists, often with pre-selected questions or topics that have been shared with the participating schools in advance.
- The symposiums then conclude with a question and answer session followed by vote of thanks remarks.

c) Accelerated learning programme

Many pupils are disengaged from learning at quite young age, and as such, they do not reach their full human potential. Their disengagement is strongly associated with the home and family context and the extent to which parents can economically, socially and emotionally support their children to engage at school (Hancock & Zubrick, 2015). In Kenya, social-economic gap has made the marginalized pupils suffer the most (Okilwa, 2015). This has led to concerted efforts by the Ministry of Education, civil societies, parents and school communities to convene a learning space under Accelerated Learning Programme – championed by Zizi Afrique Foundation. Accelerated Learning Programmes can be defined as education programmes that compress a formal curriculum by a certain *rate of acceleration* (Longden, 2013) and in the words of The Accelerated Education Working Group (AEWG, 2020, p. 9), Accelerated Learning Programme – which is sometimes referred to as Accelerated Education Programme can be defined as:

> A flexible, age-appropriate programme, run in an accelerated timeframe, which aims to provide access to education for disadvantaged, over-age, out-of-school children and youth. This may include those who missed out on or had their education interrupted due to poverty, marginalization, conflict and crisis. The goal of Accelerated Education Programmes is to provide learners with equivalent, certified competencies for basic education using effective teaching and learning approaches that match their level of cognitive maturity.

The Accelerated Learning Programme has successfully been implemented in three counties in Kenya: Bungoma, Turkana and Tana River and as of December 2020, between 6,800–7,000 learners had benefitted from the literacy and numeracy programmes conducted in the camps/community schools (Cherotich et al., 2020). The learning camps draw students from different schools – in the three counties – and offer them a range of learning support after school. In reaching pupils who are farthest behind, the programme brings joy and happiness to the learners as they 'learn how to learn' in an interactive environment with their teachers. Besides the three counties aforementioned, pilot programmes in Samburu, Nairobi, Migori and Kajiado counties have already been conducted.

Enablers of School-to-School Collaboration

The emerging learning networks are increasingly getting noticed. When schools collaborate, educators are able to deeply engage with one another in search of knowledge to fill the already existing learning gaps. Deep collaborative cultures take root when everyone – at the policy, county/district and the school levels – does their part and as Armstrong et al. (2021) contend:

> School leaders and other educational stakeholders all gain from working collaboratively with colleagues outside of their institutions and that this is (indirectly) to the advantage of the educational experiences and outcomes of the young people within their schools and classrooms.

The following initiatives have acted as enablers of school-to-school collaboration in the Kenyan school system:

a) Progressive curriculum
The competence-based curriculum – 2-6-3-3-3 – is gradually being rolled out, giving great emphasis to student-centred teaching. The curriculum envisions providing every learner with world-class standards in skills and knowledge needed in the twenty-first century with collaboration being explicitly explained as a core competence. The country is moving away from conventional teaching curriculum characterized by hand raising question and answer, teaching and learning in silos, learners learning in an often-silent classroom to a curriculum that emphasizes on crossing schools' borders in search of new knowledge. Teacher education curriculum has not been left out, as the core competences have been infused into the pre-service training – because teachers cannot teach what they do not know. Upskilling of in-service teachers has also started in earnest, with an aim of ensuring that teachers are well prepared to effectively and collaboratively implement the curriculum. Through such efforts, teachers acquire competences, skills and confidence necessary for curriculum change (Voogt et al., 2016).

The conventional approaches under the 8:4:4 system of education were inadequate to develop a whole student and his or her character. Competence-based curriculum creates a space for seamless and competence-based learning that nurtures every learner's potential, not in isolation, but within a community of schools. The seedlings of collaboration are starting to take shape, and if well watered, it is expected that 'cross-pollinated learning' – learning from each other – will pervade across the whole-school system. The curriculum challenges teachers and students alike to stretch themselves, make learning exploratory and continually engage – bearing in mind that high social capital is a powerful strategy to leverage human capital (Fullan, 2011).

b) Consistency and creativity

The growth of school symposiums – especially in boarding schools – has taken place over decades even without policy guidelines. Students and their patrons have been innovative, creative and consistent enough to design the structure of their symposiums. The patrons – teachers in this case – play the role of a collaborator and activator, while the students play the critical role of organizing and running the symposiums. The symposiums have proved to be genuinely collaborative. Both teachers and students are comfortable with what they are doing – building relationships, sharing ideas, challenging one another – and have a strong believe that together, they learn better. They develop truly memorable experiences of learning. The students see themselves as active partners in schools' life, and this increases their focus and attention and promotes meaningful learning experiences and high-order thinking skills. They are able to put into practice what they have been learning in the classroom – and therefore learning builds on and flows from experience and in the words of Boud et al. (1993, p. 8), 'learning can only occur if the experience of the learners is engaged, at least at some level'.

Symposiums expand students' imagination – making it possible for them to engage and reflect on their learning. Creativity – a core competence alongside collaboration – requires not only knowledge and understanding of the domain being investigated in these symposiums but also willingness to challenge the answers coming out during the discussions. Teaching and learning are not isolated but interactive activities (Kupers et al., 2018). Direct and constructive feedback is promptly provided to addresses faulty interpretations. Learning occurs in such a way that concepts, ideas and theories are delivered in constant interaction with the environment. Teachers and students share what they can learn from the visiting schools and celebrate learning together. There is no external force that pushes learning into one direction or another. It emerges through creative and socially embedded interactions. Most symposiums majorly take place in boarding secondary schools, and this disadvantages day schools.

c) Leadership – threads, knots and nets

Leadership is about creating a culture of improvement through building the capacity of teachers and working and reflecting together for better students' outcomes (Day & Hadfield, 2004; Robinson, 2018). A few schools – as explained in the two collaborative designs, i.e. Accelerated Learning Programmes and symposiums – in the country have been driven by a sheer willpower to network with other schools. The growth and sustainability of the already existing and new innovative networks of practice in and between schools is in part attributed to effective leadership. Symposiums are majorly student led, while the success of Accelerated Learning Programmes can be attributed to concerted efforts of teachers, Ministry of Education, parents as well as school communities. Concerted effort creates opportunities for an ongoing exchange and collaboration of educational practitioners (Sliwka, 2003).

Leading for improvement and collaborative cultures are intertwined. Collective leadership has been imperative in running of the current and emerging networks. Interactions among the network members are characterized as threads, knots and nets. Threads stand for relationships, communication and trust while activities represent the knots. The net is the resulting structure of activities and threads (Church et al., 2002). Threads give life to communication, shared ideas, relational processes, information, trust and conflicts. Collective leadership purposes to ensure that conflicts – moderate in this case – do not divert the attention of the teams from the shared vision and norms, and as Fullan (2010) notes, leadership at all levels makes the education system go.

Even though school-to-school collaboration can be clear to those who conceptually comprehend it, its implementation has been met by the following barriers:

a)   Competition
The marketized nature of the education system in Kenya has promoted competition over collaboration. The society is more concerned with grades – and this has the potential to make pupils anxious, easily irritated and overwhelmed and a feeling of frustration which could interfere with their concentration. Competition can create a little space for learners to share their talents and resources as compared to learning as a network. Though a fundamental part of human nature, the way pupils are taught to view and respond to competition needs to change. Competition has high stakes, as top-performing teachers have high chances of getting rewards such as promotion. As such, having a development policy that provides equal and positive learning opportunities for all pupils becomes untenable. In societies where competition is encouraged, pupils tend to associate it with greater self-esteem and the same applies in those societies that praise collaborative teaching and learning.

Competition can lead to negative interdependence between students, teachers and even schools as the success of one student, teacher or school is dependent on the failure of the other. As such, negative interdependence will likely inhibit collaborative behaviours (Johnson & Johnson 2014). Competition motivates only high-achieving students (Murray, 2019) and who could be in the minority. When students learn in a context without competition, they do better than their peers who learn in a competitive environment (Mukuka et al., 2019). Competition has the potential to hinder collaborative inquiry process – characterized by transparency, reflection and seeking alternatives – and this can create a gap between tacit and explicit knowledge, and so, moving beyond competition mental models is a fundamental pre-requisite to knowledge construction and new learning (Katz et al., 2008).

b)   Pupil:teacher ratio
The high pupil–teacher ratio in Kenyan schools is worrying. The Ministry of Education Science and Technology (2013) report showed a total shortage of 82,000 teachers in both primary and secondary schools by 2013, and with the 100% transition directive, the number of teachers needed could even be higher. directive is part of global campaign by the Kenyan government to give access to 12 years of basic learning and also show the government's commitment to the constitutional imperative of the right to education (Otieno & Ochieng, 2020). The directive enforces equity of enrolment opportunity for all children including disadvantaged and vulnerable groups. The government is implementing measures to improve transition rate from primary to secondary schools. Following its implementation, the transition rate from primary to secondary school increased from 76% in 2013 to 86% in 2018. The number of secondary schools increased from 7,834 to 10,665, while enrolment in secondary education grew from 1.9 million students in 2012 to 2.8 million in 2017 (Ministry of Education, 2019).

The workload of teachers has gone up and in many ways hindered collaborative teaching and learning as the government struggles to build more classrooms and recruit more teachers. High student enrolment coupled with low teacher recruitment equate to high pupil:teacher ratio, and with the many lessons to teach in the already overstretched infrastructural resources, it increasingly becomes hard for the teachers to cultivate, upload and download the best educational practices in meaningful groups. Teachers' effectiveness in meeting students' needs is largely dependent on the conduciveness of the environment in which they are operating from.

c)   Lack of clear policy guidelines
The low social cohesion in Kenyan school system can partly be attributed to lack of clear policy guidelines on school-to-school collaboration. For school-to-school collaboration to be realized, unwavering support from the state is obligatory. All the seven core competences as explained under the Basic Education Curriculum Framework (Republic of Kenya, 2017) – communication and collaboration, critical thinking and problem-solving, creativity and imagination, citizenship, learning to learn, self-efficacy and digital literacy – are only realizable in the presence of clear policy guidelines. In clear policy guidelines, schools establish rules, procedures and standards needed for students to effectively learn and achieve their goals. Without them, there is inconsistency in decision-making – since schools lack the necessary structure needed to meet educational needs of their students.

Collaboration is work. For example: a shift from institutional leadership, characterized by the head teacher being responsible for a single school, to educational leadership that focuses on a multiple of schools and educational well-being across wider geographical boundaries opens doors for the much-needed professional development of teachers (Armstrong, 2015). Policy design and implementation on collaborative learning is expected to connect range of actors vertically and horizontally across the whole-school system – with its success being dependant on the system leaders and the frontline workers, who are the teachers (Bob et al., 2019). Policy-makers and implementers are expected to be critical analytical thinkers, well-integrated personalities, highly developed egos, highly initiative, high level of leadership, above-average creative potential and instigators of constructive social action (Roberts & King, 1996). Failure to collaboratively work together has the potential to erode the strength and satisfaction of relationships.

Key Lessons for Practice and Policy

• Social capital plus human capital equal better learning outcomes
Research evidence has shown conventional wisdom and political sloganeering will be of little help in developing competencies and skills, if teaching and learning continues to be done in isolation (Leana, 2011). Students whose teachers have high human capital and high social capital have registered better learning outcomes. The converse is also true.

• De-privatised teaching builds teacher confidence
When teachers prepare, teach and analyze their lessons together, they develop trust, respect and openness to improvement within their community (Kruse & Loise, 1993). Their confidence is also strengthened as it becomes possible for them to share leadership, staff and resources (Armstrong, 2015).

• Clarity in policies and procedures is important
Policies help schools establish rules and procedures and create standards for quality teaching and learning. Without clear policies, collaborative teaching and learning is seen as a waste of time, or worse, a sign of low teacher efficacy – even when research evidence has shown positive effects of collaboration even in the rural schools (Muijs, 2015).

• Tapping the massive untapped potential
The untapped schools' joint energy need to be tapped and renewed. This has the potential of motivating teachers to rediscover their full potential and collaboratively work together – which is considered as a key strategy for strengthening the overall capacity of the school system (Ainscow et al., 2016).

References

AEWG. (2020). *The case for accelerated education.* Education in Conflict and Crisis Network/USAID. https://inee.org/system/files/resources/AEWG_Accelerated%20 Education%20Evidence%20Review.pdf

Ainscow, M., Dyson, A., Goldrick, S., & West, M. (2016). Using collaborative inquiry to foster equity within school systems: Opportunities and barriers. *School Effectiveness and School Improvement, 27*(1), 7–23.

Ainscow, M., Muijs, D., & West, M. (2006). Collaboration as a strategy for improving schools in challenging circumstances. *Improving Schools, 9*(3), 192–202.

Armstrong, P. (2015). *Effective school partnerships and collaboration for school improvement: A review of the evidence.* Department for Education.

Armstrong, P. A., Brown, C., & Chapman, C. J. (2021). School-to-school collaboration in England: A configurative review of the empirical evidence. *Review of Education, 9*(1), 319–351. https://doi.org/10.1002/rev3.3248

Bob, H., David, H., & Stephen, P. (2019). Policy failure and the policy-implementation gap: Can policy support programs help? *Policy Design and Practice, 2*(1), 1–14. https://doi.org/10.1080/25741292.2018.1540378

Boud, D., Cohen, R., & Walker, D. (1993). Introduction: Understanding learning from experience. In D. Boud, R. Cohen, & D. Walker (Eds.), *Using experience for learning* (pp. 1–17). Society for Research into Higher Education.

Chapman, C. (2019). *Making sense of education reform: Where next for Scottish education?* Association of Directors of Education in Scotland/The Staff College.

Cherotich, W., Ngindiru, V., & Ali, A. (2020). Adaptation of solutions from South Asia: Experiences of improving Learning outcomes in Africa: PAL Network. https://palnetwork.org/wp-content/uploads/2020/12/2020_PAL-Presentations_Africa-Knows-Conference.pdf

Church, M., Bitel, M., Armstrong, K., Fernando, P., Gould, H., Joss, S., Marwaha-Diedrich, M., de la Torre, A., & Vouhé, C. (2002.) *Participation, relationships and dynamic change: New thinking on evaluating the work of international networks.* University College.

Conner, L., & Sliwka, A. (2014). Implications of research on effective learning environments for initial teacher education. *European Journal of Education, 49*, 165–177. https://doi.org/10.1111/ejed.12081

Day, C., & Hadfield, M. (2004). Learning through networks: Trust, partnerships and the power of action research. *Educational Action Research, 12*(4), 575–586.

Fullan, M. (2010). *All systems go.* Corwin Press.

Fullan, M. (2011). *Choosing the wrong drivers for whole system reform.* Seminar series 204. Center for strategic education.

Fullan, M., & Langworthy, M. (2014). *A rich seam: How new pedagogies find deep learning.* Pearson. https://www.pearson.com/content/dam/one-dot-com/one-dot-com/global/Files/about-pearson/innovation/open-ideas/ARichSeamEnglish.pdf

Hancock, K. J., & Zubrick, S. R. (2015). Children and young people at risk of disengagement from school: For the Commissioner for Children and Young People Western Australia. https://www.ccyp.wa.gov.au/media/1422/report-education-children-at-risk-of-disengaging-from-school-literature-review.pdf

Hargreaves, A., & O'Connor, M. T. (2017). Collaborative professionalism. Monograph prepared for the World Innovation Summit for Education, Qatar, Qatar Foundation. www.wise-qatar.org/2017-wise-research-collaborative-professionalism

Hood, C. (1998). *The art of the state, culture rhetoric and public management.* Clarenden Press.

Johnson, D. W., & Johnson, R. T. (2014). Cooperative learning in 21st century. *Anales de Psicologia, 30*(3), 841–851.

Katz, S., Earl, L., Ben Jaafar, S., Elgie, S., Foster, L., Halbert, J., & Kaser, L. (2008). Learning networks of schools: The key enablers of successful knowledge communities. *McGill Journal of Education, 43*(2), 111. https://doi.org/10.7202/019578ar

Kruse, S. D., & Louis, K. S. (1993). An emerging framework for analyzing school-based professional community. Paper presented at the annual meeting of the American Educational Research Association, Atlanta, GA.

Kupers, E., Lehmann-Wermser, A., McPherson, G., & Geert, P. V. (2018). Children's creativity: A theoretical framework and systematic review. *Review of Educational Research, 89*(1), 93–124. https://doi.org/10.3102/0034654318815707

Leana, C. R. (2011). 'The missing LINK in School Reform'. *Stanford Social Innovation Review, 9*(4), 30–35.

Longden, K. (2013). *Accelerated Learning Programmes: What can we learn from them about curriculum reform? Background paper prepared for the Education for All Global Monitoring Report 2013*. UNESCO. https://www.eccnetwork.net/sites/default/files/media/file/225950eng.pdf

Maaske, R. (1949). The symposium method in high-school teaching. *The School Review, 57*(4), 217–222. http://www.jstor.org/stable/1082697

Ministry of Education. (2018). *National education sector strategic plan, 2018–2022.*

Ministry of Education. (2019). *Sessional Paper No. 1 of 2019 on a policy framework for reforming education and training for sustainable development in Kenya towards realizing quality, relevant and inclusive education and training for sustainable development.* Government Printer.

Ministry of Education Science and Technology. (2013). *National education sector plan. Volume 1: Basic education programme rationale approach 2013–2018.*

Muijs, D. (2015). Collaboration and networking among rural schools: Can it work and when? Evidence from England. *Peabody Journal of Education, 90*, 294-305. https://doi.org/10.1080/0161956X.2015.1022386

Mukuka, A., Mutarutinya, V., & Balimuttajjo, S. (2019). Exploring the barriers to effective cooperative learning implementation in school mathematics classrooms. *Problems of Education in the 21st Century, 77*(6), 745–757. https://doi.org/10.33225/pec/19.77.745

Murray, A. (2019). Competition as a teaching strategy. *Journal of Graduate Studies in Education, 11*(1), 13–16.

Needle, D. (2004). Business in context: an introduction to business and its environment (4th ed.). Australia, London: Thomson. ISBN: 978-1-86152-992-3.

Okilwa, N. S. A. (2015). Educational marginalization: Examining challenges and possibilities for improving educational outcomes in Northeastern Kenya. *Global Education Review, 2*(4), 5–18.

Otieno, M. A., & Ochieng J. A., (2020). Impact of 100% transition on public secondary schools in Machakos sub-county, Kenya: Focusing on coping strategies. *Journal of Education and Practice, 11*(24), 69–77.

Republic of Kenya. (2010). *The constitution of Kenya.* Government Printer.

Republic of Kenya. (2013). *Executive order no. 2/2013. Organization of the Government of the Republic of Kenya.* Issued by the Office of the President. Government Printer.

Republic of Kenya. (2013). *Basic Education Act, 2013.* Government Printers.

Republic of Kenya. (2017). *Basic education curriculum framework.* Government Press.

Roberts, N. C., & King, P. J. (1996). *Transforming public policy: Dynamics of policy entrepreneurship and innovation.* Jossey-Bass.

Robinson, V. (2018). *Reduce change to increase improvement.* Corwin Press.

Sliwka, A. (2003). Networking for educational innovation: A comparative analysis. In *Networks of innovation: Towards new models for managing schools and systems* (pp. 49–63). Paris: OECD.

Voogt, J. M., Pieters, J. M., & Handelzalts, A. (2016). Teacher collaboration in curriculum design teams: Effects, mechanisms, and conditions. *Educational Research and Evaluation, 22*(3–4), 121–140. https://doi.org/10.1080/13803611.2016.1247725

Section 3

Egalitarian Systems

Chapter 9

School Collaboration in a Divided Society: Shared Education in Northern Ireland

Tony Gallagher, Gavin Duffy and Gareth Robinson

Abstract

Northern Ireland is a society divided by political, national and religious identities. Between 1968 and 1998, there was a violent political conflict in which 3,700 people died. Throughout the conflict, many looked to schools to work to improve community relations, even though the school system itself was divided on largely religious grounds. This chapter looks at education interventions in Northern Ireland aimed at promoting conflict transformation, with a particular focus on the shared education work of the 2000s which is based on collaborative networks of schools from the different communities. The collaboration involved in the shared education initiative is based on a participatory approach which emphasises teacher-led innovation and locally tailored school partnerships. This is in contrast to the defining features of the Northern Ireland school system which has always had a hierarchist character, even when education reforms in the 1990s introduced market principles and school competition. This chapter analyzes education policy and practice in light of these frameworks and considers the potential tension between the shared education approach given the prevailing ethos of the Northern Ireland education system. It suggests that the consequences of this potential tension remain unclear.

Keywords: Education; collaboration; networks; Northern Ireland; comparative; policy

Introduction

In June 2020, the Department of Education in Northern Ireland reported that a total of 716 education settings were participating in 'shared education'

School-to-School Collaboration: Learning Across International Contexts, 157–168
Copyright © 2022 by Tony Gallagher, Gavin Duffy and Gareth Robinson
Published under exclusive licence by Emerald Publishing Limited
doi:10.1108/978-1-80043-668-820221010

activities involving collaboration between Protestant, Catholic and Integrated schools. A total of 87,385 pupils were involved in shared education classes in which they undertook classes with pupils from other schools, normally in each other's schools. These figures represented a rise in participation of 408 schools and 65,349 pupils from June 2016 (Department of Education, 2020). The pilot programmes which launched work on shared education began in 2007 with 12 schools (Gallagher, 2016). In this chapter, we will consider the development of the shared education initiative within the framework provided by Hood (1998) and suggest that it is best represented as lying somewhere on the egalitarian–fatalist axis of the framework, but that it developed within an education system that is aligned with the hierarchist–individualist axis of the framework. We will further argue that this apparent dislocation may provide the basis for tensions as the shared education model becomes a more mainstreamed part of the education system in Northern Ireland.

The Churches and Divided Schools

In order to understand the significance of the shared education model, it is necessary to understand some of the dynamics of the history of education in Ireland and Northern Ireland (Akenson, 1970, 1973; Farren, 1995). The first development of a mass education system on the island began in the 1830s with the establishment of the National Schools system. Prior to this, a variety of school types existed, many run by different religious denominations in what was already a society riven by religious, political and national divides. The framers of the National Schools system indicated a preference for proposals to establish schools within the system that were presented collaboratively by Catholic and Protestant clergy. The ambition was not realised and the emergent system quickly took on a denominational character.

In response to growing political demands from Irish, mainly Catholic, nationalists for independence, in the face of opposition from British, mainly Protestant, Unionists, the island of Ireland was partitioned in 1921/1922: this reflected the demographic pattern on the island such that Protestants were a minority on the island as a whole, but a majority in the north-eastern part of the island (Darby, 1997). The Irish Free State, later Republic of Ireland, became an independent state with an overwhelming Catholic majority. The Catholic Church had a dominant civic role in the Irish Free State, most marked by its control of the education system: the new Irish government did not so much provide education as 'provide for' education by paying the Catholic Church to run the system in schools which it owned and managed.

The Development of a Hierarchist System

Northern Ireland had a number of important differences in circumstance. It became a self-governing region within the United Kingdom, with its own parliament and government. Northern Ireland continued to send MPs to the Westminster Parliament in London, but apart from a list of reserved matters, most domestic issues were the responsibility of the Northern Ireland parliament in Belfast and were rarely, if ever, discussed at Westminster. Unlike the Irish government, which essentially continued with the model of education provided by the National Schools system, the first Northern Ireland government sought to shift the administration away from the Churches towards new local authorities, largely on the model developed in England and Wales in the latter part of the nineteenth century. This attempt was unsuccessful.

The Catholic Church declined to hand its schools over to local authority control, despite incurring a de facto financial penalty as this meant the Church had to contribute to the costs of the schools. It had been expected that the Protestant Churches would hand over their schools to the local authorities to become fully funded 'state' schools, now that the State was firmly under the control of the Unionist government which was mainly supported by the Protestant community. In fact, this did not happen for almost a decade, during which time the Protestant Churches mounted a campaign for greater control and influence over the new 'state' schools. This campaign was ultimately successful and the schools were duly handed over to local authority control, but with the Protestant Churches given guaranteed rights of representation on school committees, control over the appointment of teachers and the establishment of religious education, as 'simple Bible teaching', enshrined as the only statutory element of the curriculum.

In other words, by the mid-1930s, the school system in Northern Ireland had settled into a pattern it would retain for many years in which there were parallel systems of schools largely based on denominational interest. All schools received some level of public grant, but only the local authority, or 'state', schools were fully funded. The Catholic Church owned and managed its own schools and, at least initially, a significant number of staff in these schools were drawn from the clergy. The wider Catholic community had to contribute towards the costs of their schools. The local authority schools were in public ownership, but they were Protestant in all but name. Unlike the Southern States of the United States, there were no segregationist laws which provided legal proscriptions on which categories of children could attend which schools, but the pupil and teacher composition of the schools were, for all practical purposes, denominationally homogeneous.

In terms of Hood's framework, the education system that emerged displayed a 'light' hierarchist character, albeit with the operation and evolution of the system involving the interrelationships between three different interests: the Catholic Church, the Protestant Churches and the growing administrative apparatus of the local authorities overseen by the Ministry of Education. As the administrative apparatus of education scaled upwards, particularly after the major education reforms which can in the wake of the Second World War, the influence of the Protestant Churches was to diminish, slowly, but inexorably. By far the most intriguing relationship was that between the Ministry of Education, or rather the Northern Ireland government, and the Catholic Church.

Northern Ireland was born in the midst of violence in the aftermath of a war of independence between the Irish Republican Army (IRA) and the British armed forces between 1919 and 1921, which resulted in an estimated 1,400 deaths. After a truce was declared in July 1921, the violence continued in Northern Ireland through 1921 and 1922 with an estimated further 554 deaths. Northern Ireland now had a Catholic minority of about 30% and a society divided by the overdetermination of religious, political and national identities: this has been the dominant feature of Northern Ireland throughout its history (Darby, 1997). In this context, the operation of a separate Catholic school system was significant as, apart from the Church itself, this represented the main civic institution of that community. Furthermore, as the teaching role of the clergy diminished over time, teaching positions in Catholic schools became one of the most important sources of middle-class occupations for Catholics in a society where many felt they faced discrimination in many areas of the labour market.

Education in Northern Ireland is often compared to the segregationist system operating in the Southern States of the United States before the 1954 Brown versus Board of Education decision. This analogy is incomplete and, in all likelihood, fallacious (Gallagher, 2007). A more appropriate analogy is provided by the Northern cities of the United States where there were no formal segregationist laws, but high levels of community separation as a consequence of residential segregation and informal discriminatory practice. In the northern cities of the United States, middle-class occupations were available to minorities largely in areas where they provided services to their own, separate, communities but not in occupational sectors providing services to society as a whole, and so it was in Northern Ireland. There were plenty of Catholic small shopkeepers, but few managers in large-scale businesses; plenty of Catholic general practitioners, but few Catholic surgeons; plenty of Catholic teachers, but few Catholic education administrators (Aunger, 1975, 1983).

In this respect, the relationship between the Catholic Church and the Northern Ireland government was fundamentally linked to the relationship over education and schools. It is therefore interesting to note that for all the tensions and conflicts that existed between the Catholic community and the Northern Ireland state, barring one exception Unionist prime ministers invariably appointed political figures from the more moderate part of the Unionist Party to the role of Minister of Education, almost as if it recognised the need to develop some form of rapprochement with the Church. Two examples seem to point to the outworkings of this.

In her consideration of the teaching of history in Northern Ireland, Smith (2005) pointed out that textbooks for use in the schools had to be approved by the Ministry of Education. Given the contentious nature of the past in Northern Ireland, this regulation had the potential to become a source of conflict, but in fact only once was a history textbook banned for use in Northern Irish schools, and only then because of an illustration rather than because of content. As Smith (2005) points out, it was not just that the Ministry trod lightly in its use of its power to ban textbooks in Catholic schools, but the Catholic Church itself seems to have tried to ensure that it did not seek to use overtly partisan or oppositional textbooks.

A second example arises from the fact that the apparent Prime Ministerial imperative to appoint moderate figures as Minister of Education created regular friction with backbench Unionist MPs in the Northern Ireland Parliament as they tried to encourage the government to take a more robust and hostile attitude to Catholic schools. This came to a head when the 1947 Education Act was passed by the Northern Ireland Parliament (Walker, 2017). This Act mirrored the 1944 Butler Act in England by creating free secondary education. The Northern Ireland Act included a small rise in the level of public grant going to Catholic schools, but this was fiercely opposed by a section of backbench Unionist MPs and only the intervention of the Prime Minister calmed the situation sufficiently to allow the legislation to pass. Two years later, however, the backbench MPs took 'revenge' on the Minister of Education by blocking the passage of an unrelated piece of legislation and forced his resignation. In response, the Prime Minister appointed the leader of the rebellion as Minster of Education, making him responsible for overseeing the massive construction programme for new schools and effectively neutralizing the backbench opposition on education matters.

What emerged, in other words, was a parallel form of hierarchist management in which schools were locally administered either by the local authorities, or by the parish or diocesan authorities of the Catholic Church, and strategic discussions were held between the Ministry of Education and the Catholic bishops (see Fig. 1). This arrangement reached its apogee in the mid-1960s when the Catholic Church made a formal agreement with the Northern Ireland government to allow, for the first time, government-appointed representatives onto the Boards of Governors of Catholic schools in return for an increase in the level of public grant. Such an offer had been on the table as far back as 1923 but had never before been considered. This new climate was not to flourish, however, as a growing civil rights campaign seeking an end to discrimination against Catholics gathered pace and would lead, in a few short years, to civil disorder and widespread political violence.

The background and outworking of the Northern Ireland Troubles is well documented (Darby, 1986, 1997). For the moment, the most relevant aspect was the abolition of the Northern Ireland Parliament in 1972 and the establishment of 'direct rule' from Westminster. Under this arrangement, MPs from Westminster were appointed to run a number of government departments in Northern Ireland which had two countervailing effects: one was an inclination on the part of some ministers to suggest that policies developed for England and Wales ought to be transferred to Northern Ireland; or alternatively, it could enhance the power of the civil servants in a Ministry if an individual 'direct rule' Minister evinced little or limited interest in a specific portfolio. The system of local authorities had also been reformed by this point so that only five now existed for different regions of Northern Ireland. All-in-all it distanced the administration and oversight of education policy from democratic accountability and enhanced its hierarchist character.

The Introduction of Education Markets

The next major shift in the system resulted from the 1989 Education Order (Northern Ireland). This was the Northern Ireland equivalent of the 1988

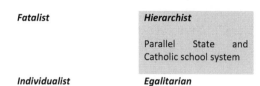

Fatalist   **Hierarchist**

Parallel   State   and
Catholic school system

Individualist   *Egalitarian*

Fig. 1.   The Northern Ireland Education System Before 1989 With Parallel
State and Catholic School Systems.

Education Act in England which introduced an education market and parental choice and weakened the role of local authorities. It also shifted the axis of the education system towards an individualist orientation. The Northern Ireland legislation largely followed the pattern of the English legislation, with a number of local modifications. It provided the basis for parental choice of schools for their children, devolved some administrative and financial autonomy to schools, introduced annual performance tables, a statutory curriculum and a new form of school inspection. In England, there was an intention to encourage greater diversity in school types to widen choice, but a wide variety of school types already existed in Northern Ireland and only a minority of schools were under local authority control. In addition, the education authorities in Northern Ireland had much less power and responsibility in comparison with England anyway.

Prior to the 1987 UK General Election, there had been discussions between the Department of Education in Northern Ireland and the Catholic Bishops with the view to establishing a Council for Catholic Maintained Schools (CCMS) to act as a type of managing authority for Catholic primary and secondary schools. As it turned out, these discussions ran counter to the market principles embedded in the 1989 Order, so when the draft Order appeared, the Bishops felt they had been blindsided as the proposals for CCMS were very much lighter than they had been led to expect. The situation wasn't helped by emerging research for the Standing Advisory Commission for Human Rights (SACHR) that seemed to show systemic underfunding of Catholic schools for many years (Osborne et al., 1992/1993).

The net effect of all of this was a shift in the focus of the education system from a hierarchist to an individualist direction, but with a market-based system that was somewhat skewed. As noted, there was already a diversity of school types, and local authorities had more limited power. The marketplace for pupils was skewed as a consequence of the system of academic selection as parental choice now left open the possibility that grammar schools would simply increase the proportion of pupils in their intake, a pattern that was to occur within a decade when overall pupil enrolment numbers started to fall. And while the corporatist-style relationship with the Catholic Church was somewhat disrupted by some of the changes, there were efforts made to restore the rapprochement. Hence, the conclusion that while the system did shift towards an individualist position, it did not quite cast off its hierarchist features.

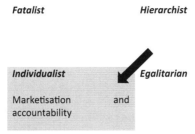

Fig. 2.   The Northern Ireland Education System After 1989 and the Introduction of Markets.

Shifting Towards Collaboration

This then takes us to the next stage of the analysis where we return to the shared education initiative and the formalization of school collaboration within the education system. The origin of this lies in the educational response to the Northern Ireland Troubles from the late 1960s up to the peace agreement in 1998. When the political violence broke out in Northern Ireland, some commentators focussed on the denominationally divided school system and suggested it may have been responsible for fomenting societal divisions (Heskin, 1980). For some years, there was a debate on this issue, and three views can be discerned: first, there was a view that segregated schooling had encouraged religious divisions to such an extent that a shift towards common, religiously integrated schools would make a significant contribution to restoring peace and calm; second, there was a milder view that while separate schools had not created societal divisions, they did help to fuel them and so some measures should be taken through education to address community relations and reconciliation; and third, there was a view that the conflict in Northern Ireland had little to do with community attitudes and more to do with discrimination and inequality in a majority–minority situation. In this view, what was needed was a drive towards equality and social justice, and in that vein, the issue of separate schools was largely irrelevant and may even be a distraction.

There was no consensus in this debate, and in practical terms, the second view became the working assumption for education policy. Over the next quarter century, a variety of education interventions were put in place to address community relations issues, including contact programmes that brought young Protestants and Catholics together for joint activities; curriculum initiatives on such areas as the teaching of history, religious education, mutual understanding or citizenship; and efforts to establish a sector of religiously mixed integrated schools. In a gesture towards the equality agenda, and arising from research carried out for SACHR, Catholic schools were provided with a means to receive 100% public funding and all of them availed of the opportunity (Cormack et al., 1991).

With the signing of the peace agreement in 1998 and the establishment of new shared political institutions, there was also an opportunity to take stock of all the measures that had been put in place to address community relations throughout the conflict. In a comparative analysis of the role of education in divided societies, including Northern Ireland, Gallagher (2004) suggested that the measures in Northern Ireland had been worthy but limited. Contact programmes tended to be short term, often lacked any sustained focus on development, also tended to avoid dealing with difficult or controversial issues and were peripheral to the core curriculum or activities of schools (Hewstone et al., 2008). Some of the curriculum initiatives had been impressive, but in many cases, it seemed that the 'received curriculum' for pupils often fell short of the 'planned curriculum' of the planners (Arlow, 2004; Richardson & Gallagher, 2010). A new sector of religiously mixed integrated schools did emerge, largely as a consequence of the commitment and effort of parents, but despite official government support, the sector grew to comprise about 7% of the pupil population and then seemed to stall. Gallagher (2004) concluded that what may be required was not so much changing education structures in the hope they would somehow or other solve the problem, but rather to focus on ways to encourage greater levels of participative dialogue within and between institutions and to do so in a more sustainable way.

There were plenty of examples of school collaboration to support improvement processes, but none in a context where the schools served different communities on political sensitive social dimensions (Atkinson et al., 2007). Support from two major funders, Atlantic Philanthropies and the International Fund for Ireland, allowed pilot programmes to start in 2007 and 12 schools in Northern Ireland were invited to participate. The invitation was to support them in trying to develop a network of partner schools which would provide shared education classes in which pupils from the schools would take classes in each other schools. The schools would be supported in developing partnership activity through resources, professional development activities and other activities across the network of participating schools. The research team would collect data on the progress of the partnerships and try to identify the elements of an effective partnership.

The first set of pilot projects ran from 2007 to 2010, and new funding allowed for additional, more focused pilot work from 2010 to 2013. Additional funding from The Executive Office (the prime ministerial office in Northern Ireland) allowed for the examination of a different type of school partnership which also engaged with a number of statutory and non-statutory agencies (Duffy & Gallagher, 2017). A Ministerial Advisory Group was established by the Minister of Education to consider the emerging evidence from these pilots and related projects and recommended that shared education be mainstreamed across the education system (Connolly et al., 2013). Legislation to rationalise the administrative support system for education was supported by the Northern Ireland Assembly in 2014 and made it a statutory duty of the new single Education Authority to facilitate, encourage and promote shared education. This statutory duty was extended to the Department of Education in the Shared Education Act (2016). The department is required to report to the Northern Ireland Assembly on progress on shared education, and the most recent (Department of Education, 2020) included the participation figures cited at the start of this chapter.

A more detailed consideration of the development of the shared education initiative and the body of evidence upon which it was based is provided by Gallagher (2016). The Northern Ireland model of shared education which emerged from the work contains three core elements. The first is to empower teachers to lead the development of each school partnership, which also means that each partnership will take on some distinctive features linked to its local context. We will consider the significance of this in more detail below. The second is that the partnership should seek to realise multiple benefits, rather than target a singular purpose. The rational was that a contribution to reconciliation was only one among a number of goals for schools in Northern Ireland and schools would be more likely to engage in collaboration with other schools if it helped them might a range of different goals, including school improvement. The third element was that shared education classes should not focus solely on school subjects that had traditionally been the focus for reconciliation work but should include core curricular areas when possible. Linked to this was the encouragement of multiple levels of engagement across the partnership schools. The key purpose of this was to ensure the partnership work was visibly important to the schools and the communities they served, with the aim it would eventually become a 'taken-for-granted' aspect of the schools' normal activities.

The issue of teacher empowerment and locally tailored partnerships emerged in the pilot programmes with the realization that the people best placed to identify the challenges and opportunities for shared education were the teachers working in the schools. We knew from social network theory that there were potentially multiple routes to successful outcomes, while the traditional educational reliance on best practice was difficult when there was so little practice of any kind to draw on (Robinson et al., 2020). Drawing instead on the concept of 'next practice' (Hannon, 2008), we encouraged the teachers in the schools to identify and try out possible solutions to barriers they identified as placing constraints on effective collaboration. Given that we were trying to encourage a spirit of innovation in developing next practice solutions, we also made it clear to the teachers that it was okay to try out potential solutions even when they did not work, as that provided additional data on which to develop and try alternative solutions. This also meant that the character of each school partnership differed in some of the detail of their outworking: they all involved sustained collaborative relationships across the partnership, with shared classes involving pupils from different schools in the same classroom and increasing levels of teacher engagement across the partnerships. The specific disciplinary or subject areas on which shared activity was based varied across different partnerships, as did the year groups of pupils who were involved, but within a broad common framework of shared activity, the specific activities were distinctive.

This concept was later extended in an initiative from the Education Authority to establish the network for shared school improvement (NSSI) in which teacher-led professional development programmes are identified and implemented, and expertise developed within one school partnership can be shared with other schools and school partnerships (Gallagher et al., 2020). The goal is to use social

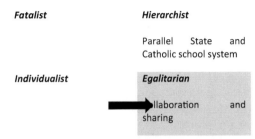

Fig. 3.   The Northern Ireland Education System After 2014 and the Implementation of Collaboration and Shared Education Partnerships.

network principles to encourage the development of a self-sustaining school improvement process.

Key to all of these processes is that they are teacher-led and locally tailored and avoid the rigidity of top-down processes that often seek to impose common templates or evaluate activity under a uniform set of criteria. Local teacher participation is central to making the partnership activities work, reflecting key elements of the egalitarian dimension of Hood's (1998) framework. In addition, and largely as a consequence of the reliance on social network principles, this type of collaborative partnership shares some features of the fatalist dimension on Hood's (1998) framework to the extent that the partnership is not working towards some prescribed endpoint, for example, that the schools must commit to working towards eventual merger into a single integrated school. Rather the schools, their teachers, parents, pupils and local communities are free to develop the extent of their own collaboration, their rate of change and their final location, which also implies that a range of possible outcomes are likely to occur.

One of the challenges facing the future of the shared education school partnership model is that it is occurring within an education system that remains heavily imbued with a hierarchist/individualist ethos. The current Northern Ireland government policy for school improvement is largely based on the General Education Reform Model (Hargreaves, 2012; Sahlberg, 2012) which uses market principles and relies on targets, competition and top-down systems of accountability, much of which may be inimical to partnership and collaboration on an enduring scale. The Northern Ireland model of shared education is now firmly established in our education system and a majority of schools are participating in collaborative partnerships. Furthermore, aspects of the model are being adapted for use in other divided societies, most notably Israel and North Macedonia, with plans to extend it further into other jurisdictions (Gallagher, 2017; Loader et al., 2018; Payes, 2013). There is not yet any significant evidence of tensions between these approaches in Northern Ireland, but it seems unlikely that an approach based on an egalitarian/fatalist axis can function within a policy ethos characterised by hierarchist/individualist principles for too long. But neither is it yet clear which framework will be set aside.

Key Lessons for Practice and Policy

This example from Northern Ireland shows the fluidity of education policy in a polity where stable government is challenged by long-standing political divisions. The shared political institutions created by the peace agreement were designed to encourage cooperation between the leaders of the different communities, though the practical reality is that some major policy debates in education have failed to achieve consensus precisely because the issues became embroiled in the older divisions (Gallagher, 2021). The shared education initiative, by contrast, did achieve a high level of political consensus, but it seems mainly because it emerged from the bottom up, and by the time the point was reached for formal policy decisions, a strong level of consensus had already been formed.

Hood's (1998) framework provides an interesting mechanism for framing education policy in this context even if the primary conclusion is that the shared education initiative seems to be based on a set of dimensions that are inconsistent with the long-standing ethos of the education system itself. The more interesting policy question, however, is whether this dislocation acts as a creative tension which produces further innovation in future or a disruptive contradiction which must be resolved one way or the other.

References

Akenson, D. H. (1970). *The Irish Education Experiment: The national system of education in the nineteenth century*. Routledge and Kegan Paul.

Akenson, D. H. (1973). *Education and enmity: The control of schooling in Northern Ireland 1920–1950*. David and Charles.

Arlow, M. (2004). Citizenship education in a divided society: The case of Northern Ireland. In S. Tawil & A. Harley (Eds.), *Education, conflict and social cohesion*, (pp. 255–313). International Bureau of Education.

Atkinson, M., Springate, I., Jonhson, F., & Halsey, K. (2007). *Inter-school collaboration: A literature review*. NFER.

Aunger, E. A. (1975). Religion and occupational class in Northern Ireland. *Economic and Social Review, 7*(1), 1–18.

Aunger, E. A. (1983). Religion and Class: An analysis of 1971 census data. In R. J. Cormack & R. D. Osborne (Eds.), *Religion, education and employment*, (pp. 24–41). Appletree Press.

Connolly, P., Purvis, D., & O'Grady, P. J. (2013). *Advancing shared education: Report of the Ministerial Advisory Group*. Department of Education (Northern Ireland).

Cormack, R. J., Gallagher, A. M., & Osborne, R. D. (1991). *Educational affiliation and educational attainment in Northern Ireland: The financing of schools in Northern Ireland. Annex E, sixteenth report of the Standing Advisory Commission on Human Rights, House of Commons Papers 488*. HMSO.

Darby, J. (1986). *Intimidation and the control of conflict in Northern Ireland*. Gill and Macmillan.

Darby, J. (1997). *Scorpions in a bottle: Conflicting cultures in Northern Ireland*. Minority Rights Group.

Department of Education. (2020). *Advancing shared education report to the Northern Ireland Assembly*. Department of Education.

Duffy, G., & Gallagher, T. (2017). Shared education in contested spaces: How collaborative networks improve communities and schools. *Journal of Education Change, 18,* 107–134.

Farren, S. (1995). *The politics of Irish education 1920–65.* Queen's University Institute of Irish Studies.

Gallagher, T. (2004). *Education in divided societies.* Palgrave/MacMillan.

Gallagher, T. (2007). Desegregation and resegregation: The legacy of Brown versus Board of Education, 1954. In Z. Bekerman & C. McGlynn (Eds.), *Addressing ethnic conflict through peace education,* (pp. 9–20). Palgrave/Macmillan.

Gallagher, T. (2016). Shared education in Northern Ireland: School collaboration in divided societies. *Oxford Review of Education, 42*(3), 362–375.

Gallagher, T. (2017). Co-existence and education: General principles and some lessons from Northern Ireland. In I. Psaltis, N. Anastasiou, H. Faustmann, M. Hadjipavlou, H. Karahasan, & M. Zackheos (Eds.), *Education in a multicultural Cyprus* (pp. 30–47). Cambridge Scholars.

Gallagher, T. (2021). Governance and leadership in education policy making and school development in a divided society. *School Leadership & Management, 41*(1–2), 132–151. https://doi.org/10.1080/13632434.2021.1887116

Gallagher, T., Duffy, G., Robinson, G., & Hadfield, M. (2020). *Attitudes towards, and experiences of, the Network for Shared School Improvement: A survey of teachers and school leaders.* Queen's University.

Hannon, V. (2008). *'Next practice' in education: A disciplined approach to innovation.* Innovation Unit.

Hargreaves, A. (2012). *The Global Fourth Way: The quest for educational excellence.* Corwin Press.

Heskin, K. (1980). *Northern Ireland: A psychological analysis.* Gill and Macmillan.

Hewstone, M., Tausch, N., Hughes, J., & Cairns, E. (2008). *Can contact promote better relations? Evidence from mixed and segregated areas of Belfast.* OFMDFM.

Hood, C. (1998). *The art of the state: Culture, rhetoric and public management.* Clarendon Press.

Loader, R., Hughes, J., Petroska-Beshka, V., & Tomovska Misoska, A. (2018). Developing social cohesion through schools in Northern Ireland and the former Yugoslav Republic of Macedonia: A study of policy transfer. *Journal on Education in Emergencies, 4*(1), 114–140.

Osborne, R. D., Gallagher, A. M., & Cormack, R. J. (1992/1993). The funding of Northern Ireland's segregated education system. *Administration: Journal of the Institute of Public Administration of Ireland, 40*(4), 316–332.

Payes, S. (2013). Separate education and hegemonic domination: Civil society challenges in the Arab-Jewish city of Jaffa. *Intercultural Education, 24,* 544–558.

Richardson, N., & Gallagher, T. (2010). *Education for diversity and mutual understanding.* Peter Lang.

Robinson, G., Gallagher, A., Duffy, G., & McAneney, H. (2020). At the boundaries: School networks in divided societies. *Journal of Professional Capital and Community, 5*(2), 183–197.

Sahlberg, P. (2012). *Finnish lessons: What can the world learn from educational change in Finland?* Teachers' College Press.

Shared Education Act (Northern Ireland). (2016). Available at https://www.legislation.gov.uk/nia/2016/20/contents. Accessed on May 22, 2022.

Smith, M. (2005). *Reckoning with the past: Teaching history in Northern Ireland.* Lexington Books.

Walker, G. (2017). The 1947 Education Act – A landmark in Northern Ireland's history. Queen's Policy Engagement blog posted August 7, 2017. http://qpol.qub.ac.uk/1947-education-act/

Chapter 10

Moving Beyond a Narrative of School Improvement: How and Why Should We Create Purpose-driven and Impactful Collaboration for Educators?

Sian May and Kevin House

Abstract

This chapter argues we should not regard school-to-school collaboration as simply a mechanism for outcome-driven improvement but rather consider the establishment of teacher relationships as the necessary priority when building highly effective collaborative networks. By revisiting the research of Sandra Kruse, Amanda Datnow and Andy Hargreaves, we develop an additional tool to Hood's matrix of regulation and cohesion in an effort to position collaborative networks in the context of international private fee-paying schools. The tool visualizes the collaborative network development as a relationship continuum in which time is the necessary driver of a network's success. The 12 Asian private international schools in the case study were given collaborative framework guidance drawn from multiple sources. Subsequently, the enablers and hindrances reported by the collaboration leads highlight the need for trust and teacher agency development to be prioritized by leadership. Finally, on sharing some lessons learned from the case study, we close by arguing the value of collaboration lies in opening the door to allow for agenetic cultures that build reflexive practitioners.

Keywords: Teacher agency; trust; reflexive practice; assemblage; collective efficacy; collegiality

School-to-School Collaboration: Learning Across International Contexts, 169–185
Copyright © 2022 by Sian May and Kevin House
Published under exclusive licence by Emerald Publishing Limited
doi:10.1108/978-1-80043-668-820221011

Introduction

Much that has been written recently in the United Kingdom about how the English state school sector contextualizes collaboration in terms of school-to-school partnership. Furthermore, from a policy perspective, its primary benefit is seen as a tool for 'school improvement' and not as a strategy for developing teacher relationship capabilities or a sense of agency. 'Collaboration is a vital tool in the school improvement arsenal. It can be used to improve teaching and learning, leadership, and the use of data and assessment' (Sumner & Wespieser, 2017). We argue this narrative means key drivers like teacher agency and trust take a backseat to central policy and outcomes, and this has significant consequences on building the intrinsic motivation required to guarantee successful school-to-school collaboration. Moreover, the competitive realities of the English state sector's relatively narrow definition of 'school improvement' brings extrinsic pressures, which further jeopardize the building of trust among teachers working in different school contexts.

We believe this view of the purpose of collaboration is of limited value when examining the private international school-to-school collaboration described in this chapter. Generally, this is because private international schools have a regulatory agility that allows them to be more responsive to their contexts. International school education strategy is often developed independent of central policy and can utilize methods like collaborative inquiry, which appear to have been less used in the English public school system. Furthermore, and in line with the English state sector understandings of collaboration's purpose and value proposition, the UK research community, with some notable exceptions (Brown et al., 2016), has largely focussed on interrogating the English government's desire to build a 'self-improving' education system. Whereas we aim to offer an alternative perspective, one that argues that relational trust is a core driver for collaborative networks in an international context. Moreover, the development over time of such trust between educators is a fundamental step towards a deeper sense of both individual and collective teacher agency. It is, therefore, these elements that need to be regarded as the purpose of fostering international school-to-school collaboration rather than vaguely defined notions of school improvement.

Furthermore, we suggest a school-to-school 'partnership' approach entrenches forms of cooperation and collegiality that do little to develop the deep trust necessary to nurture teacher agency.

> In contrived collegiality, collaboration among teachers [is] compulsory, not voluntary; bounded and fixed in time and space; implementation – rather than development-oriented; and meant to be predictable rather than unpredictable in its outcomes. (Hargreaves, 1994, p. 209)

In the example of the English state sector, where collaboration is held to be a 'partnership' between schools, there is clearly a power dynamic centred on improvement that requires scrutiny. An assumption that one school might mentor another is, in the context of this chapter, interesting for two reasons. First, the English state sector's notion of partnership bears little resemblance to the intentions behind the private international school-to-school collaboration presented in this chapter. Second, in defining the purpose of teacher collaboration in private international schools, one must remain cognisant of diverse cultural, lingual and geographical realities. Therefore, we argue there needs to be a more elaborate understanding of what constitutes a collaborative culture when faced with a varied range of teacher identities and educational goals.

The aim in this chapter is to make the case for understanding the international school-to-school collaborative network presented in this chapter as a complex social system, which we identify as an *assemblage* (DeLanda, 2006; Deleuze & Guitarri, 1988). We draw on this heuristic because it best captures the dynamic structural, temporal and relational amalgam found in the international school collaboration groups we present. Made up of individuals from multiple cultures and speaking numerous languages, these collaborative groups represent an assemblage in that each is more than the sum of its disparate parts. Therefore, beyond Hood's regulation–cohesion matrix, there is need for an additional conceptual model to reflect how trust and agency in such networks only develops over an extended period. Failure to conceptualize the timeline of collaborative culture development runs the risk of only understanding these social assemblages in terms of top-down leadership and externally derived purpose and values.

> Collaborative cultures comprise of evolutionary relationships of openness, trust, and support among teachers where they define and develop their own purposes as a community. Contrived collegiality consists of administratively contrived interactions among teachers where they meet and work to implement the curricula and instructional strategies developed by others. (Hargreaves & Dawe, 1990)

In other words, even though we might identify international school-to-school collaboration as 'egalitarian' using Hood's matrix, this is only one piece of the picture. Alongside this, we need to understand the role time plays in the establishment of trust and agency. For this reason, and before sharing our case study and conclusions drawn from the experience, we review some early literature on collaboration to develop an addition tool for understanding the complex nature of international school-to-school collaborative networks.

In 1990, Hargreaves and Dawe suggested,

> collaborative cultures may need administrative support and leadership to help them grow and to facilitate their development, but their evolution – depending as it does on vulnerable human qualities like trust and sharing – will inevitably be slow. (1990, p. 238)

Moreover, in his book *Teacher Agency* (2015), Gert Biesta argues that agency must be encouraged if we are to build lasting educational improvement. For him, the dominant trends in contemporary education involve 'systems of bureaucratic accountability, invasive and often oppressive regimes of inspection and control, performance-related pay, standard setting, league tables, naming and shaming, and so on', which are all efforts to improve education by introducing 'systemic solutions for alleged problems' (Biesta, 2015, p. 147). In this context, he argues, it is necessary to force teacher agency back into educational discourse in response to the increasingly 'truncated development of future aspirations and expertise' within the profession. In his view, a key social mechanism for building greater teacher agency is for school leaders to 'carefully consider the relational conditions through which teachers achieve agency' (Biesta, 2015, p. 104). He argues that a tactfully nurtured 'collaborative culture' can go a long way towards strengthening teacher agency across the profession.

Even though Hood's matrix might, at first glance, appear as adequate for understanding collaborative school-to-school partnerships in the context of current UK government-led initiatives in England, we argue it lacks the multidimensionality required to grasp international collaborative networks. Consequently, we have reviewed research that focuses more on the relationship dynamics of collaborative networks to see if we can develop a conceptual model that shows how relationships and agency grow over time.

In trying to make sense of the impact of education's 'age of accountability' on the 'culture of teaching' (Datnow, 2011, p. 148), Amanda Datnow revisited Andy Hargreaves' early work (1994). In her paper, she returns to Hargreaves' distinctions of between 'collaborative culture' and 'contrived collegiality' (Datnow, 2011, p. 148) to see which is the most likely outcome for collaboration in an age of such accountability. Her conclusion is that relationships often described as professional collaboration are in fact examples of contrived collegiality because they are 'administratively regulated, compulsory, implementation-orientated, fixed in time and space, and predictable' (Datnow, 2011, p. 148). Indeed, early experiences from the collaborative groups formed in our international schools would indicate that such contrivance is a necessary step on the journey towards successful collaboration. Therefore, we have adapted Datnow's interpretation of Hargreaves' 'contrived collegiality' to be a centre point in our relational continuum timeline, which we use in conjunction with Hood's matrix.

In *Collaborate* (1999), Sharon Kruse builds on earlier distinctions made between cooperation and collaboration by introducing the term 'collegiality'. She argues that these are the three fundamental forms of teacher interaction, and that each is markedly different from the other. First, cooperation 'is best described as the most basic social and intellectual interaction amongst teachers' (Kruse, 1999, p. 15). Second, collegiality is 'characterized by mutual learning and discussion of classroom practice and student performance' (Kruse, 1999, p. 15). Finally, collaboration is when 'teachers engage in mutual decision-making to resolve their problems of practice' (Kruse, 1999, p. 15). In the context of international private school collaborative networks, rather than see these as simply three interchangeable forms of teacher interaction, we argue they describe three developmental stages. In other words, each represents a distinct point in a developmental relationship continuum timeline. The continuum identifies three points (cooperation – collegiality – collaboration) in teacher relationship development as international school collaboration networks mature over time. Moreover, we have noted that as groups move through these stages, the need for contrivance subsides as individual and collective agency develops.

In essence, we argue that our relationship continuum recognizes three points in a collaborative group's journey towards greater teacher-to-teacher trust and a collective sense of agency. In the early days of forming a collaborative group, there is inevitably evidence of contrivance such as centrally mandated meeting times because these are beneficial in protecting the individual participant's time as the network gets off the ground. In the language of Hood's matrix, such a 'regulatory' approach encourages initial cohesion by protecting teacher time and thus creating space for teachers to begin building trust. However, soon into its formation, and once some level of trust has been established, teachers require the agency to move beyond any initial administrative contrivance.

By leveraging both Hood's regulation and cohesion matrix and our relationship continuum timeline, we can better account for contextual variety caused by hierarchy, micro-politics, language, culture, pedagogy, place and space. Furthermore, this approach avoids reductionism by offering a more complex way of understanding of how collaborative networks develop. It encourages us to be cognisant of the evolutionary stages of a collaborative group and recognize its organic nature. Fundamentally, it enables us to see collaborative networks as assemblages because each group matures into something more than a sum of its parts. Understanding collaborative networks in such an *ecological* way supports our closing remarks on the fundamental purpose of school-to-school collaboration in an international context.

Our Case Study Methodology

Our strategic principles at the creation of the network drew on the work of Jenni Donohoo (2016) on collective teacher efficacy, Richard DuFour (DuFour, DuFour, & Eaker, 2015) on the establishment of Professional Learning Communities, Bandura (2000) on concepts of collective agency and Amy Edmondson (2018) on cultures of organizational trust for innovation.

Donohoo's work, with the weight of Hattie's (2012) rigorous analysis of effect sizes on student achievement behind it, establishes the value of collective efficacy as a defining attribute of effective practitioners. Collective efficacy achieves 1.57 in effect size in Hattie's work (2016, p. 12) making the link clear between teacher beliefs and student outcomes. Teacher's judgement of their ability and agency to positively impact student achievement is therefore highly desirable, if not vital. Our collaboration network aimed from the outset to have at its core the opportunity to develop a shared sense of collective efficacy. Our position on collective efficacy was further informed by Bandura, 'collective efficacy is not simply the sum of the efficacy beliefs of different members. Rather it is an emergent group-level property' (2000, p. 75). This was a key component in establishing the values of the network and ensuring that groups remained purpose driven. Furthermore, there was recognition that to build on such values and create collective efficacy, participants needed to establish norms of trust and respect the agency of group members.

In addition to this, the network also drew on DuFour's more pragmatic approach, which offers frameworks teachers can utilize to become a collaborative community who decide their own focus and who work through their results together: 'To create a professional learning community, focus on learning rather than teaching, work collaboratively, and hold yourself accountable for results' (DuFour et al., 2014, p. 521). Elsewhere, DuFour identifies the contradictory role leaders play considering traditional hierarchies. 'In our earlier work we refer to this paradox of strong and forceful principals empowering teachers as simultaneous loose/tight properties' (DuFour et al., 2004, p. 147). This antithetical tension was anticipated at the outset of our network. At the start, we placed norm-building tools in the hands of our collaboration leads in order to orchestrate a structure as teacher groups navigated the psychodynamics of hierarchy, trust and agency.

Our method was further underpinned using Edmondson's (2018) analysis of the impact of hierarchical cultures which can and do reduce a learning culture. 'for jobs where learning or collaboration is required for success, fear is not an effective motivator' (Edmondson, 2018, p. 21). This insight informed the levels of autonomy and trust groups operated within. For example, a central team member would receive frequent feedback from the network as a form of 'reverse mentor' model in which traditional top-down lines of communication are reversed so that the central team member gets formal and informal feedback in non-hierarchical, non-threatening ways.

Furthermore, planning was informed by the specific needs of our private international schools and a strategic focus designed to leverage group expertise in a dispersed way. Primarily, the focus of this network was empowering teachers and their practice rather than centralized outcomes, and as such, the commitment was for long-term teacher capacity building and the creation of culture. In terms of Hood's matrix, the network most closely resembles the 'egalitarian' domain, but the essential time needed still requires elaboration using the relationship continuum timeline.

Teacher Principles of Collaboration

These were established based on a synthesis of the above research and the findings from our group-wide schools[1]:

1. Collaboration allows us to build collective efficacy through peer learning and increase our capacity to meet student learning needs.
2. Collaboration can respond to our collective needs.

---

[1]The school review encompassed qualitative interviews with several hundred educators, parents and thousands of senior school-aged students. This was then triangulated to draw out themes, some of which were localised and others which were shared across the group.

3. Collaboration can support wider professional practice and strategic plans.
4. Our collaboration network can provide colleagues with a means of sharing practice across our group and create a support network for new and existing teams and colleagues.
5. Collaboration can be led by any teacher and sits outside hierarchical structures within and across our schools.

A Case Study in International School-to-School Collaboration

As was outlined earlier, the collaboration network was designed to develop trust, enable and recognize agency and harness collective efficacy. This was further complemented by the school group's strategic focus on profiling teacher growth with a tool developed by Dr House and Dr Calnin. This tool was informed by an extensive literature review, which identified potentially malleable teacher dispositions, values and beliefs. The profiler, combined with the work of the collaborative groups, aims to create reflexive practitioners. Teachers who can explore not only their experiences of teaching but also their dispositions, values and beliefs *about* teaching in an international context. Fundamentally, understanding about how they learn develops teacher lifelong learner capabilities because it requires engaging with research and reflecting on the cultural complexities faced in private international schools. Our long-term goal is to build a cadre of future changemakers in international education who shape learning culture rather than submit to existing norms. This approach, therefore, stands in contradiction to the earlier example wherein the English state sector's partnership-focussed collaboration becomes a mechanism for trying to attain a self-improving school system.

Background and Characteristics of Collaboration Network

1. Education in Motion (EiM) is a group of schools in Korea, China and Southeast Asia. The group was founded in 2003 when a partnership was formed between Dulwich College, London, and the first international college in Pudong, Shanghai. Over the next decade, more K-12 colleges were added to the group in the Chinese cities of Shanghai, Beijing and Suzhou, in Seoul, Korea, in Yangon, Myanmar, and most recently in Singapore. Historically, the colleges educated the children of expatriates with over 50 nationalities following an internationalized version of the English National Curriculum and International (IB) Diploma Programme. In recent years, this demographic has begun to shift as more and more returning Chinese expatriates and local wealthy Chinese families have gained government permission to send their children to a private international school. In addition, two Dulwich High Schools were established to offer a British-style international education to local Chinese parents whose children have been granted permission to leave the Chinese National Curriculum after sitting the compulsory Zhongkao examination in grade 9. Once at a Dulwich High School, students pursue a range of IGSCEs and A levels with the aim of attending a university

overseas. All these schools participated in our collaboration network. The broad scope of the network encompassed highly complex organizational dynamics, and perceptions of what collaboration was and should be varied from person to person as much as culture to culture.

2. As stated earlier, the collaboration network was in part established as a response to feedback from colleagues collected in data sets drawn from a schools review process. The qualitative data were collected by the EiM's central Education Team during academic year 2018–2019. Interviewed colleagues identified a desire to overcome the isolation of working in an international school, enhance their own practice by making 'critical friends' and tap the reservoir of expertise there is across the group.

3. The coordination of the Senior School collaboration group network used a centralized 'service model'. This consisted of centrally appointing leads to each collaboration group and then drip-feeding them the approaches discussed earlier (Donohoo, 2016; Hattie, 2016; Bandura, 2000; Edmondson, 2018). This drip-feed involved scheduled network sessions for collaboration leads, keynote speakers and shared frameworks and tools. The distinction between schools and the centre means that our interpretation of collaboration in such schools remains fundamentally an 'outsider' view and thus means the biases from the centre possibly permeate our reading of enabling and hindering factors.

4. The scope of the Senior School network was devised to include Middle Leaders and classroom teachers and therefore atypical of the traditional hierarchical culture of leadership across the group.

5. Four core languages, multiplicity of cultures and diversity were reflected in our collaboration network as a result of the geographical spread of the group.

6. The central Education Team office neighboured one school. This school participated disproportionately more than other schools, and proximity might have been a driving factor.

7. Cross-group collaboration might have some of the advantages which are not found in entrenching practice within a school culture that professional learning communities (PLCs) go through. For example, the first part of getting to know another school and trusting expertise and building relationships is asking questions which may be more revealing when working between schools rather than within. This can be observed at the cooperative and collegial stages in the relationship continuum (see Fig. 2), colleagues moved from focused and often closed questions to becoming 'outsider' view mentors/coaches who were more open and curious.

8. The collaboration network referred to in this case study is present in Senior Schools only, even though most schools were K-12.

9. Each collaboration group led their own prioritization of needs and were not directed centrally. This did mean that priorities were divergent but also frequently categorized into short-, medium- and long-term plans for collaboration.

10. The network's development was charted by following our group leads through their experience in a podcast series developed in conjunction with

Evidence-Based Education (EBE). There were four episodes in total which provided insightful reflections for all EiM teachers by drawing on the experiences of individuals in the collaboration groups (Scott, 2021).

11. A centrally coordinated review cycle ran continuously during the two years via focus groups and surveys of collaboration leads. Collaboration leads also coordinated their own reviews of their own groups and shared the results with peers.

12. All collaboration before and following COVID was online with a few rare exceptions which occurred in Shanghai/Suzhou area of China and between colleagues in Singapore.

Due to there being a structure of schools and a central office with Education Team, there are multiple potential layers of application of the Hood matrix (Fig. 1):

13. The structure of our head office resembles Hood's Fatalist Way (refer to the matrix) in cultural norms and hierarchies. This was the coordination centre for the network.

14. Each individual school culture varied considerably depending on the leadership and the contextual norms. In some cases with evidence of all four manifestations on Hood's matrix.

15. The concept behind the establishment of the collaboration network most closely fits the egalitarian way.

However, the observations above appear inadequate without the relationship development continuum timeline we have created because the introduction of group-wide collaboration for Senior School took place over two years in deliberately planned stages. During our first year of the network, eight specialized

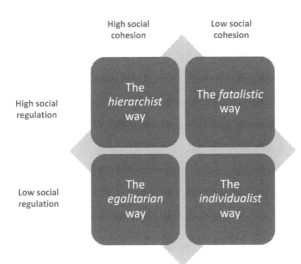

Fig. 1.   Hood's Matrix. *Source*: From Malin et al. (2020; used with permission).

groupings were identified and established based on school review processes and clear strategic needs. This included, English Language Learning, Social and Emotional Counselling and groups of leaders including Assistant Heads of School. In the second year of the network, this was expanded to include subject groupings which broadened the network to 49 collaboration groups and included approximately 400 participants. These subject-specific groups were for educators in academic subjects offered for students aged 11–18.

Finally, the process of identifying collaboration leads in each specialist or leadership area was driven as an open apply process which was supported by Heads of School in each and using volunteers with an interest in developing their own skills portfolio further. Each group met online for six hours in one-hour slots throughout the academic year.

Frameworks for Collaboration

All collaboration leads were given access to a variety of tools to use, evaluate or set aside depending on the needs of the group including but not limited to:

1. DuFour's framework for establishing Professional Learning Communities. This links to a variety of structures and activities which can be used (DuFour et al., 2012). The toolkit provides a useful starting point to scaffold the norming process of each group. Many collaboration leads wanted structure to support their own confidence and development in the role. Many had no leadership experience within traditional structures. Therefore, this kit provided strategies to help develop trust and expertise recognition.
2. EBE's Problem Identification Methodology. Our group of schools partnered with EBE for a range of professional learning, which was very well received. Particularly popular was EBE's problem identification and solution identification process, which guides participants through data, evidence and critical discussion in their school context.
3. Harvard's Teaching and Learning Lab's Discussion Protocols. Many groups were new and had never met online or in-person, and this framework created a basis for starting the relationship and trust-building process (Harvard, 2021).

A key objective for providing the frameworks as above was to build efficacy and the individual agency of the collaboration leads as a first step towards creating collective agency. Collaboration leads were able to discern which frameworks fit their context and purpose or were able to choose an alternative methodology. Many used one or more of the above as a catalyst to move beyond Hargreaves' 'contrived collegiality'.

Beliefs and Enabling and Hindering Factors

The enabling and hindering factors found below were identified via surveys and focus groups with collaboration group leads and capture a wide range of experiences:

Beliefs

Further, our network leads formulated some shared beliefs regarding effective collaboration based on their experiences which acted as enablers during the process and set the future direction for the network:

1. The basis of authentic collaboration is human connection and relationships. Meaningful and focussed professional dialogue is essential to individual, team and organizational development.
2. In the early stages of collaboration trust building is essential. As soon as possible, the network must be supportive in the sharing of effective practice and welcoming of both individual and collective needs.
3. Collaboration is a process, not a product. It takes time to develop cycles of reflection and realize that learning is continuous, and that forming a clear purpose is more important than simply defining outcomes.

Enabling Factors

1. Understanding each other's school and professional development contexts is critical and takes time and trust. Trust both in terms of psychological safety and confidence in one another's expertise.
2. Peer support is critical to the perceived value of collaboration. Reduction in teacher isolation and a sense in which all teachers could impact the system in which they were working was an invigorator. For example, collaboration lead feedback shaped digital architecture across the group and specific groups impacted effective safeguarding practices due to their knowledge of the group and their expertise having the time and space to explore current processes. Therefore, a responsive structure where a teacher can be made visible to a community of teachers is essential.
3. Accessing Middle Leaders and classroom teachers allowed rich horizontal discussions across the organization and consequently produced different messaging and perceptions. This in turn created experiences for development which were free of traditional hierarchies. For example, the value of collaboration as an end in itself rather than simply a mechanism for school improvement started to emerge as cultural rhetoric. Many teachers embraced the agency that the network provided in order to analyze group-wide data.
4. Innovation arose in the space created in the groups due to the lack of restrictions placed on the processes. For example, strategic working groups with a targeted focus emerged that will continue to impact the norms regarding specialist areas across all of our schools.
5. Cohesion and a desire for shared visions started to emerge between schools as they familiarized themselves with each other's cultures and processes. The desire to test what practice worked in one location quickly spread to emerge as informal action research.

6. The central coordination was an enabler; however, it requires regular review to ensure that the network remains autonomous and a vehicle for trust and agency amongst the teachers.

Hindering Factors

1. The context of our other cultural norms and outcome-driven cultures was potentially the biggest hindering factor. For example, there was, on occasion, a lack of alignment regarding an outcome focus vs an intelligent network built on agency and trust. Additionally, some groups perceived pressure to deliver a product or a task. The network was a culture within a broader multifaceted culture, therefore greater time is required for Bandura's 'collective agency entity' to emerge. If time is lacking, then the network can become a vehicle for driving central directives and priorities. This can result in too many competing priorities and a transactional approach for participants.
2. Time poor colleagues and different contexts valuing collaboration to varying degrees and a myriad of competing priorities created a challenge. For some, this was compounded by time-zone differences or lack of calendar synchronicity.
3. Depth of collaboration between schools could arguably have detracted from collaboration vertically in colleges and within schools. Intra-school priorities must also be examined to see whether a culture is ready to take on partnerships between schools. One can be a catalyst to the other; however, many practitioners emulate their home school in terms of culture and environment. This can be further exacerbated by a potential cultural divide between local home nation and expatriate staff.
4. Leading a new collaboration group is complex and challenging, therefore supportive professional learning for those leading/coordinating is needed alongside this. A spread of experience can impact trust as people scrutinize the variety of expertise within the group. Some colleagues guide other teachers rather than perceiving their own needs are met through the collaboration. Large group sizes also proved challenging for coordinators because trust and agency appear far more likely to happen with groups of less than eight people.
5. Online collaboration can create gaps in trust and visibility between colleagues in terms of both relationship building and expertise. In-person collaboration is the best kick-start approach to later online meeting.
6. System-ness in its early stages can amplify 'contrived collegiality' and feelings of duty rather than inclination which are self-defeating in developing agentic collaboration.

The Relationship Continuum

The aim of this diagram (Fig. 2) is to capture the stages by which practitioners, for the most part, developed greater levels of trust and agency within an established

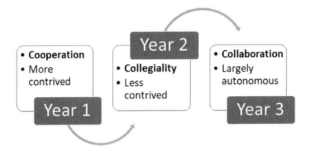

Fig. 2

timeframe. We would suggest that this continuum largely occupies the 'egalitarian' quadrant in Hood's matrix by year 3 because this most accurately reflects the long-term aims of our school-to-school collaborative network. We identify trust and agency as the core relational elements necessary to building intrinsic practitioner motivation. Both need significant time to establish themselves, but they are essential if a network is to feel empowered to work autonomously and have meaningful educational discussions without recourse to accountabilities established by existing managerial hierarchies.

Below, using the relationship continuum, are examples of what can surface over time across dedicated collaboration groups. The examples are drawn from the network's reflections, surveys and our own literature review. Fig. 2 serves as a useful reference point when gauging the changes in norms and individual practitioners as collaborative culture starts to emerge.

Key Lessons for Practice and Policy

In summary, we suggest Hood's matrix is (Fig. 1) only one of two conceptual models necessary when trying to understand the functioning components required for successful teacher collaboration because such a complex social network is fundamentally an assemblage. While Hood's matrix does provide a structural taxonomy when positioning collaborative networks, we argue this offers only one piece of the puzzle because truly collaborative networks require relational capital that can only accrue over time. Therefore, we propose the reductionism of the regulation–cohesion matrix needs to be mitigated with the addition of a relationship continuum (Fig. 2), which combines Kruse's 'three Cs' with Hargreaves' 'contrived collegiality'. This offers a second piece of the puzzle because it captures the dynamism of the relationships found in these highly sophisticated, problem-solving systems. Moreover, we contend *the* core reason for nurturing teacher collaboration is to bring together colleagues to identify collective needs and problems to be solved. This work requires a burgeoning trust in one another's ability to identify such needs and problems and then the agency to feel empowered to make a difference. To aid relationship development and mutual trust in expertise, we suggest leadership consider the following approaches when establishing school-to-school collaboration networks:

Relationship Evolution	Cooperative Examples (0–12 Months)	Collegial Examples (12–24 Months)	Collaborative Examples (24–36 Months)
Trust is defined here using Amy Edmondson's (2018) work on psychological safety and additionally Hargreaves and O'Connor's (2018) exploration of shared trust in one another's expertise.	• Clear frameworks and norms are used to structure discussion and promote membership inclusion. • Nominated lead coordinates the collaboration. • Skills mapping and bio sharing between colleagues to create shared understanding of each other's expertise. • Needs-based analysis in each school is made visible to other members.	• Specific areas of focus emerge which align to shared professional learning goals. • Sub-groups emerge aligned challenges to investigate. • Greater number of coordinators.	• Layers of collaboration create coaching networks among colleagues. • Teams and sub-teams who can select their focus. • Distributed leadership model, i.e. flat leadership structure.
Agency as defined in Bandura's (2000) work on collective agency informs the stages here.	• Freedom to determine the focus of collaboration following professional dialogue. • Developing shared values and beliefs about their ability to make an impact on student learning and each other's professional development.	• Individual members of the collaboration begin to self-reflect on their contribution to driving the collaboration. • Further the group aggregates its own reflections on the group's capability in collaboration (Bandura, 2000).	• All members of the group become proactive agents versus onlookers. All members are actively shaping the direction and review cycle of the group, holding each other to collective account, using the beliefs and values of the group and reviewing their perceived capability in collaborating.

1. Develop a culture of collaborative spiralled inquiry (Timperley et al., 2020) where all members of each school are engaged in collaboration into their own school contexts as a cultural norm. This might better empower colleagues to meaningfully partner between schools and solidify a stronger basis for growing efficacy and agency within the collective. This should also include the development of a robust peer review process which reflects any learning that can be drawn from a school evaluation process.
2. Explore change leadership tools. For example, a systems thinking approach could prove very useful in identifying the leadership strategies required to shift perceptions via transparent communications and implementation planning. Examples might include Donohoo's (2016) reflective tools which include methods for pulse-checking teachers' perceptions of their impact or building a teacher growth profiler to create positive changes in practitioner behaviour.
3. Schools where this is significant cultural shift might prefer to start small with a proto-type group and use their peer insights to grow the network and draft a contextual guiding framework.
4. It appears wise, if collaboration is a key priority, to actively encourage school leadership to connect it to all teacher training and have a clear plan for early careers' teacher development. This then enables the next generation of teachers to develop collective efficacy and agency with the right level of guidance and resource in place.

A Closing Thought on Reflexivity

We believe our foregrounding of the importance of relationship development in building trust-based and agentic school-to-school collaboration in an international context returns us to asking the core purpose of teacher collaboration. The point made at the opening of this chapter is that in certain contemporary contexts, collaboration is being touted as the latest silver bullet for creating a 'self-regulating' education system. And, as such, collaboration's value and success gets evaluated in the context of often ill-defined notions of school improvement. Conversely, we have shown how Biesta (2015), Hargreaves (1994; Hargreaves & Dawe, 1990) and others argue that the real long-term purpose of collaboration is more intrinsic, personal and in many ways reminiscent of Donald Schön's definitions of practitioner 'reflection-in-action' and 'reflection-on-action' (1983).

However, Alan Bleakley argues that practitioners must go beyond these 'interiorities' to become 'eco-logical not ego-logical' (1999, p. 324). In his 1999 paper, *From Reflective Practice to Holistic Reflexivity*, Bleakley argues that education practitioners must embrace 'engaged agency' (p. 324), which we interpret as *the* collective output of collaboration. In turn, such an exteriorization of agency shifts a collaborative teacher from being merely reflective in a 'technical' sense and towards what Bleakley calls 'holistic reflexivity' (p. 326). In other words, through collaboration practice evolves both 'aesthetic and ethical' qualities and thus carries ontological and epistemological significance. Seeing international school-to-school collaboration as an assemblage means that individual practitioners begin to appreciate their own cultural, linguistic or geographical incongruities. Such heightened self-awareness of difference is a form of 'holistic reflexivity' that encourages aesthetic and ethical practice in every international educator. In an 'age of accountability', perhaps collaboration's greatest value is as a tool to develop teacher reflexivity, which may prove to be the ultimate school improvement strategy.

References

Bandura, A. (2000). Exercise of human agency through collective efficacy. *Current Directions in Psychological Science, 9*(3), 75–78.

Biesta, G. (2015). *Teacher agency: An ecological approach*. Bloomsbury.

Bleakley, A. (1999). From reflective practice to holistic reflexivity. *Studies in Higher Education, 24*(3), 315–330,

Brown, C., Daly, A., & Liou, Y.-H. (2016). Improving trust, improving schools: Findings from a social network analysis of 43 primary schools in England. *Journal of Professional Capital & Community, 1*(1), 69–91.

Datnow, A. (2011). Collaboration and contrived collegiality: Revisiting Hargreaves in the age of accountability. *Journal of Educational Change, 12*, 147–158.

DeLanda, M. (2006). *A new philosophy of society: Assemblage theory and social complexity*. Continuum.

Deleuze, G., & Guatarri, F. (1988). *A thousand plateaus: Capitalism and schizophrenia*. Continuum.

Donohoo, J. A. M. (2016). *Collective efficacy: How educators' beliefs impact student learning* (1st ed.). Corwin.

DuFour, R., & DuFour, R. (2012). *The school leader's guide to professional learning communities at work (essentials for principals)*. Solution Tree Press.

DuFour, R., DuFour, R., & Eaker, R. (Originally Published 2008; Updated 2015). In Revisiting Professional Learning Communities at Work (pp. 1–9). Bloomington, IN: Solution Tree.

DuFour, R., DuFour, R., Eaker, R., & Karhanek, G. (2004). *Whatever it takes: How professional learning communities respond when kids don't learn*. Solution Tree Press.

Edmondson, A. C. (2018). *The fearless organization: Creating psychological safety in the workplace for learning, innovation, and growth*. Wiley.

Hargreaves, A. (1994). *Changing teacher, changing times: Teachers' work and culture in the postmodern age*. Teachers College Press.

Hargreaves, A., & Dawe, R. (1990). Paths of professional development: Contrived collegiality, collaborative culture, and the case of peer coaching. *Teacher & Teaching Education, 6*(3), 227–241.

Hargreaves, A., & O'Connor, M. T. (2018). Solidarity with solidity. *Phi Delta Kappan, 100*(1), 20–24.

Hattie, J. (2012). *Visible learning for teachers: Maximizing impact on learning* (1st ed.). Routledge.

Hattie, J. (2016, July 11–12). Mindframes and maximizers. In *Proceedings of the 3rd annual visible learning plus conference*. Corwin. http://www.sagepublications.com/images/eblast/CorwinPress/PDF/AVL-program-2016.pdf

Kruse, S. D. (1999). Collaborate. *Journal of Staff Development, 20*(3), 14–16.

Schön, D. A. (1983). *The reflective practitioner*. Basic Books.

Scott, J. (2021, July 9). *Teacher collaboration: Episode 4* [Audio podcast]. https://eviden cebased.education/teacher-collaboration-episode-4/

Sumner, C., & Wespieser, K. (2017, November 1). Successful school-to-school collaboration. https://www.sec-ed.co.uk/best-practice/successful-school-to-school-collaboration/

Teaching & Learning Lab. (n.d.). *Discussion protocols*. https://www.gse.harvard.edu/sites/ default/files/Protocols_Handout.pdf. Accessed on July 2021.

Timperley, H., Ell, F., Fever, L. D., & Twyford, K. (2020). *Leading professional learning: practical strategies for impact in schools*. ACER Press.

Chapter 11

From Professional School Networks to Learning Ecosystems: The Case of Networks for Change in Barcelona

Jordi Díaz-Gibson, Mireia Civís Zaragoza and Marta Comas Sabat

Abstract

Today, education shows an urgent need for transformation to better respond to the complex and interdependent nature of current learning and social challenges we are facing. This chapter is based on the evidence of schools and district initiatives that claim for systemic change with a strong focus on wider interconnection and collaboration between learners, professionals and organizations.

Networks for Change is a programme launched in 2017 by the Barcelona Education Consortium that intends to create professional networks of schools in the city. The programme seeks a deep change in the whole system: to influence how teachers learn from one another to lead a collective transformation of schools, moving towards inclusive, significant and profound learning of all students. To achieve this, the programme articulates 25 territorial networks of schools, spread over the 10 districts in the city of Barcelona, grouping a total of 283 schools (ages 3–18), 1,700 leadership teams and 10,000 teachers. The network sessions are facilitated by one district leader, existing a team of 13 facilitators in the programme. Each school assigns an internal and volunteering leadership team that is responsible to assist to the network meetings, so as to empower internal change processes in schools.

The present study evaluates the impact of the programme on the development of territorial networks, as well as on the changes emerged in school communities. The instruments used combine a quantitative and qualitative approach including a questionnaire for teams of leaders involved in the programme, a questionnaire for teachers from schools and a focus group with programme facilitators of the 25 networks.

School-to-School Collaboration: Learning Across International Contexts, 187–207
Copyright © 2022 by Jordi Díaz-Gibson, Mireia Civís Zaragoza and Marta Comas Sabat
Published under exclusive licence by Emerald Publishing Limited
doi:10.1108/978-1-80043-668-820221012

The main results show that the Networks for Change programme is already becoming a response to the widely contrasted need to weave sustainable relationships between teachers from different schools in the system at the same time that it is strengthening the collaborative capacities of educational actors in the city's neighbourhoods and territories. Likewise, and to take a step further in the development of the programme, it is suggested emphasizing the increase of transversality in the networks as cross-sector collaboration, distributing the leadership of the programme through its actors and establishing direct ways for the impact to schools and their transformation. Right now, the network mainly fulfils a function of generating learning among its participants, although the desired horizon is to extend this learning to the entire ecosystem and at the same time generate systemic change in the neighbourhoods in order to enhance and document real impact on learners.

Keywords: Learning ecosystems; collaboration; professional networks; educational transformation; school networks; educational leadership and social capital

Assessment of the 'Networks for Change' Programme

This chapter aims to share the insights and learning from the 'Networks for Change' programme evaluation process. Networks for Change is a programme promoted by the Barcelona Education Consortium that intends to create professional networks of schools in the city in order to enhance significant, meaningful and inclusive learning environments in schools. As any research and survey project, it has been developed in a social context that conditions its meaning and frames it in a chain of interdependent and systemic realities. First, we have found out evidence that a large number of schools in the education system in Catalonia are seeking the renewal of their pedagogies and practices (Carbonell, 2015; Díaz-Gibson et al., 2019; Martínez-Celorrio, 2016). At the same time, in the middle of this research process, we experienced the COVID-19 pandemic, an unprecedented health and economic crisis with a notorious social and educational impact, which deconstructed our ordinary learning environments and consolidated practices and led us to a transitional and uncertain space. In this sense, research shows that the most resilient education systems are those that show greater capacity for collaboration between teachers, families and other community actors (Azorín, 2020; UNESCO, 2020). Thus, with no doubt, the dense relationships in the programme, the relationships of support and the purpose-driven networks have undergone the research process in times of high individual isolation and collective uncertainty.

Also, it is relevant to mention that we have an educational scenario characterized by balanced doses of regulation and cohesion (Hood, 1998), influenced at the same time by the unique political reality of Catalonia. In relation to the Catalan competence framework, despite the fact that the Autonomous Community of Catalonia has its own government (the Generalitat) with full competence in the field of education (Catalonia, 2009), the curricular organization and the regulation of both the educational offer and financing continue linked to the Spanish legislation. And it is precisely in the Spanish Parliament where education has been politically used with a historical record of eight education laws approved and repealed over the 40 years of democracy in the country, in accordance with the alternation of more progressive or more conservative governments. Progressive laws have typically increased the level of supply regulation, limiting the family's right to choose a certain centre and regulating the education market, as opposed to a more competitive and pro-private initiative driven by conservative regulations. Likewise, progressive education laws impose an inclusive school model and greater community participation where the role of the educational environment and local governments is more prominent, and conservative laws establish meritocratic models of individual excellence more prone to segregation (Comas et al., 2014; Viñao, 2017).

However, it is important to point out that in the Catalan context, the approval of the LEC was an attempt to overcome partisan tensions and reached a broad social consensus. In this way, the various governments that Catalonia has had recently have tried to promote school autonomy in combination with a hierarchical model where the relevant decisions are taken centrally without delegating to areas of proximity.

In this framework, the case of the Barcelona Education Consortium also becomes unique and, despite the centralized model of the Catalan Department of Education, governance in Barcelona is different. In this city, thanks to the Municipal Charter Act (1998), the local government participates as an education administration in the management of the city's education and is competent to implement its own public policies. This exceptionality has given a relevant role to the local administration that, from the institutional formula of the Consortium, has worked for territorial cohesion and equity. Thus, it has promoted cooperation between all schools supported with public funds to ensure that all of them have equivalent quality characteristics.

All in all, we are talking about a model halfway between the quadrant of the egalitarian and the hierarchical model (Hood, 1998) (Fig. 1).

Thus, public administration (local government and education administration) leads a process of network transformation by collecting initiatives and proposals that the educational scene is already generating and ensuring that no school supported with public funds is left out (egalitarian quadrant). However, and to ensure equal opportunities, there is an institutional appeal to all schools from the hierarchy, but one that is deemed necessary to preserve the ultimate purpose: educational success for all.

In this context, the Networks for Change programme began in 2017 and seeks a systemic change: to influence how teachers learn from one another to lead a collective transformation of schools, moving towards inclusive, significant and profound learning of all students. To achieve this, the programme proposes the articulation of 25 territorial networks of schools, spread over the 10 districts in

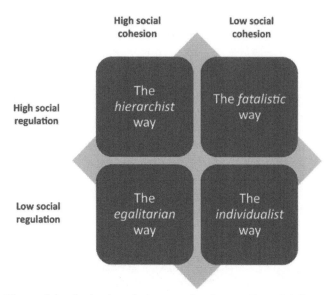

Fig. 1   The social cohesion/regulation matrix. *Source*: From Malin et al. (2020; used with permission).

the city of Barcelona, grouping a total of 283 schools (ages 3–18), 1,700 leadership teams and 10,000 teachers. Thus, the 25 networks are formed by a range of 8–14 schools in a specific territory in the city, that get together four times per year. The network sessions are facilitated by one district leader, existing a team of 13 facilitators in the programme. Each school assigns an internal and volunteering leadership team, a team that ranges from 3 to 10 teachers that can hold or not formal leadership positions and is responsible to assist to the network meetings, so as to empower internal change processes in schools. Therefore, the aim of this study is to evaluate the impact of the programme on the development of territorial networks, as well as on the changes facilitated in schools.

Learning Ecosystems: The Network of Relationships and Educational Change

Today, education shows an urgent need for transformation in order to adequately prepare the new generations that must live in this world with the will to change it. This transformation is reflected in the many initiatives by schools, pedagogical movements and educational policies aimed at innovation and change that are emerging everywhere. With the urgency of overcoming the education model of the industrial age (Senge, 2017), educational transformation has become a clear priority worldwide as a result of the need to adapt educational structures and professional skills to today's reality (Schleicher, 2016), marked by multiple complexities such as the pandemic itself, social inequalities, economic globalization, systemic racism, climate change, the ubiquitous role of technologies or the challenge of authoritarianism. Thus, the complex and interdependent nature of current socio-educational challenges requires a systemic approach, and innovation and transformation in education is increasingly configured as a process of collaboration between multiple actors (Díaz-Gibson et al., 2020; Eggers & Singh, 2009), overcoming fragmentation and tackling issues that are difficult to address from the individual (Harris et al., 2017). We therefore overcome the walls of classrooms and schools, and commit society as a whole:

> Schools must work together and with other partners in a more intelligent and intentional way instead of doing on their own, they need to learn from each other and give each other mutual support. (Brown & Flood, 2020, p. 130)

In this way, education is increasingly based on the power of collaboration between educational and social actors for continuous improvement from an ecosystem perspective, which frames the network of relationships at the community level. The idea of ecosystem refers to interconnections between educational actors that include internal interdependencies – between professionals, students, families and so on – and external ones – between organizations in the community, such as schools, extracurricular entities, social services, families, universities, companies, etc. – (Díaz-Gibson et al., 2016). As Brown and Flood (2020) rightly point out,

> (…) highly successful professional learning activities often involve three key guidelines: teachers collaborating between schools; teachers who collaborate persistently over time; and teachers who collaborate with other actors in the community or neighborhood. (p. 131)

In the same direction, numerous international studies addressing the need to reform the education system highlight the importance of these collaborative ecosystems aimed at responding to emerging educational and social challenges. These papers argue that the systematization of relations between educational and social professionals in the community, the formal articulation of the project around common goals and sustainable collaboration between educational organizations lay the foundations for which these initiatives become effective (Clayton, 2016; OECD, 2020; Rincón-Gallardo & Fullan, 2016; UNESCO, 2020).

In terms of leadership, this is a crucial issue in any project directly involving its direction and success, and in terms of educational leadership, we see how it is becoming an increasingly critical issue in educational agendas confirming a direct impact on educational improvement (Martínez et al., 2013; OECD, 2013; Schleicher, 2012). Thus, and understanding that many education systems are beginning to establish networking as a way to improve both teaching and learning, educational leadership has the function of ensuring the balance and connection between various parts of the system recognizing their interdependence and coordination around a shared project (Díaz-Gibson et al., 2015). Leadership is understood here from a holistic and networked perspective as the concept has clearly evolved from more instructive to more distributive conceptions (Daly, 2010; Díaz-Gibson et al., 2020; Maureira et al., 2014; Murillo, 2006).

Thus, and focussing on our object of study, it is clear that professional networking grounds the theory of change of the analyzed programme, understanding it as those collaborative, intentional and regular actions that occur between teachers and/or other professionals from different schools in the same district of Barcelona in the framework of the Networks for Change programme, with the aim of learning and sharing a horizon of pedagogical change to then promote changes in their own schools. Thus, in order to investigate and deepen the collaborative work carried out in the programme, we have established four parameters that, inspired by previous work and validated with the project's leading team, will help us better understand the quality of the work done from a collaborative and systemic perspective. These parameters become key intangibles and are trust, horizontality, co-responsibility and transversality, which we will deploy later. To measure these values, we have used validated scales (Daly, 2010; Díaz-Gibson et al., 2020) and adapted them for an emerging learning network with less than five years of life such as Networks for Change.

Methods

The assessment has the participation and testimony of three diverse actors involved in the programme but at three different levels of the ecosystem: macro-meso-micro. The instruments used combine a quantitative and qualitative approach, distributed in the following stages: (1) Questionnaire for teams of leaders involved in the programme (April and May 2020), which analyzes the type of relationships that occur in the network, satisfaction with the project and the perception of the impact on the school, as well as the dimensions of horizontality, transversality, trust, co-responsibility and transformation – micro- and meso-levels of the ecosystem; (2) Questionnaire for teachers from schools involved in the programme (June 2020), which analyzes project satisfaction and the perception of impact on the school – microlevel of analysis; and (3) Focus group with the facilitators of the 25 networks (July 2020), from the results obtained in the previous instruments, contrasting and assessing the impact and improvement of the programme. It is an 'ad hoc' instrument that ends up focussing on network values through three key issues: network facilitation, transversality in local networks, and enacting more practical and applicable support – macro level of analysis.

Teams of School Leaders Involved in the Programme

The survey has 217 valid answers corresponding to schools in all 25 Networks for Change, representing almost 80% (76.7%) of responses. It is therefore a high percentage that ensures a good representativeness and reliability of results, also taking into account that sample and universe are equated in this case.

With regard to the type of centres, the diversity of the set of Networks for Change is included: publicly owned, subsidized schools, infant and primary education, primary and secondary, secondary and special education schools. However, there is a predominance of primary schools (59% IE and PE and 19% PE-SEC)*, as we can see in Fig. 2.

Furthermore, the level of participation of these centres in the sessions is also very consistent as 80% have attended more than 80% of sessions, which gives greater validity to the results, as they are people who speak knowingly about the operation and dynamics of each of the sessions. This distribution is also homogeneous in the different types of centres.

Teachers of the Schools Participating in the Programme

To collect the teachers' views, we have analyzed the satisfaction with the programme and the perception of the impact on the school. At the same time, we have collected some contextual data in relation to the training done by teachers as a result of participating in Networks for Change.

In relation to response rates, there are 1,139 valid responses, corresponding to 10% of the universe, which we consider a satisfactory percentage for being an online questionnaire at a difficult time as explained in the introduction (end of academic year in confinement). In addition, these are the second-level participants of the programme (teachers who are not part of the leading team and therefore have not participated in the Networks for Change sessions). However, and as mentioned above, despite knowing that the response rate would not be high, we did not want to pass up the opportunity to ask the teachers and contrast the results of the previous target group.

Among the centres represented, we have IE, PE, secondary and special education centres. Thus, there is a predominance of primary schools (52% IE and PE and 27% PE-SEC). In this case, there is a slightly lower proportion of IE-PE centres than in the leading teams and instead quite a bit more PE-SEC. We have the response rates in Fig. 3.

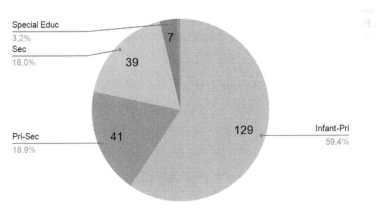

Fig. 2   Type of sample centers. *Source*: Author's elaboration.

---

* IE - Infant Education; PE - Primary Education; PE-SEC - Primary Education and Secondary Education

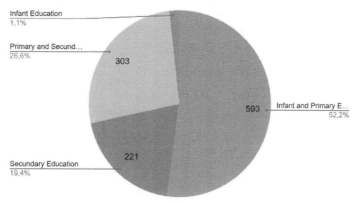

Fig. 3   Sample centers. *Source*: Author's elaboration.

Likewise, the number of teachers who respond per school is very diverse and ranges from schools where there is only one answer to more than 10. However, the predominant ones are between 1 and 4 people per school.

The Team of Facilitators of the Programme

The programme has a team of 13 facilitators who guide and energize the network sessions. These are people with educational experience who are currently developing their professional role in Pedagogical Resources Centers (CRP), as Language and Social Cohesion (LIC) advisers or within the Barcelona Education Consortium itself. We have had their opinion through a focus group in which 11 of them have been able to participate.

Discussing Key Results

As main results, we can highlight high levels of satisfaction with the programme and the creation of collaborative climates among members of the networks, typical of a first moment and level of development of a successful professional network. Thus, these emerging climates have to do with the intangibles of the networks corresponding to co-responsibility, horizontality and trust, which have been consistently increased by the programme. However, we have identified a path for improvement in relation to transversality, as diversity of community actors' involvement, and in this sense, the recommendations are aimed at incorporating new educational agents into the networks beyond schools and basic educational services and at better linking with other existing networks and programmes with shared objectives. Being able to make transversality a successful pillar of the Networks for Change programme would strengthen the local educational ecosystem by making the idea of the Educating City a reality insofar as the whole educational fabric connects and vertebrates while recognizing the educational potential that goes beyond school. Here we share three conditions for systemic change where the most relevant results are summarized, discussed with specialized theoretical references and, finally, specific improvements are proposed.

From School Networks to Co-responsible Ecosystems for Educational Change

The global programme is becoming a connecting and weaving space for new and better relations between schools in the same neighbourhood or district. The results provide evidence of how the networked educational work promoted by the programme in these first three years is affecting both the construction of new human capital and social capital in the territory. The new human capital generated refers to the learning achieved by the participants in the programme, and the new social capital takes shape with the new relationships established. We understand the increase in social capital as the quantity and quality of relationships between educational actors, and it is related to literature with a more effective educational and social response, laying the foundations for more inclusion, more equity and more innovation, at the territory and city levels (Daly, 2010; Díaz-Gibson & Civís, 2011; Liou et al., 2019).

In this sense, we understand that the programme is being successful in generating three of the four pillars of networking for the generation of social capital: trust, horizontality and co-responsibility, but it still has a long way to go to finish building the last of the pillars: transversality.

The levels of trust achieved throughout the programme become one of the three intangible pillars intentionally generated by the programme. These results are especially relevant as trust becomes an essential seed for the sustainability and cohesion of the actors in a professional network. Trust is a fundamental relational value that sustains mutual obligations and expectations between people. The more I trust someone, the more I am able to be vulnerable and authentic

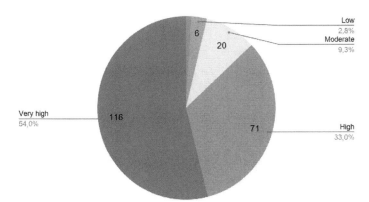

Fig. 4   Global level of trust. *Source*: Author's elaboration.

(Díaz-Gibson et al., 2016; Daly, 2010), feeling a sense of safety and the opportunity to share all our human and social potential. In this sense, the vast majority of participants state that in their own network: they feel safe and secure in sharing opinions, disagreements and doubts with others; they feel respected by others; they perceive that colleagues are open to sharing expectations, experiences, achievements, doubts or difficulties about their processes of change in the network; and they especially value their contributions and reflections. In this sense, the literature tells us that trust between educational actors plays a critical role in improving the educational success and educational innovation of a territory (Clayton, 2016; Daly, 2010) and facilitates the development and sustainability of community collaborations by fostering effective communication and knowledge exchange (Daly & Liou, 2018). Thus, existing trust weaves social relationships into networks and becomes a crucial intangible foundation on which to grow the programme (Fig. 4).

A second intangible pillar of networking in the programme materializes with the high levels of horizontality in social relations in networks. The horizontality achieved brings to light the inclusive, active and dynamic role of social relations, which promotes the added value and resilience provided by the existence of multiple and diverse leaderships throughout the collaborative process (Díaz-Gibson et al., 2020; Earl & Katz, 2007). Therefore, horizontality refers to the empowerment of participants to feel the space as their own, where the facilitators of the network assume a role of facilitating the relationships within the framework of teams leading change. One of the challenges of the programme in the near future will be to continue to cultivate these levels of confidence and horizontality in order to expand and strengthen the capital generated (Fig. 5).

A third pillar built has been the achievement of relevant levels of co-responsibility. Although the programme promotes professional networks where participants do not jointly implement the same initiative or project, it has sought co-responsibility of the centres around learning for educational transformation

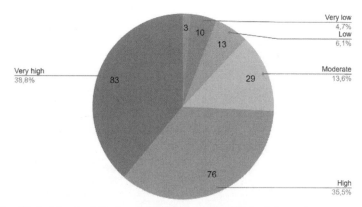

Fig. 5   Global level of horizontality. *Source*: Author's elaboration.

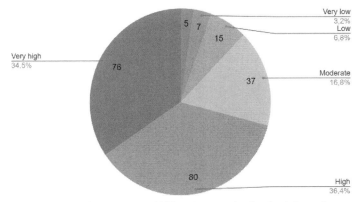

Fig. 6   Global level of Co-responsibility. *Source*: Author's elaboration.

with an emphasis on its systemic and city character. In this sense, the lead-ing teams show a high degree of alignment and commitment to the network, first as a learning space between schools, and second on its interdependence in the face of the challenge of educational transformation at the present time. Co-responsibility becomes a key element from a networking perspective that incorporates collaboration between schools or educational organizations, as it indicates an alignment that integrates diverse expertise, interests, perspectives and expectations among the actors in the ecosystem, around a shared purpose (Díaz-Gibson et al., 2016; Leithwood, 2019). An interesting value that rein-forces networked educational work in the programme is the fact that the leading teams perceive that the challenge of educational transformation is a challenge shared by all schools. This evidence also shows us that the programme estab-lishes a positive balance between the individual benefit – teacher or school – and the collective benefit – network and programme – that the leading teams obtain by participating in the programme, turning the Networks for Change into something more than a shared space where each member seeks their own benefit exclusively (Fig. 6).

Therefore, the challenge of co-responsibility increases with the diversity and heterogeneity of members, meaning that it is easier to align shared commitments between similar educational actors, such as teachers or schoolteachers, than to do it with different educational agents such as psychologists from the Psycho-pedagogical Guidance Team (EAP), leisure monitors, psychologists from social services or social educators from the neighbourhood centre, among others. In this sense, there is an important path to follow in the future of the programme in terms of sustaining levels of co-responsibility in more transversal and heterogeneous networks. And these ideas lead us to the final pillar of transversality (Fig. 7).

The participants in the programme have shown more discreet results around the levels of transversality achieved. Transversality values diversity in net-works, understood as the involvement of diverse educational actors in terms

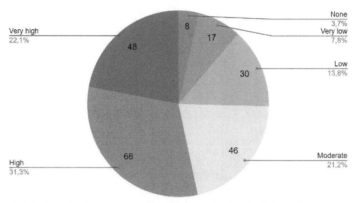

Fig. 7   Global level of transversality. *Source*: Author's elaboration.

of organizations, areas, disciplines or sectors. Research on transversality in educational networks tells us that the greater heterogeneity in the participation of socio-educational agents and therefore the greater inclusiveness of community actors, the more capacity to generate equal opportunities in the territories (Marschall & Stolle, 2004), the more capacity for systemic innovation (Clayton, 2016) and the more potential for systemic impact (Díaz-Gibson et al., 2020). The Networks for Change programme proposes work in professional networks of schools, very focussed on transforming educational practices within schools.

In this sense, the leading teams show divergences around the level of involvement of other educational actors at a district level involved in some of the networks, such as the Center for Pedagogical Resources, Psychological and Pedagogical Advice Services or the Inspection. At the same time, there are also divided opinions regarding the value provided by the different profiles of existing schools in the network, regarding the fact that the schools in the network are in different times of a change process. In this sense, the facilitators emphasize that one of the keys to generate appropriate learning climates and motivation for networking has been the territoriality of the networks, indicating that those facilitators who were part of the Center for Pedagogical Resources contributed a plus knowledge of the territory and underpinned a sense of belonging necessary for the proper functioning of the network.

However, a short-term challenge facing the programme refers to the levels of transversality desired to meet the challenge of educational transformation, understanding that transversality fosters a deep and complex interdisciplinary dialogue that contributes to responding in a more comprehensive, effective and holistic way to the educational and social challenges we face – such as equity, inclusion or environmental sustainability – by crossing the boundaries between organizations, areas, disciplines and sectors (Díaz-Gibson et al., 2020; OECD, 2018; UNESCO, 2020).

Weaving Connections Between Teachers Beyond the Territorial Networks

In terms of satisfaction, this is shown as relevant by the participants, and especially by all the leading teams that are those who have enjoyed the sessions of the network and shared dynamics and relationships between teachers from diverse schools. It is clear that the programme has generated new human capital in the city that is sustained by high levels of satisfaction with the programme and the levels of learning acquired. Thus, we detect that the programme responds directly and satisfactorily to the need for relationships between schools and between diverse teachers in order to learn together and share a common horizon of educational change. The need to build professional networks of teachers as a tool for educational improvement is one of the emerging local educational change strategies globally (Azorín et al., 2020; Brown & Flood, 2020; Díaz-Gibson et al., 2020; Pino-Yancovic & Ahumada, 2020). Thus, the results of the survey show us that Networks for Change is perceived by schools and teachers as a good opportunity to open and share their own classroom experiences beyond the centres themselves, expanding team learning and exploring a shared educational advancement.

The leading teams' satisfaction with the programme indicates that the Networks for Change has found a good professional network format for learning, optimal both in terms of investment and use of teachers' time and in relation to the dynamics and participation in the sessions. In this sense, the work of the project facilitators is an element directly related to the high levels of satisfaction with the sessions. Thus, the dynamics and climates generated in the networking sessions are a priority vector for the proper functioning of the networks and for their consolidation (Harris & Jones, 2017), an aspect especially relevant in the initial phase of the networks (Díaz-Gibson et al., 2016). As the facilitators point out, some of the key aspects in facilitating the sessions have been the attitude of empathy and support for teachers; shared pre-design and good preparation of sessions; pedagogical leadership and the construction of shared sense; collaborative work by the network of facilitators; and, finally, the territorial character of the networks.

In a way, we understand that this first stage of the programme has played a more distributive, equalizing and scaling role, also from a more 'top-down' or designated networks perspective (Díaz-Gibson & Civís, 2011). That is, Networks for Change has ensured that conceptions of the theory of desired change reach everyone and that all centres have the potential to make it possible. Disseminating change and innovation is clearly a role for networks but not the only one (Beresford, 2017). Beyond escalating change, which would be a more 'technical' issue, these networks seek a more significant change at a cultural and relational level (Beresford, 2017).

However, if we focus on the networking sessions, the leading teams highlight an element of improvement in their development that could increase the learning of all. Although, as we have stated above, the teams are satisfied with the network work carried out, and with the climate of the network, they state that they would like to know the various schools and their initiatives better, which would further strengthen relationships between teachers and between schools. In this sense, the interest shown in getting to know the other centres better goes beyond the territory itself, and some of the teams share the idea of also connecting with centres in the city with which they share challenges, projects, methodologies or moments of change. In this sense, with the aim of making the learning more meaningful for the leading teams, the need emerges to better connect the centres while establishing a balance between the territorial connection of centres and a more intentional connection of these centres. We quote a response from a leading team that surely reflects a balance in this direction:

> Perhaps it would have been a good group to guarantee diversity but also to be able to think and collaborate with schools that are at similar times in their process of change. That would have been more stimulating.

On the other hand, a significant part of the teachers surveyed shows a certain distance and a lack of commitment around the dynamics of the programme. Teachers argue that the low involvement evidenced in the results is mainly due to the lack of time and spaces to connect the majority of teachers with the programme. At the same time, teachers feel that the leading teams in the school are the only link between them and the programme, which also limits the impact on the learning of other teachers in schools in the city, as well as in action and change practices in centres. Teachers often perceive that the programme is more for the leading teams and less for the centre as a whole. These results, therefore, show some difficulties in making the theory of change underlying the programme effective, where the leading teams are expected to be the representatives and ambassadors of change in the centres.

Likewise, an interesting result is that, despite the distance identified, the schoolteachers themselves have expressed their willingness to participate in the programme in a more active way, repeatedly pointing out the interest in connecting with other schools and other teachers beyond their own faculty. We understand this call as a natural adjustment of the network at a microlevel (school) that calls for more horizontality in exchange for greater involvement.

Thus, one of the challenges in advancing the programme is to find a first balance between network models, territorial and thematic, and a second balance between a representative or horizontal network model. The representative model is the current one where the leading teams are the 'brokers' of the relationships between what happens in the programme and what happens in the centre, and a horizontal model is a model where teachers also feel called to participate directly in some of the initiatives of the general programme or the territorial network. It is clear that the desired balance is to measure forces and resources allocated to the programme but at the same time also to explore the possibilities and limitations of a more systemic design of the network, accepting that each territorial network will acquire an authentic and different nature based on the actors involved and the relationships established; at the same time, it becomes interesting to explore new connections within the network understanding that there is life beyond territorial networks, moving from Networks for Change to a change that is interwoven in the network space.

From a Professional Learning Network to a Network of Action and Educational Change in Schools

Networks for Change in its first three years of life show, beyond the impact on networks, significant impacts on joint reflection and learning mainly from the members of the leading teams. At the same time, the results show a clear limitation on the incidence of the programme in the centres themselves, either in the field of reflection and learning of all the teachers of the centres, as in the field of support and accompaniment to new practices in the classroom (as shown in Fig. 8). In this sense, Brown and Flood (2020), among others, express how one of the main challenges of school leaders is to know how to transfer the work done in the network to a work plan for the school, giving time and space to the faculty to work on the proposals.

Thus, most leading teams see in the pedagogical approaches shared in the networks the present levers of change and claim that they are working in this direction. At the same time, the teachers surveyed argue that while the programme has focussed on determining managing teams to promote change, most centres were already more or less immersed in their own process of change. Therefore, participation in the programme has become another contribution to sustain and add to some dynamics already in progress.

Thus, as Fig. 8 indicates, evidence of this survey is that, at the beginning of the programme, the leading teams have not sufficiently transferred the learning generated in the networks to the centres, and, at the same time, have not clearly affected changes to the educational practices of the faculty. However, as the literature explains, this fact can be explained in part by the very nature of the networks and the evolutionary moment of the programme: first, because the construction of relational pillars and the social capital of territorial networks – trust, horizontality, co-responsibility and transversality – require time and effort to weave and grow (Daly, 2010; Díaz-Gibson et al., 2016); second, because the programme is in an initial phase and has three years of life; and third, for the depth and scope of the change pursued, a change that, to be lasting and impact on the organizational

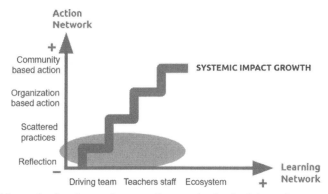

Fig. 8   Networks for change impact. *Source*: Author's elaboration.

cultures of the centres – and not just a superficial and rapid change – also takes time: 'Recognize that the profound transfer of practices culturally complex that meets complex needs takes time' (Beresford, 2017).

Likewise, this result pushes us to deepen the orientation of the programme in order to, while maintaining the high doses of learning at the level of the networks, promote and accompany both the learning and the processes of change in the centres. In a way, it points to the need to move from so-called learning networks to so-called action networks, a complex path to follow as the literature and international experience point to effective or successful networks (Kallio & Halverson, 2019; Rincón-Gallardo & Fullan, 2016).

In this same direction, Mas (2020) tells us about the double role of the network: on the one hand, it becomes a collaborative space to submit the educational fact itself to critical analysis, and on the other hand, it is configured as a space to test action hypotheses and effective actions resulting from the analysis made.

Bearing in mind the data obtained by the leading teams, teachers of the schools involved and the facilitators of the programme, we identify three aspects of the programme that can strategically address the impact of networks on action and practice in schools: the first aspect refers to work within networks, where the need to address more practical content adapted to the needs expressed by each of the networks is highlighted; the second refers to the commitment of the centres to provide space and time for the leading teams to be able to connect learning and accompany changes; and the third refers to the evaluation of the impact of the programme.

In this sense, the evaluation of networks becomes a crucial element for their progress, sustainability and success. As we said in the introduction, the proliferation of networks as a strategy for change has not always guaranteed effective networks. Thus, clearly establishing the desired effects and then being able to evaluate their achievement in terms of impact is essential to move the network forward and make decisions about its operation. It will be interesting to highlight the impacts generated by this new capital promoted intentionally by the Networks for Change in the city of Barcelona in the coming years. In fact, the literature indicates how, in general terms, we need more evidence of the functioning of networks (Ion & Brown, 2020, Rincón-Gallardo & Fullan, 2016). Having evidence on the impact of networks would mean a benefit for the networks themselves and for the practice of networks in general, helping to connect what is known about effective networks and what school networks do (Rincón-Gallardo & Fullan, 2016).

Key Lessons

The present study shows us that the Networks for Change programme is already becoming a response to the widely contrasted need to connect teachers from different schools in the system (OECD, 2018); at the same time, it is strengthening the need for collaboration between educational actors in the city's neighbourhoods and territories (UNESCO, 2020). Likewise, and to take a step further in the development of the programme, it is suggested emphasizing the increase of transversality in the networks, and distributing the leadership of the programme through its actors, and establishing direct ways for the impact to schools and their transformation. Right now, the network mainly fulfils a function of generating learning among its participants, but we know that the desired horizon is to extend this learning to the entire ecosystem and at the same time generate systemic change, which will ensure a real impact on schools. Therefore, we would like to conclude with three propositive lessons for network improvement with detailed efforts. First, in order to enhance transversality and involve various community actors in the network:

- The progress of the programme should provide for levels of transversality with regard to the territorial network. It will therefore be necessary to make an initial map of possible alliances that include relevant actors in the ecosystem such as those already mentioned by the facilitators: Inspection, EAPs, territorial coordinators, Social Cohesion and Interculturality (SCI) agents, families, students, basic and specific educational services or municipal educational technicians. Identifying actors and drawing alliances also means exploring the nature of the relationships that are given or can be given, always looking for ways to increase the quantity, but above all the quality of the relationships.
- Given this map, it will be relevant to detect those actors who are really interested in collaborating and being part of the networks to achieve the purpose of educational change. At this point, the facilitators identified two key agents that can really impact on the achievement of the objectives of the programme: the first agent is the inspection, as connecting with the evaluation action can help to share horizons and provide the system with greater coherence; and the second actor would be the district education technician(s), as they have great knowledge of the territory and represent the entire non-formal sector of education, in addition to the formal one.
- Stimulating networks with greater diversity involves some relevant issues to keep in mind, such as the flexibility and ability to adapt one's own objectives at the territorial level, or one's own ability to align the shared purpose. As the facilitators pointed out, we need to be prepared for the involvement of diverse actors to involve greater complexity in management and involve changes and adaptations of the views and actions designed so far. Thus, it will be essential that the new actors participate in the climate already generated mostly in the networks of the territory based on horizontality, trust, co-responsibility and collaboration in the face of a shared purpose.
- Likewise, it is essential to seek synergies with other networks and parallel programmes that share objectives such as the Network of Basic Competences, the Laboratory for Educational Transformation, the Futures of Education, Changemakers Schools or the Network of Innovative Institutes, among others. Doing so will bring order to the network of existing networks and, at the same time, help professionals know where to join.

Second, with the purpose of distributing leadership across the whole network:

- Think of a leading team where its members gather greater diversity and representation of the centres – such as including one teacher per cycle in the teams; or design a leading group for each centre that includes the different school actors, such as teachers, families, students and/or administrative staff. Especially the idea of including children and young people in the processes of change seems very relevant to us since they are too often disregarded and we end up working for children and young people without children and young people.
- Maintaining territorial networks as a basis for proximity and territorial educational change is a success. At the same time, it will be necessary to promote more informal networks that arise from shared needs and that are developed in parallel, led by teachers from schools interested in advancing on specific topics such as the personalization of learning, the prevention of bullying or problem-based learning. Thus, the exploration and learning we are all currently experiencing about collaborative work and e-learning environments can shed some light on the development of a more horizontal and sustainable networking model. Online meetings can facilitate access to teachers, the management of large and diverse groups and at the same time collaboration in the various spaces of the network.
- Deepen in a distributed leadership in the networks that will be the same that the leading teams will have to distribute in their own centres to achieve synergies between teachers. Again, we see the leading teams not as network speakers but as weavers of opportunity for schoolteachers, being able to both facilitate relevant discussions and make teachers part of the programme by offering learning spaces, beyond the centres, to connect needs, to generate complicities between centres of the networks and to look for possible collaborations between teachers of diverse schools that contribute to expand the learning and impel the changes in the centres.
- This same path to follow could be strengthened with some specific leadership training, as we have advanced above. Thus, the training could be multilevel, either for the network of leading teams, facilitators or more institutional government of the programme, encouraging learning that questions the strategies used and proposing new ones (Liou et al., 2019; Pino-Yancovic & Ahumada, 2020).
- Establishing specific and personalized support for the most unstable, fragile or novice leading teams can help to accompany and facilitate the generation of the capital needed to move forward in networking. Other more experienced and established leading teams could act as tutors for those who need timely support to get started.

And third, willing to turn substantial learning into real practice:

- The development and growth of the programme requires that the sessions of the networks be oriented to practice and respond more to the needs of each territory and centre. This priority is initially to provide the programme with greater internal coherence that facilitates this more practical approach. To do this, a systemic map of actions of the Barcelona Education Consortium can be intentionally created to help us generate coherence, integrating the offer of programmes such as the area and centre training plan, align the main objectives of the course with seminars and other spaces for reflection, the action of the Educational Services or greater coordination with the mentoring programme in schools.

- It is necessary to strengthen the time of reflection in the centres to accompany the transfer of learning, structuring a feedback between the network and the centre with a dynamic character. This implies an explicit commitment from the participating centres to allocate a monthly space for the faculty to stop, share and reflect on their own practice and start planning the changes that make the expected transferability real. Advancing in the culture of reflection involves planning workspaces during school hours that are not intended for action or classroom work, and this also implies a commitment on the part of the administration that must provide resources to do so, where possible (Pino-Yancovic & Ahumada, 2020). The leading team could use this space to move relevant discussions from the network to the centres themselves, distribute the leadership and thus extend the scope of the programme.
- An operational and practical advance of the work with the centres can be the development of a work plan or portfolio by centre, where objectives, specific tasks for courses and people involved are reflected, and where at the same time the advances can be documented dynamically throughout the process. This instrument can become a tool for development and inter-centre reflection, which allows a greater transfer of learning, and at the same time a tool for documenting changes that can help both to share the process on the network and to pilot the accompanying processes.
- Finally, with the aim of enhancing the support of change processes in schools, while weaving the quality of links between teachers, we could seek collaborative strategies such as tutoring between schools, where two schools or two related teachers – from the same territory or not – would become pairs during an academic year with the aim of sharing projects, workspaces, observations between teachers and at the same time they could co-evaluate their own work plans and the changes implemented. The proposal of 'critical friends' made by Mellado et al. (2020), which provide feedback and a different look, would also go in this direction.

Finally, the Networks for Change programme has produced a fruitful path of collaboration between the researchers and policymakers that we will surely continue to explore and promote as a driver of change in our educational ecosystems.

References

Azorín, C. (2020). Beyond COVID-19 supernova. Is another education coming? *Journal of Professional Capital and Community*, 5(3–4),381–390.

Azorín, C., Harris, A., & Jones, M. (2020). Taking a distributed perspective on leading professional learning networks. *School Leadership & Management, 40*(2–3), 111–127.

Beresford, T. (2017). *Human-scale at scale. Cultivating new education cultures.* Innovation Unit.

Brown, P. C., & Flood, J. (2020). Conquering the professional learning network labyrinth: What is required from the networked school leader? *School Leadership & Management, 40*(2–3), 128–145.

Carbonell, J. (2015). Pedagogías del siglo XXI. Alternativas para la innovación educativa. *Educatio Siglo XXI, 33*(2), 325–328.

Catalonia. (2009). Llei 12/2009, del 10 de juliol, d'educació (LEC). *Diari oficial de la Generalitat de Catalunya,* 16 de juliol 2009, núm. 5422, pp. 56589–56682.

Clayton, R. (2016). *Building innovation ecosystems in education to reinvent school: A study of innovation and system change in the USA.* Winston Churchill Memorial Trust.

Comas, M., Abellán, C., & Plandiura, R. (2014). *Consells escolars i participació de les famílies a l'escola: Una lectura marcada per la LOMCE.* Fundació Jaume Bofill.

Daly, A. J. (2010). *Social network theory and educational change.* Harvard Education Press.

Daly, A. J., & Liou, Y. (2018). The lead igniter: A longitudinal examination of influence and energy through networks, efficacy, and climate. *Educational Administration Quarterly, 55*(3), 363–403.

Díaz-Gibson, J., & Civís, M. (2011). Redes Socioeducativas promotoras de capital social en la comunidad: Un marco teórico de referencia. *Cultura y Educación, 23*(3), 415–429.

Díaz-Gibson, J., Civís, M., Cortada, M., & Carrillo, E. (2015). El liderazgo y la gobernanza colaborativa en proyectos educativos comunitarios. *Pedagogía social: Revista interuniversitaria, 26*, 59–83.

Díaz-Gibson, J., Civís, M., Daly, A. J., Longás, J., & Riera, J. (2016). Networked leadership in educational collaborative networks. *Educational Management Administration & Leadership, 45*(6), 1040–1059.

Díaz-Gibson, J., Civís, M., Fontanet, A., López, S., & Prats, M. A. (2019). La visión de los directores de escuela sobre el impulso de la innovación educativa en Cataluña/School head teachers' views of the drive towards educational innovation in Catalonia. *Cultura y Educación: Culture and Education, 31*(3), 655–670.

Díaz-Gibson, J., Daly, A., Miller-Balslev, G., & Civís, M. (2020). The SchoolWeavers tool: Supporting school leaders to weave learning ecosystems. *School Leadership & Management, 41*(4–5), 429–446.

Earl, L., & Katz, S. (2007). Leadership in networked learning communities: Defining the terrain. *School Leadership & Management, 27*(3), 239–258.

Eggers, W. D., & Singh, S. K. (2009). *The public innovator's playbook: Nurturing bold ideas in government.* Ash Institute.

Harris, A., & Jones, M. S. (2017). Professional learning communities: A strategy for school and system improvement? *Cylchgrawn addysg cymru/Wales Journal of Education, 19*(1), 16–38.

Harris, A., Jones, M., & Huffman, J. (2017). *Teachers leading educational reform: The power of professional learning communities.* Routledge Press.

Hood, C. (1998). *The art of the state.* Oxford University Press.

Ion, G., & Brown, C. (2020). *Redes entre escuelas para la mejora educativa. ¿Qué prácticas són las más efectivas?* Fundació Jaume Bofill. *Document no publicat.*

Kallio, J. M., & Halverson, R. R. (2019). Designing for trust-building interactions in the initiation of a networked improvement community. In N. Kolleck (Ed.), *Frontiers in Education* (Vol. 4, p. 154). Frontiers.

Leithwood, K. (2019). Characteristics of effective leadership networks: A replication and extension. *School Leadership & Management, 39*(2), 175–197.

Liou, Y. H., Bjorklund, P., Jr., & Daly, A. J. (2019). Climate change in Common Core policy context: The shifting role of attitudes and beliefs. *Educational Policy, 35*(6), 908–948.

Malin, J. R., Brown, C., Ion, G., van Ackeren, I., Bremm, N., Luzmore, R., ... & Rind, G. M. (2020). World-wide barriers and enablers to achieving evidence-informed practice in education: what can be learnt from Spain, England, the United States, and Germany?. *Humanities and Social Sciences Communications, 7*(1), 1–14.

Martínez, M., Badia, J., & Jolonch, A. (2013). *Lideratge per a l'aprenentatge. Estudis de cas a Catalunya*. Fundació Jaume Bofill.

Martínez-Celorrio, X. (2016). Innovación y reestructuración educativa en España: Las escuelas del nuevo siglo. In A. Blanco & A. M. Chueca (Eds.), *Informe España 2016* (pp. 43–84). Universidad Pontificia Comillas.

Marschall, M. J., & Stolle, D. (2004). Race and the city: Neighborhood context and the development of generalized trust. *Political Behavior, 26*(2), 125–153.

Mas, M. (2020). Una estratègia democràtica de canvi professional. Les xarxes i el seu context. *Revista Catalana de Pedagogia, 17*, 133–157.

Maureira, O., Moforte, C., & González, G. (2014). Más liderazgo distribuido y menos liderazgo directivo: Nuevas perspectivas para caracterizar procesos de influencia en los centros escolares. *Perfiles Educativos, 36*(146), 134–153.

Mellado, E. M., Rincón-Gallardo, S., Aravena, O. A., & Villagra, C. P. (2020). Acompañamiento a redes de líderes escolares para su transformación en comunidades profesionales de aprendizaje. *Perfiles Educativos, 42*(169), 52–69.

Municipal Charter Act. (1998). Llei de la Carta Municipal de Barcelona de Catalunya (Llei 22/1998, de 30 de desembre).

Murillo, F. J. (2006). Una dirección escolar para el cambio: del liderazgo transformacional al liderazgo distribuido. Revista Electrónica Iberoamericana sobre Calidad. *Eficacia y Cambio en Educación, 4*(4), 11–24.

OECD. (2013). *Leadership for 21st century learning. Educational research and innovation*. OECD Publishing.

OECD. (2018). *The future of education and skills: Education 2030*. OECD Publishing.

OECD. (2020). *TALIS 2018 results (Volume II): Teachers and school leaders as valued professionals*. OECD Publishing.

Pino-Yancovic, M., & Ahumada, L. (2020). Collaborative inquiry networks: The challenge to promote network leadership capacities in Chile. *School Leadership & Management, 40*(2–3), 1–21.

Rincón-Gallardo, S., & Fullan, M. (2016). Essential features of effective networks in education. *Journal of Professional Capital and Community, 1*(1), 5–22.

Senge, P. (2017). Entrevista: 'El profesor del siglo XXI tiene que enseñar lo que no sabe'. Diari El País.

Schleicher, A. (2012). *Preparing teachers and developing school leaders for the 21st century: Lessons from around the world*. OECD Publishing.

Schleicher, A. (2016). *Teaching excellence through professional learning and policy reform: Lessons from around the world*. international summit on the teaching profession. OECD Publishing.

UNESCO. (2020). *Education in a Post-COVID world: Nine ideas for public action international commission on the futures of education*. UNESCO.

Viñao, A. (2017). El modelo neoconservador de gobernanza escolar: Principios, estrategias y consecuencias en España. In J. Collet & A. Tort (Eds.), *La gobernanza escolar democrática* (pp. 41–65). Morata.

Chapter 12

Germany: School-to-School Collaboration at the Interface of Bureaucracy and Autonomy

Anke B. Liegmann, Isabell van Ackeren, René Breiwe,
Nina Bremm, Manuela Endberg, Marco Hasselkuß and
Sabrina Rutter

Abstract

School networks are of increasing importance in Germany. Despite not being formally anchored in the structure of the school system, school networks are promoted via a wide variety of programmes. These initiatives have varying aims such as the systemic promotion of school development and the identification of key factors for success. Some programmes even provide for accompanying research into the impact of networks on their success. Following the classification of the German school system according to the cohesion/regulation matrix by Chapman, and suggesting an emphasis on 'egalitarian culture', this chapter then focuses on the topic of school-to-school collaboration. Doing so, we shall define our understanding of school networks, present a typology of commonly found networks in Germany and provide systemic examples of some of the larger school networks. The review of the national state of research in this field including experience from two of our research and development projects shows desiderata especially concerning processes of school-to-school collaboration. The role of school leadership, which will be expanded upon further, has proven to be a driver of success in school networks.

Keywords: School networks; network initiators; school leadership; school development; transfer; school governance

School-to-School Collaboration: Learning Across International Contexts, 209–225
Copyright © 2022 by Anke B. Liegmann, Isabell van Ackeren, René Breiwe,
Nina Bremm, Manuela Endberg, Marco Hasselkuß and Sabrina Rutter
Published under exclusive licence by Emerald Publishing Limited
doi:10.1108/978-1-80043-668-820221013

In Germany, school networks have come into focus for the role they play in catalysing innovation through the initiatives of external stakeholders, most frequently charitable foundations. The '*Netzwerk innovativer Schulen in Deutschland*' [Network of Innovative Schools in Germany] programme, which was sponsored by the Bertelsmann Foundation between 1998 and 2003,[1] has often been cited as a hub for facilitating collaboration among school networks (Rürup et al., 2015, p. 91). The relationship between school network activity and changes in management strategy was also evidenced by the project '*Eigenständige Schule*' [Semi-Autonomous Schools] which was also funded by the Bertelsmann Foundation between 2002 and 2008. In this network, schools were able to explore the scope and practices of school autonomy. Despite not being formally recognized by the structures of the school system, networks continue to attract support and funding through programme initiatives.

These initiatives have a number of aims such as the systemic promotion of school development and the identification of key factors for success that can be applied across the wider school system. Some programmes also provide for accompanying research into the impact of networks on their success. Nevertheless, the fundamental question regarding which function school networks should play within school management remains unresolved. Rürup et al. (2015) claim, to a greater or lesser degree, that external actors such as foundations and businesses seek to gain more influence over schools through their promotion of network initiatives, in which participation is conditional upon adherence to predetermined terms and objectives. However, as long as school participation in networks remains voluntary, any attempt by stakeholders to realize a social innovation agenda across the board may not be sustainable.

A full-scale examination of the function of networks is beyond the scope of this chapter. Instead, we shall focus attention on the frameworks within which school networks operate. Following the classification of the German school system in the cohesion/regulation matrix (Chapman, 2019), while placing an emphasis on 'egalitarian culture' (along with elements of other facets of the matrix), this chapter focuses on the topic of school-to-school collaboration from the German perspective. We define our understanding of school networks, present a typology of commonly found networks in Germany, provide systemic examples of some of the larger school networks in Germany and review the national state of research in this field. In so doing, we shall reference experience from two of our research and development projects with respect to the topic of school networks. The role of school leadership, which will be expanded upon further, has proven to be a driver of success in school networks. Our chapter ends with an overall assessment of the German situation with regard to school-to-school collaboration.

---

[1]https://www.bertelsmann-stiftung.de/de/unsere-projekte/abgeschlossene-projekte/projekt?
tx_rsmbstcontent_projectlist%5Baction%5D=show&tx_rsmbstcontent_projectlist%
5Bcontroller%5D=Projectlist&tx_rsmbstcontent_projectlist%5Bproject%5D=403&cHash=
0b0cee4b47a91c1147e81a04d704a68e

Structure and Management of the German School System in the Context of the Cohesion/Regulation Matrix

The German school system is organized federally and is, therefore, characterized by a great deal of diversity between, and even within, federal states. During primary education, which typically lasts four years, almost all children are taught together and inclusively, unless they have special educational needs which are being met in a dedicated school. The structure of the school system, in which children progress from primary to lower secondary education, is based on the tripartite model. Secondary schooling is divided between three pathways of general education (*Hauptschule, Realschule* and *Gymnasium*), which lead to three distinct types of qualification. Pupils can obtain these qualifications in schools dedicated to just one pathway or in schools that offer all or multiple learning tracks. Learning pathways vary according to a pupil's anticipated cognitive attainment level and differ, therefore, in the opportunities they provide to progress to upper secondary education which, in Germany, includes vocational education. As a result, after primary education, schooling can vary greatly between federal states. Throughout the history of schooling in Germany, this heterogeneity of provision has been a long-standing topic of debate in education policy. However, structural issues have rarely been the focus of discussion when it comes to viewing individual schools as self-improving organizations.

To ensure quality and equivalence of standards across the country, the Standing Conference of the Ministers of Education and Cultural Affairs – also known as the KMK – is responsible for coordinating the provisions of education policy between all federal states (KMK, 2019). As well as agreeing the fundamental structural elements of the school system, the conference produces resolutions on quality assurance primarily through establishing shared, empirically monitored educational standards in certain subjects. Most of the measures and management strategies for school development are generally organized by the individual states and, increasingly, with the involvement of local authorities in quality improvement. Some states have greater levels of external accountability than others (e.g. with regard to central exams and school inspections, which do not take place in every state). Other states have greater degrees of autonomy at the school level than others over issues such as staff recruitment, for example.

The social cohesion/social regulation matrix, introduced by Chapman (2019) to address 'socio-cultural perspectives on reform and unintended outcomes', provides a reference point for assessing Germany's development. A clear categorization is not straightforward in the German context because of differences between federal states and the degree of crossover between development targets and the *status quo.*

The German school system is characterized by the following three factors when it comes to social cohesion frameworks: it is predominantly organized by the state; the private school market is insignificant in scale (and requires state approval); and elements, such as competition and the market, are barely apparent. Teachers or employees working for educational authorities tend to be classed as 'civil servants' who are paid according to statewide terms and conditions. Civil servants often enjoy their status for life and have a close relationship to the state and to the federal constitution. Despite the selective nature that underpins much of the German school system (which simultaneously perpetuates social inequality), equal opportunities and achievement have taken on greater significance in education policy as a result of the findings of international attainment studies. Greater importance is placed on interventions at the individual school level, such as more differentiated resource allocations or targeted support and guidance measures.

In Germany, social regulation can be considered relatively weak. Although most federal states have established their own quality assurance systems, few consequences are incurred in cases of poor performance during school inspections or central testing. Poor results do not lead to school closures or even to a change in staffing, because civil servants tend to enjoy lifelong tenure. Furthermore, while teaching staff are granted a high degree of autonomy (KMK, 2019, p. 50) when it comes to how they approach their pedagogical responsibilities, strong management capabilities are often lacking when it comes to leadership at the school level.

This development goes hand in hand with an understanding of the school as a learning organization that has been partially strengthened in its scope for decision-making and action. Schools should be able to adapt to local changes continuously, with the help of data, and be able to monitor their actions – and their impact – themselves.

Nevertheless, the coupling of the development of the overall system with that of the individual school and its personnel is complex, since German schools and the individual actors within them can decide independently how to deal with external interventions. The idea of managing development processes still encounters

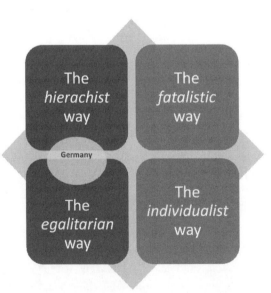

Fig. 1.   Mapping the German School System Within the Social Cohesion/ Social Regulation Matrix.

a bureaucratic administrative context, in which an institutional culture has developed over a long period of time where the interpretive sovereignty over school quality lies with the pedagogical professionals (Klein & Bremm, 2020). For these reasons, cooperation between teaching staff is described as deficient (e.g., Baum, 2014).

Against this background, the German governance model could be classified in the upper left quadrant of the social cohesion/social regulation matrix: 'hierarchical culture: bureaucratic, managed organizations'. At the same time, frameworks that support egalitarian culture are emerging amidst increasing cases where educational policy encourages partnerships and cooperation among schools and in collaboration with other educational stakeholders. In order to capture the diversity of frameworks across the German federal states, we have assigned the German landscape its own spatial field in the matrix, with a hybrid position that combines elements of both hierarchical and egalitarian systems placing more emphasis on 'egalitarian culture' (see Fig. 1). In so doing, we recognize the tensions between hierarchical and bureaucratic culture that arise from the contradictory policy frameworks at work in Germany, such as scrutiny without consequences and tight guidelines for administration contrasted with a high degree of teacher autonomy, for example.

A weakness of the German school structure is that it is not responsive at the systemic level to changing needs. Ultimately, it is up to individual schools to decide what to do if they do not achieve set standards. School authorities often do not see themselves as managers or are at least reluctant to take on this role (Klein & Bremm, 2020). In this way, pressure and unintended side effects are largely avoided, but systemic initiation of and support for fundamental change is still lacking. It is in this arena that school networks offer a promising support structure to foster systemic improvements.

A Classification of School Networks

We begin by exploring how networks can be categorized in the German school system from a governance theory perspective. This chapter focuses on school networks as a format for organizing cooperation between schools and other institutions such as school administrations, for example. From a governance perspective – taking account of school autonomy and the function of the individual school as an organizational entity – school networks are a format that sits between top-down hierarchical management, on the one hand, and market-driven competition, on the other hand. Such networks enable indirect strategic impulses to be given through cooperation, coordination and reciprocal learning (Rürup et al., 2015, p. 161).

Based on the different definitions found in the German and international literature (e.g., Boos et al., 2000; Czerwanski, 2003; Hadfield et al., 2006; Jungermann et al., 2018, p. 10; Kools & Stoll, 2016; Muijs et al., 2010), school networks are taken to mean structures of cooperation between schools and other stakeholders that are established intentionally by certain actors in order to achieve given objectives. These networks provide a forum for (mostly time-bound) thematic cooperation on the basis of common interests and shared goals. They facilitate reciprocal learning, cooperation and collaborative development towards new opportunities or objectives which are better realized through coordinated efforts rather than isolated activities. As structures they can be more readily activated than informal collegiate cooperation and tend to enjoy a more binding format and programme of activities thanks to their institutionalized framework. Furthermore, these networks are characterized by their voluntary nature, mutual trust, consideration and interdependence.

Research has defined several forms of network that are relevant for school development and improving school quality. These include collegiate cooperation (described and analyzed from a network perspective by Moolenar, 2012, for example), professional learning networks among teachers (e.g., Brown, 2019) and dedicated inter-school networks (e.g. Jungermann et al., 2018; Muijs et al., 2010). Rürup et al. (2015) distinguish between different types of school networks according to their overarching objectives:

- **Exchange networks:** focussed on mutual learning/exchange and experience-based reflection;
- **Development networks**: also centred around mutual learning processes, but with a stronger emphasis and orientation towards shared outputs, such as the joint creation of learning modules or the introduction of school development processes;
- **Transfer networks**: here mutual exchange and learning processes are complemented by a focus on promoting wider adoption of innovative methods by facilitating the dissemination of knowledge from schools with relevant prior experience to schools that are new to this innovative way of working. Consensus-driven, hierarchy-free cooperation acts as a vehicle of implementation for innovations in the education sector (Gräsel & Fussangel, 2010); and
- **Cooperation networks**: these are long-term cooperative relationships that extend beyond individual network meetings and may include a shared identity, such as their regional educational landscape.

The authors of this chapter point out that different types of network do in fact overlap in a number of dimensions (Rürup et al., 2015). This must be viewed critically, especially when addressing issues of development and knowledge transfer. From a theoretical perspective, as well as in the context of practical experience, it is of central importance that the creation of educational innovations is not confined to one type of environment while restricting other actors to 'mere implementation' of what has been developed elsewhere. Solutions – and the experiences that accompany them – are only transferable to other schools up to a certain point and cannot simply be adopted on a like-for-like basis (e.g. Rolff, 2019). From a governance theory perspective, this poses the question of whether there is a shared core of educational innovations whose objectives will be not be compromised by varying circumstances. Despite the challenges that remain unresolved at the theoretical level, the degree of network cooperation among German schools has increased notably in the last two decades. The research conclusions stemming from these experiences will be outlined briefly below.

Literature Review: The Impact of Networks and the Conditions for Their Success

School-based network activities are generally considered to be conducive to innovation, as joint work in a network promotes the learning processes of the actors involved (see Berkemeyer et al., 2008). The positive effects of networks are manifold: they provide the participants with a space for knowledge exchange and enable participation in new and different practices (see Berkemeyer et al., 2009; Järvinen & van Holt, 2011). By working together on shared topics, goals and projects, synergy effects can be used for one's own work, so that networking thus contributes to the further professionalization of teachers (Czerwanski, 2003; Hameyer & Ingepaß, 2003). At the level of student learning, early studies occasionally found positive effects of cross-school networking, such as the development of subject-specific competence and the learners' convictions and attitudes relevant to learning (for example, Adler et al., 1995). Here, however, the findings are ambiguous (Berkemeyer et al., 2009). Thus, positive effects of cross-school networks on teaching competencies and strategies could be found in recent studies. For example, an increase in application relevance and a broader range of teaching methods could be shown, which allows for the cautious assumption that school networks can be associated with improving students' skills (Glesemann & Järvinen, 2015). In order for school networks to harness such positive effects, some conditions must be met (Manitius et al., 2015).

First, both the support and the acceptance of all staff and school leaders are important factors for effective collaboration in networks, the transfer of network innovations and the sustainability of improvements (see Järvinen & van Holt, 2011). In order to ensure the success of cross-school networks, it is essential that all participants have clear, shared goals; coherence in network activities between participants; as well as a recognizable structure of network participation (Müthing et al., 2009). Furthermore, focal points of work must be created cooperatively, and responsibilities must be clearly and precisely divided. In addition to mutual recognition and trust between network participants (Brown et al., 2016), it appears important that schools within cross-school networks do not perceive each other as competitors for certain groups of pupils, for example. In this context, a combination of schools within cross-school networks due to spatial proximity can negatively impact cooperation if internal competition undermines mutual trust (see Jungermann et al., 2015). The composition of networks (based on themes, proximity or school type) is a factor that is considered, 'decisive for the success of networking' (Otto et al., 2015, p. 68). Excessive differences and even too few similarities between schools in a network can hamper networking or at least make network management much more difficult (Otto et al., 2015, p. 68). Based on the brief overview of cross-school networks outlined above, it can be seen that networks between schools can have a positive effect on school improvement (see also Brown & Poortman, 2018).

Whether networks are more effective than individual schools at implementing innovation has not yet been investigated in the German literature, because research has been focussed on goal attainment instead. Similarly, little is known about the way in which networks and their stakeholders work together. These perspectives are being explored further in the DigiSchulNet project (see Box).

Methods of Analysing School Networks: A Case Study from the 'DigiSchulNet' Project

In accordance with the assumptions of social network analysis, networks are defined as a group of actors and their relationships to one another (Wasserman & Faust, 1994). This definition allows for the analysis of all social contexts from a relational perspective. In this way, explanations of individual behaviour or social phenomena are determined less by their individual features and more in terms of the characteristics of networks and the position of actors within them.

The research project 'DigiSchulNet–Digitale Schulentwicklung in Netzwerken' [Digital School Development in Networks] has examined several school networks (using, among other things, social network analysis) to discover the conditions that contribute to successful cross-school cooperation in digital transformation (Gageik et al., in press). The project is carried out by the Working Group on Educational Research and the Learning Lab at the University of Duisburg-Essen. The aim of the project is to investigate cooperation within school networks with a focus on school development in the context of education in the digitalized world, education for sustainable development and schools in challenging circumstances.

In order to track the communication, cooperation and transfer processes and strategies that make up network activities and school development processes, school networks undergo an ego-centric network analysis as part of a longitudinal study (Perry et al., 2018). Information is gathered from teaching staff via online questionnaires. To account for the relational perspective, an online tool is used (based on the work of Stark & Krosnick, 2017) that provides participants with a visualization of their own network while completing an online questionnaire. This visualization is referred to during the course of the survey (when referencing contacts, for example), which not only improves clarity for participants but also serves to enhance motivation and enthusiasm for the process. Not only are cooperative relationships within the school and network (cf. Gräsel et al., 2006) recorded from a first-person (ego) perspective, but relationships of the cooperation partners to one another are also evaluated from a first-hand ego perspective. The data obtained in this way are analyzed using Netdraw software (Borgatti, 2002), which supports a visual mapping of cooperative relationships as ego-centric networks. This visual rendering also highlights the diverse plurality of the cooperation partners in terms of their organizational affiliation, function, thematic content and channels of communication, for example. The data are evaluated through a longitudinal comparison, which explores not only the typical network metrics such as size and density,[2] but

---

[2]Network density = proportion of theoretical (and sometimes empirically observable) relationships in ego networks.

also allows findings to be reached about the homogeneity or heterogeneity of the network constellations with regard to different features of various groups. Using this approach, a deeper understanding of transfer processes between school networks and the individual school as well as of cooperative developments within schools can be obtained.

School Networks: Examples from Germany

School networks are not formally recognized in the 16 school laws that comprise the most important formal legal governance instruments of the federal states. This leaves open the potential for other stakeholders to convene their own structures and networks (see Table 1). In this context, more and more large foundations with an interest in education have emerged as initiators of school networks, sometimes in cooperation with state education ministries. The introduction of school networks through *political* initiatives occurs at both *federal* and *state levels* through funding programmes, for example. The latest funding programme of the *Bundesministerium für Bildung und Forschung* [Federal Ministry of Education and Research] (BMBF) underlines the relevance of networks and cooperation, especially between research and practice. At the state level, there are school network projects that are initiated by state ministries. Furthermore, *civil engagement activities*, such as through registered associations, play an important part in supporting network structures.

Table 1 shows different stakeholders which have set up school networks. They might follow different approaches when it comes to management and implementation of networks. In Germany, there remains, however, a gap in the research when it comes to charting a systemic overview of school networks, their initiators and thematic content.

A great deal of thematic diversity can be seen in the activities of school networks, especially with respect to issues such as the environment, digitalization, political education, individual support and working with schools in deprived areas.

Interconnectedness Between Schools in the Context of the Research and Development Project 'Potenziale Entwickeln– Schulen Stärken' (PeSs)

The experience of the network project '*Potenziale entwickeln–Schulen stärken*' [Developing potential–strengthening schools] (PeSs) yields many examples of opportunities and challenges that arise in collaborations between different stakeholders and also present themselves at the school leadership level. PeSs was one of the research and development projects sponsored by the Mercator Foundation and was carried out by the Universities of Duisburg-Essen and Dortmund (2014–2020) (Ackeren et al., 2021). The project focussed on quality improvements for lower

Table 1.   Examples of School Networks in Germany Grouped By Their Various Initiators.

Initiating Body	Project Example	Themes	Start Date
Association: Aktion Courage e.V. (https://aktioncourage.org/startseite/)	*Schule-ohne-Rassismus/Schule-mit-Courage* [School without racism – school with courage] (SoR/SmC)	Political education	1995
State authorities: Ministry for Schools and Education, North Rhine-Westphalia (https://www.schulministerium.nrw)	*Zukunftsschulen NRW* [Schools of the future]	Individualized support	2013
Foundations: Deutsche Kinder- und Jugendstiftung, Stiftung Mercator [German Children and Youth Foundation, Mercator Foundation] (https://www.dkjs.de/en/home/; https://www.stiftung-mercator.de/en/)	*Lernen im Ganztag* [Full-day school learning] (LiGa)	Individualized learning in a full-day setting	2016
Universities: University of Duisburg-Essen; University of Siegen (funded by the Federal Ministry of Education and Research, BMBF) (https://digi-ebf.de/udin)	*Unterrichtsentwicklung in der Sekundarstufe I digital und inklusiv durch Research Learning Communities* [Development of digital and inclusive teaching in lower secondary schools in research learning communities] (UDIN)	Digitalization, inclusion	2020
KMK, federal and state governments: Federal Ministry of Education and Research (BMBF); state ministries (https://www.empirische-bildungsforschung-bmbf.de)	*Schule macht stark* [School makes you strong] (SchuMaS) (https://www.schule-macht-stark.de)	Developing schools in socially deprived areas	2021

secondary schools in socially deprived parts of the Rhine–Ruhr region ($N = 36$), whose activities were systematically accompanied and supported for three years. *The Qualitaets- und UnterstuetzungsAgentur NRW* [North Rhine–Westphalian State Institute for the Quality and Support of Schools] (QUA-LiS) also joined the consortium and acted as an interface between schools and the educational administration.

This constellation of actors – researchers, school practitioners, the state institute and a non-profit foundation – provided a format in which mutual learning could occur through cooperative exchange of knowledge management (Manitius & Bremm, 2019). At the same time, the combination of different actors brought with it inherent challenges when it came to the division roles and responsibilities, because the groups contained such a diversity of interests, objectives, working styles and timelines (Rutter et al., 2020).

Conclusions regarding the aims and objectives of the project are, in part, sobering because minimal change in school performance could be attributed to the project when assessed against the central indicators of quality improvement such as school environment and teaching quality, for example (Holtappels & Brücher, 2021). However, useful indications about the factors which precipitate successful school network projects can be drawn in terms of the format arrangements of a project and the relevance of its membership. With regard to the transfer of network activities in participating schools, it can be seen that the degree of involvement and support from school leaders is strongly correlated with not only the effectiveness of the cooperation within the network but also with the degree of network content that is transferred down to the individual school level (Brücher et al., 2021, p. 238). In cases where the project was not supported by school leadership, or where there was an absence of strong participants in the network, any success in gathering support and momentum within the peer group tended to bring the innovation activities of individual participants to their limits (Brücher et al., 2021, p. 238). Another important factor was driven by changes in school leadership (towards a bottom-up approach) that were not anticipated at the beginning of the project. For sustainable development and a successful translation of knowledge about school operations, it was crucial that school leaders used and encouraged wide dissemination of the complementary knowledge readily available in individual schools and the network itself. School leaders who followed a 'leadership for learning' approach in terms of this perspective shift were able to take an active role in shaping knowledge management and the necessary frameworks that promote and disseminate innovations in their schools (Brücher et al., 2021, p. 238). A further necessary factor for successful knowledge transfer proved to be the flexibility and adaptability of the internal support efforts provided by each school.

Networks, Management and Leadership

Based on the findings of the research accompanying the PeSs project, as well as the results of wider school improvement research, the following challenges can be identified with regard to implementing reforms in the context of the plurality of actors involved in the multilayered school system. Depending on the internal logic of their systems (e.g. schools vs supervisory bodies or schools vs. education authorities), stakeholders may recontextualize the motivating factors driving their activities in terms of government guidelines or network-based objective setting, for example (Asbrand, 2014; Dietrich, 2017). This approach is reinforced by the weak or absent accountability structures as described in reference to the cohesion–regulation matrix in Chapter 1. Under these conditions, German schools can be understood as self-referential systems that define their identity, autonomy and functionality independently from the outside world and tend to be resistant to change. In order to initiate change processes externally through network activities, it is necessary to have a knowledge of the organizational operating principles and/or the development strategies of schools and their employees, especially their leaders.

School leadership occupies two key functions within the management structures of the German school system. From a top-down management perspective, school leaders serve as an interface between individual schools and the administrative system that encourages and structures a recontextualization of central policy incentives for individual schools. Findings show that a greater significance should be attributed to the role of school leaders within the multilayered education system, especially in the context of profound changes to Germany's educational policy framework in the wake of *Neue Steuerung* [New Governance] (Dubs, 2019; Scheerens, 2012). In recent years, this has revealed itself in the form a tendency towards reappraising the role of school leaders as management and executive authorities in individual schools, although they still have relatively weak decision-making authority when compared with their international counterparts (Schleicher, 2020). Nonetheless, school leaders are framed as change agents and catalysts for raising standards and implementing policy programmes in schools.

Viewed from a bottom-up perspective, by contrast, school leaders and leadership networks can be ascribed the following functions: gathering, evaluating and systematizing schools' innovations and successful development strategies and reporting these back to education authorities and policymakers, most frequently in the form of 'best practices'. In this scenario, school leaders are not merely interface managers who carry out reform measures independently on behalf of educational policymakers and administrators and recontextualize them for the school level. Instead they are leaders who shape the conditions and climate in which innovations can be developed and implemented at the school level.

In order to be able to fulfil the responsibilities of this executive function, school leaders need to go far beyond the traditional top-down understanding of their role in school improvement commonly found in Germany (cf. the Anglo-American context, e.g., Armstrong & Ainscow, 2018; Brown & Poortmann, 2018; Ehren & Perryman, 2018; Gilbert, 2017; Glenn et al., 2017; Mitterlechner, 2019). When leadership of this kind is seen to be a fundamental factor for effective networking and successful cooperation in educational networks, then closer attention is owed to role of these leaders in school network activities in Germany. The concept of distributed leadership seems promising in this context, because it accounts for the management patterns found in flat organizational structures while capturing the presence of bottom-up management practices.

A Summary of School Networks in Germany

School-to school collaboration networks are not systemically anchored in the German educational landscape. In the past, certain large-scale school networks tended to be initiated by actors from outside of the school system, who typically created time-bound projects. Often elements of these projects go on to be picked up by educational stakeholders (policymakers, administrators, etc.) later, who carry forward relevant themes into further programmes and projects that tend to have longer time horizons. Permanent structural changes are not introduced, and any additional resources are temporary. It remains to be seen whether such programmes have the potential to function as educational development programmes that can leave a sustained impact.

Network initiatives are not driven by competition, because the German school system is not designed along the principles of free-market competition. Instead, networks are an attempt to respond at a professional level to specific challenges such as digitalization or improving the performance of schools in socially deprived areas. On the one hand, it can be seen as positive that in a relatively egalitarian system (by international standards), with a high degree of teacher autonomy, school network initiatives are sustained through intrinsic motivation rather than as a response to additional pressures. On the other hand, however, this environment creates a dilemma when it comes to the impact of development-related network activity. Although extending the high degree of structural autonomy and freedom that teachers enjoy upwards to the school level may encourage more school participation in network activities, the systemic impact of this will be limited. This is because the management of the school system tends to be organized in a hierarchical pattern, which means that projects remain simply 'projects' and are, as such, rarely equipped to bring about sustainable change that impacts individual schools beyond the process level. This recognition of the need to strengthen both the internal and external roles of school leaders (as supported by the PeSs project, Chapter 5) is met with structural barriers.

From a structural perspective, network activities are unlikely to bring about significant far-reaching change because there are no structural pathways to support this within Germany's largely hierarchical system. In this framework of largely voluntary activity, it is possible that the schools and teachers who are engaged and mobilized through the process will be those who were more motivated and open to innovation to begin with, rather than those who would be in greater need of incentivization to innovate and develop.

In the German context, it is notable that education policy prioritizes the individual school level, while the structural system remains in the background of political discourse, especially when it comes to the debate on tackling social inequality. Fundamental issues of reallocating resources receive scant mention in political debates. Although programme-based school development guidelines have their limitations, they do offer policymakers the possibility to postpone or avoid taking structural decisions that would be hard to carry out publicly, especially given Germany's federal school system. Within this system, good, well-documented examples of school network activities offer only the potential for change via the 'back door' as long as they relate to teacher training and bring a positive effect by encouraging openness towards collaboration and the opportunities this can bring for the individual and to the organization.

Key Lessons for Policy

- In order for network structures to be able to transmit quality development in a widespread, sustainable manner, they will need to be formally anchored as structures within the school system in a way that empowers them beyond their typical status as time-bound programmes with only local reach.
- The high degree of freedom granted to schools – and the recognition of teachers' status as professionals – brings many advantages when it comes to motivation, social innovation and the avoidance of undesirable side effects. At the same time, however, in a system with little external accountability and unclear roles for school monitoring, this autonomous approach can make it harder to introduce change in the places where it is most severely needed. Introducing flexibility and clarity of roles is one of the central tasks of network structures.
- In this environment, the role of school leaders is of particular importance at the interface of working between hierarchical supervisory processes and schools whose operations are shaped by a context of increasing autonomy. The role of school leaders should be strengthened because research into school networks has shown them to be essential for fostering innovation-oriented practices and change processes.
- With regard to all network stakeholders, it is important to reflect on respective interests, objectives, operating principles and timelines; to make explicit their relation to the thematic agenda; and to reach agreement on the shared objectives of the network.
- To this end, tools such as network analysis and dialogue with accompanying research can offer meaningful assistance.

References

Ackeren, I., van, Holtappels, H. G., Bremm, N., & Hillebrand-Petri, A. (2021). *Schulen in herausfordernden Lagen – Forschungsbefunde und Schulentwicklung in der Region Ruhr*. Das Projekt "Potenziale entwickeln – Schulen stärken". Beltz Juventa.

Adler, L., Cragin, J., & Searls, P. (1995). *The Los Angeles area business/education partnership. A study of the impact of a community based school to work program for high risk youth*. East San Gabriel Regional Occupation Program.

Armstrong, P. W., & Ainscow, M. (2018). School-to-school support within a competitive education system: Views from the inside. *School Effectiveness and School Improvement, 29*(4), 614–633.

Asbrand, B. (2014). Die dokumentarische Methode in der Governance-Forschung. In K. Maag Merki, R. Langer, & H. Altrichter (Eds.), *Educational governance als Forschungsperspektive* (pp. 183–205). Springer VS.

Baum, E. (2014). *Kooperation und Schulentwicklung. Wie Lehrkräfte in Gruppen Entwicklungsanlässe bearbeiten.* Springer VS.

Berkemeyer, N., Manitius, V., Müthing, K., & Bos, W. (2008). Innovation durch Netzwerkarbeit? Entwurf eines theoretischen Rahmenmodells zur Analyse von schulischen Innovationsnetzwerken. *Zeitschrift für Soziologie der Erziehung und Sozialisation, 28,* 411–428.

Berkemeyer, N., Manitius, V., Müthing, K., & Bos, W. (2009). Ergebnisse nationaler und internationaler Forschung zu schulischen Innovationsnetzwerken. *Zeitschrift für Erziehungswissenschaft, 12,* 667–689.

Boos, F., Exner, A., & Heitger, B. (2000). Soziale Netzwerke sind anders. In K. Trebesch (Ed.), *Organisationsentwicklung. Konzepte, Strategien, Fallstudien,* (pp. 65–76). Klett-Cotta.

Borgatti, S. P. (2002). *NetDraw: Graph visualization software.* Harvard, Analytic Technologies.

Brown, C. (2019). Exploring the current context for professional learning networks, the conditions for their success, and research needs moving forwards. *Emerald Open Research, 1*(1), 1–19. https://doi.org/10.12688/emeraldopenres.12904.2

Brown, C., Daly, A., & Liou, Y.-H. (2016). Improving trust, improving schools – Findings from a social network analysis of 43 primary schools in England. *Journal of Professional Capital & Community, 1*(1), 69–91.

Brown, C., & Poortman, C. L. (2018). *Networks for learning. Effective collaboration for teacher, school and system improvement.* Routledge.

Brücher, L., Holtappels, H. G., & Webs, T. (2021). Schulleitungshandeln an Schulen in herausfordernden Lagen – Zur Bedeutung von Leadership for Learning für den Aufbau von Schulentwicklungskapazität. In I. van Ackeren, H. G. Holtappels, N. Bremm & A. Hillebrand-Petri (Eds.), *Schulen in herausfordernden Lagen – Forschungsbefunde und Schulentwicklung in der Region Ruhr. Das Projekt "Potenziale entwickeln – Schulen stärken"* (pp. 205–243). Beltz Juventa.

Chapman, C. (2019). *Making sense of reform. Where next for Scottish education? Association of Directors of Education in Scotland.* The Staff College.

Czerwanski, A. (Ed.) (2003). *Schulentwicklung durch Netzwerkarbeit. Erfahrungen aus den Lern-netzwerken im "Netzwerk Innovativer Schulen in Deutschland".* Verlag Bertelsmann Stiftung.

Dietrich, F. (2017). Inklusion im Mehrebenensystem. Überlegungen und explorative Analysen zur Einführung der "Inklusiven Schule" aus der Perspektive einer rekonstruktivn Governanceforschung. In J. Budde, A. Dlugosch, T. Sturm (Eds.), *(Re-) Konstruktive Inklusionsforschung: Differenzlinien–Handlungsfelder–Empirische Zugänge* (pp.181–195). Barbara Budrich.

Dubs, R. (2019). *Die Führung einer Schule.* Franz Steiner Verlag.

Ehren, M., & Perryman, J. (2018). Accountability of school networks: Who is accountable to whom and for what? *Educational Management Administration & Leadership, 46*(6), 942–959.

Gageik, L., Hasselkuß, M., & Endberg, M. (2022, in press). School Development within Networks in a Digital World: Risky Ride or Beneficial Blessing? In K. Ortel-Cass, K. Laing, & J. Wolf, (Eds.), *Partnerships in Education.* Transdisciplinary Perspectives in Educational Research 5. Springer.

Gilbert, K. A. (2017). Innovative leadership preparation. Enhancing legal literacy to create 21st century ready principals. *Academy of Educational Leadership Journal, 21*(1), 1–17.

Glenn, P. (2017). *Creating Tomorrow's Leaders. Examining Teacher Perceptions of a Systems Approach Framework to Continuous Classroom Improvement.* Gardner-Webb University.

Glesemann, B., & Järvinen, H. (2015). Schulische Netzwerke zur Unterstützung der Einführung und Konzeption des Ganztags an Gymnasien. In H. Wendt & W. Bos (Eds.), *Auf dem Weg zum Ganztagsgymnasium. Erste Ergebnisse der wissenschaftlichen Begleitforschung zum Projekt „Ganz In–Mit Ganztag mehr Zukunft. Das neue Ganztagsgymnasium NRW"* , (pp. 129–151). Waxmann.

Gräsel, C., & Fussangel, K. (2010). Die Rolle von Netzwerken bei der Verbreitung von Innovationen. In N. Berkemeyer, W. Bos, & H. Kuper (Eds.), *Schulreform durch Vernetzung Interdisziplinäre Betrachtungen* (pp. 117–129). Waxmann.

Gräsel, C., Fußangel, K., & Pröbstel, C. (2006). Lehrkräfte zur Kooperation anregen – Eine Aufgabe für Sisyphos? *Zeitschrift für Pädagogik, 52*, 205–219.

Hadfield, M., Jopling, M., Noden, C., O'Leary, D., & Stott, A. (2006). *What does the existing knowledge base tell us about the impact of networking and collaboration? A review of network-based innovations in education in the UK.* National College for School Leadership.

Hameyer, U., & Ingepaß, A. (2003). *Schulentwicklung im Netzwerk. Orientierungen für die Praxis.* Ministerium für Bildung, Wissenschaft, Forschung und Kultur des Landes Schleswig-Holstein.

Holtappels, H. G., & Brücher, L. (2021). Entwicklungen in den Projektschulen. Qualitätsverbesserungen und Aufbau von Schulentwicklungskapazität. In I. van Ackeren, H. G. Holtappels, N. Bremm & A. Hillebrand-Petri (Eds.), *Schulen in herausfordernden Lagen – Forschungsbefunde und Schulentwicklung in der Region Ruhr. Das Projekt "Potenziale entwickeln – Schulen stärken"* (pp. 128–166). Beltz Juventa.

Järvinen, H., & van Holt, N. (2011). Mit Netzwerken Schule und Unterricht entwickeln. Erfahrungen aus dem Projekt "Schulen im Team". *Journal für Schulentwicklung, 15*, 16–25.

Jungermann, A., Manitius, V., & Berkemeyer, N. (2015). Regionalisierung im schulischen Kontext. Ein Überblick zu Projekten und Forschungsbefunden. *Journal for Educational Research Online, 7*(1), 14–48.

Jungermann, A., Pfänder, H., & Berkemeyer, N. (2018). *Schulische Vernetzung in der Praxis. Wie Schulen Unterricht gemeinsam entwickeln können.* Waxmann.

Klein, E. D., & Bremm, N. (2020). *Kooperation, Unterstützung, Kontrolle? Zum Verhältnis von Schulaufsicht und Schulleitungen in der Schulentwicklung.* Springer VS.

KMK. (2019). *The education system in the Federal Republic of Germany 2016/2017.* A description of the responsibilities, structures and developments in education policy for the exchange of information in Europe.

Kools, M., & Stoll, L. (2016). *What makes a school a learning organisation?* OECD Publishing.

Manitius, V., & Bremm, N. (2019). Kooperation von Wissenschaft, Praxis und Administration als Wissenstransferstrategie. Einblicke in ein Schulentwicklungsprojekt zu Schulen in sozial-räumlichen benachteiligten Lagen in NRW. In C. Schreiner, C. Wiesner, S. Breit, P. Dobbelstein, M. Heinrich & U. Steffens (Eds.), *Praxistransfer Schul- und Unterrichtsentwicklung* (pp. 265–282). Waxmann.

Manitius, V., Junker, R., & Berkemeyer, N. (2015). Entwicklungsverläufe und Nachhaltigkeit schulischer Netzwerke. In N. Berkemeyer, W. Bos, H. Järvinen, V. Manitius & N. van Holt (Eds.), *Netzwerkbasierte Unterrichtsentwicklung. Ergebnisse der wissenschaftlichen Begleitforschung zum Projekt "Schulen im Team"* (pp. 153–187). Waxmann.

Mitterlechner, M. (2019). *Leading in inter-organizational networks.* Towards a reflexive practice. Palgrave Macmillan.

Moolenar, N. M. (2012). A social network perspective on teacher collaboration in schools. Theory, methodology, and applications. *American Journal of Education, 119*, 7–39.

Muijs, D., West, M., & Ainscow, M. (2010). Why network? Theoretical perspectives on networking. *School Effectiveness and School Improvement, 21,* 5–26. https://doi.org/10.1080/09243450903569692

Müthing, K., Berkemeyer, N., & van Holt, N. (2009). Fachbezogene Unterrichtsentwicklung in Netzwerken. Wie Netzwerke entstehen. In H. Rolff, E. Rhinow & T. Röhrich (Eds.), *Unterrichtsentwicklung - Eine Kernaufgabe der Schule. Die Rolle der Schulleitung für besseres Lernen* (pp. 194–203). Köln: LinkLuchterhand.

Otto, J., Sendzik, N., Järvinnen, H., Berkemeyer, N., & Bos, W. (2015). *Kommunales Netzwerkmanagement. Forschung, Praxis, Perspektiven.* Waxmann.

Perry, B., Pescosolido, B., & Borgatti, S. (2018). *Egocentric network analysis: Foundations, methods, and models* (Structural analysis in the social sciences). Cambridge University Press. https://doi.org/10.1017/9781316443255

Rolff, H. G. (2019). Transfer von Innovationen im Schulbereich. In C. Schreiner, C. Wiesner, S. Breit, P. Dobbelstein, M. Heinrich, & U. Steffens (Eds.), *Praxistransfer Schul- und Unterrichtsentwicklung* (pp. 49–60). Waxmann.

Rürup, M., Heinke, R., Emmerich, M., & Dunkake, I. (2015). *Netzwerke im Bildungswesen. Eine Einführung in ihre Analyse und Gestaltung.* Springer VS.

Rutter, S., Löhr, T., & Bremm, N. (2020). Schule – Schulbegleitung – Forschung. Aspekte einer erfolgreichen Zusammenarbeit. *Journal für Schulentwicklung, 3,* 29–36.

Scheerens, J. (2012). *School leadership effects revisited: Review and meta-analysis of empirical studies.* Springer Science & Business Media.

Schleicher, A. (2020). *The impact of COVID-19 on education – Insights from education at a glance 2020.* OECD Publishing. https://www.oecd.org/education/the-impact-of-covid-19-on-education-insights-education-at-a-glance-2020.pdf

Stark, T. H., & Krosnick, J. A. (2017). GENSI: A new graphical tool to collect ego-centered network data. *Social Networks, 48,* 36–45.

Wasserman, S., & Faust, K. B. (1994). *Social network analysis: Methods and applications.* Cambridge University Press.

Section 4

Fatalist Systems

Chapter 13

School-to-School Collaboration Through Teaching School Alliances in England: 'System Leadership' in a Messy and Hybrid Governance Context

Toby Greany and Paul Wilfred Armstrong

Abstract

This chapter explores school-to-school collaboration via Teaching School Alliances (TSAs) in one locality in England, drawing on governance theory (Bevir, 2011) – specifically hierarchy, markets and networks (Tenbensel, 2017). It focusses on three TSAs in detail, describing their individual development as 'school-led' networks but also how they interact with each other and with other networks in the context of wider hierarchical and market-driven pressures and opportunities. It compares these examples to the three common TSA trajectories described by Greany and Higham (2018) – *exclusive, marketized, and hierarchical* – showing how these trajectories overlap and interact in hybrid forms. It concludes by discussing these findings in relation to social regulation and cohesion (Chapman, 2019; Hood, 1991) and to the wider themes in this book. We argue that while collaboration between schools in the English system has been driven at the policy level by an egalitarian narrative, in reality, such activity is enacted within a hierarchical and individualist framework which can be in tension with the professional values and ethics of school leaders. We conclude with recommendations, which include a need to rethink national and local accountability structures in order to encompass a broader range of outcomes; encourage more ambitious levels of experimentation in how the needs of children and families can best be addressed;

School-to-School Collaboration: Learning Across International Contexts, 229–244
Copyright © 2022 by Toby Greany and Paul Wilfred Armstrong
Published under exclusive licence by Emerald Publishing Limited
doi:10.1108/978-1-80043-668-820221014

focus on place-based coherence and collaboration; and, finally, develop the skills and capacity of frontline leaders to shape productive networks.

Keywords: School-to-school collaboration; partnership; leadership; governance; networks; Teaching School Alliances

Introduction

This chapter explores school-to-school collaboration via Teaching School Alliances (TSAs) in one locality in England, drawing on governance theory (Bevir, 2011) – specifically hierarchy, markets and networks (Tenbensel, 2017). It focusses on three TSAs in detail, describing their individual development as 'school-led' networks but also how they interact with each other and with other networks in the context of wider hierarchical and market-driven pressures and opportunities. It compares these examples to the three common TSA trajectories described by Greany and Higham (2018) – *exclusive, marketized, and hierarchical* – showing how these trajectories overlap and interact in hybrid forms. It concludes by discussing these findings in relation to social regulation and cohesion (Chapman, 2019; Hood, 1991) and to the wider themes at the heart of this book. We argue that while collaboration between schools in the English system has been driven at the policy level by an egalitarian narrative, in reality, such activity is enacted within a hierarchical and individualist framework which can be in tension with the professional values and ethics of school leaders. This has implications for policy and practice, so we conclude with a set of recommendations.

Three Trajectories for Teaching Schools in the 'Self-improving School-led System'

The idea of a 'self-improving school-led school system' (SISS) has been an overarching narrative for the government's school policy in England since 2010. The associated reforms have been far-reaching, but have included new, more demanding, curriculum standards and school accountability requirements. The structure of the school system has changed radically, through an expansion in the number of academy schools and multi-academy trusts (MATs) and a parallel reduction in the role of England's 152 local authorities (LAs). Academies are funded and overseen by central, rather than local, government and have additional 'freedoms' (e.g. they are not required to follow the National Curriculum) (Greany, 2018; Greany & McGinity, 2021; West & Wolfe, 2018). The government has argued that these reforms aim to 'dismantle the apparatus of central control and bureaucratic compliance' (DfE, 2010, p. 66) by 'moving control to the frontline' (DfE, 2016, p. 8).

Policy has also stimulated collaboration between schools (Armstrong et al., 2020), often by encouraging high-performing schools and 'system leaders' to support schools that are judged to be under-performing but also through the broader Teaching Schools initiative outlined here. School partnerships have been viewed by government as 'an essential requirement' (House of Commons Education Committee, 2013, Ev46, para 3) for realising its SISS vision and it has supported their development through various initiatives, particularly TSAs (DfE, 2010).[1] Between 2010 and 2019, a school could volunteer to be designated as a Teaching School by the government if it met specified performance criteria – for example in terms of its Ofsted[2] inspection grade and pupil performance in standardized tests. Designation brought some limited core funding and a remit to provide initial teacher training (ITT), school-to-school support for schools facing challenges, and ongoing professional and leadership development for staff across its network.[3] In order to fulfil this remit, the Teaching School was required to form an alliance of partner schools, though the precise size and nature of this network was not prescribed. From the outset, Teaching Schools were expected to generate their own income, by selling services to other schools (DfE, 2010), but they could also bid for a variety of central grants to support a range of different policy priorities, such as supporting other schools with the implementation of government curriculum and assessment reforms. A particular government priority in this period was to expand the role of schools in ITT (and to reduce the role of universities), so Teaching Schools were required to develop provision in this area as a priority (Greany & Brown, 2015).

In summary, then, Teaching Schools were expected to: i) support the enactment of government policies and priorities; ii) foster the development of a commercial marketplace for school improvement-related services; iii) promote lateral networks between schools as a means of securing systemic improvement.

These three roles neatly traverse the three coordinating mechanisms identified by governance theory (Bevir, 2011; Rhodes, 1997; Tenbensel, 2017), which Greany and Higham (2018) define as follows:

- *Hierarchy* – the authority exercised by national, regional, and local government as well as formally governed school groups, through policies, guidance, bureaucratic oversight, accountability, and support
- *Markets* – incentives and (de)regulation which encourage choice, competition and commercialization
- *Networks* – the (re)creation of interdependencies that support and/or coerce inter-organizational collaboration.

---

[1]The first cohort of Teaching Schools was designated and began work in 2011, with 750 in operation by 2019. In 2019, after the data for this chapter had been collected, the government announced that Teaching Schools would be replaced by a smaller number of Teaching School Hubs. The Hubs began operating nationally in 2021 – see https://www.gov.uk/guidance/teaching-school-hubs accessed 27.8.21.
[2]Ofsted stands for the Office for Standards in Education, Children's Services and Skills. It is a non-ministerial department that inspects and regulates services that provide education and skills for learners of all ages (GOV.UK, 2021a).
[3]Teaching Schools were initially expected to work across six areas, but these were merged into three in 2015.

Each mechanism is seen to have strengths but also limitations. For example, Adler (2001) notes how hierarchy draws on formal authority to enable control, but this can weaken collaboration and lateral innovation; markets rely on price to co-ordinate supply and demand and promote flexibility, but this can corrode trust, knowledge sharing, and equity; while networks co-ordinate on the basis of trust and promote knowledge sharing but can become dysfunctional, complacent, and/or exclusive. Critically, government attempts to mix and match these mechanisms, through 'meta-governance', are not straightforward and can lead to messiness and governance failure (Ball & Junemann, 2012). In addition, this mixing of hierarchy, markets, and networks by the state can create tensions, contradictions, and confusion, which can be experienced as 'personal, professional or ethical dilemmas' (Newman & Clarke, 2009, p. 127) by leaders in frontline contexts. We return to these points in the conclusion, where we assess how the mixing of hierarchy, markets, and networks in the core remit of TSAs has created challenges and tensions for TSA leaders.

Gu et al.'s (2015) government-funded evaluation of Teaching Schools found that they were clustered in urban areas and concentrated among secondary schools. The evaluators concluded that TSAs could be conceived as 'loose partnerships' that rely on 'like-minded people' working together through a process of 'give and take' to develop collective and collaborative intellectual and social capital for improvement (2015, p. 180). Greany and Higham agreed that 'the relatively non-prescriptive and voluntary nature of the Teaching Schools initiative left scope for local adaptation and variation' (2018, p. 79). However, they argued that Gu et al.'s interpretation was a 'somewhat idealized view' (2018, p. 79), not least because Teaching Schools were also working to generate income and to enact government policy. Based on their study of four localities across England, Greany and Higham identified three common development trajectories for TSAs, arguing that in:

- *hierarchical alliances*, one or more lead schools dominated developments and was seen by alliance members to be benefitting disproportionately;
- *marketized alliances*, the lead school/s sold services in a transparent but transactional way, with limited commitment to ongoing partnership or reciprocity with 'client' schools; and
- *exclusive alliances*, a subset of higher performing schools had formed the network as a way of securing their own performance, providing relatively limited opportunities or support for schools more widely to engage.

This chapter builds on Greany and Higham's analysis, showing how these trajectories develop in hybrid ways as leaders respond to different, often competing, opportunities and requirements, and as they seek to align these with their personal and professional values. It draws on previously unpublished data from the earlier study, focussing in detail on one of the four localities studied – Eastern City. The research in Eastern City[4] involved visits and interviews in three established

---

[4]See Greany and Higham (2018) for a detailed methodology and for further details on Eastern City, which is a pseudonym.

Teaching Schools as well as a fourth school that was in the process of applying to become one. In addition, a range of staff in seven other schools across the city were interviewed along with a number of 'system informants', such as LA and Ofsted (regional) leaders and the Regional Schools Commissioner.[5]

Existing Networks as a Foundation for Many TSAs

Greany and Higham's research identified that partnerships have become more extensive and more important to schools since 2010. School leaders argued that collaboration was 'more and more something we *need* to do' (primary head). This view reflected a mix of factors, but particularly the loss of support from LAs coupled with a need for schools to respond to rapid changes in the curriculum and assessment regime and to meet the changing demands of the accountability system. Networking was also seen to provide mutual support and professional development opportunities for school leaders and staff and to offer access to expertise and additional improvement capacity for schools that required it.

Greany and Higham found that collaborative activity between schools took many forms, but that the 'local school cluster' was the most common form of partnership, especially among primary schools. These local clusters ranged widely, but the strongest examples were usually long-standing, with formalized governance and involvement from staff at multiple levels in a range of improvement-focussed activities. Secondary schools tended to collaborate in different ways, reflecting higher levels of local competition, although this did not necessarily prevent them from co-operating locally.

Many of the TSAs operating across the four localities studied by Greany and Higham had grown out of an existing local cluster. SUCCESS TSA, outlined in Box A, is one example of this kind of cluster development. However, as the SUCCESS vignette indicates, such transitions were rarely seamless. Indeed, Greany and Higham show how the decision to engage with a government-funded initiative of this sort inevitably required changes to existing cluster arrangements and ways of working. One example relates to network governance, where clusters were required to move from relatively egalitarian and informal head teacher steering groups, to a model in which one school – the designated Teaching School – became the *primus inter pares*. These changes led to wider shifts in how schools engaged with and perceived these networks, some of which could be seen as positive (e.g. enabled by increased network-level staffing capacity), while others were more problematic (e.g. if the lead school was seen to be benefitting disproportionately). Evaluations of previous government-led initiatives that required schools to work with and support other schools have typically revealed similar opportunities and barriers (see Armstrong & Ainscow, 2018).

---

[5]There are eight Regional School Commissioners who work across England. Broadly speaking, their remit is to work with existing academies and MATs in their region to address underperformance and ensure they are supported to improve (GOV.UK, 2021b).

Three TSAs in Eastern City

Eastern City has a population of around half a million and is served by about 200 schools and academies in total. The city has above-average levels of poverty and ethnic diversity but with significant differences between different parts of the city.

All of the wider case study schools visited in Eastern City (i.e. the non-Teaching Schools) had engaged with one or more Teaching Schools to support their work, though not necessarily one of the Teaching Schools we focus on here. The nature and extent of this engagement varied. At one end of the spectrum was the primary principal quoted in Box A, who had been closely involved in the development of SUCCESS TSA: even though his school was not the designated Teaching School, it had agreed to take a lead responsibility for delivering some aspects of the overall remit. Most other case study schools had much lower levels of engagement with Teaching Schools and had more transactional relationships with these schools. For example, most had bought in specific expertise and/or had participated in Teaching School-run professional development programmes and events. Nevertheless, perceptions of this support were broadly positive, as the following quote indicates:

> The LA has gone from 30 advisors to 3, so getting the person you need, when you need them, is now nearly impossible … [So last year] I went and bought time in from the City TSA, which was excellent, and cheaper than the LA now. (Principal, maintained primary school, Ofsted Good)

In Boxes A, B, and C, we provide vignettes of three established Teaching Schools visited in Eastern City. The first, SUCCESS TSA, offers a clear example of an *exclusive* alliance, as defined by Greany and Higham, but the second and third examples are less clear-cut. Coherence TSA (Box B) is seeking to achieve scale and sustainability by forming meta-alliances with other TSAs and with the City Primary Heads group, an approach that could be characterized as combining the *hierarchical* and *marketized* trajectories in hybrid form. However, these efforts are only partially successful and achieved limited benefit for the Executive Head or her Teaching School, while generating significant additional work and pressure for her and her team. Indeed, the fact that the Executive Head continues to work to build a collaborative city-wide approach, in contrast to Principal of Reluctant TSA (who decides that the additional work and risks are not worthwhile), indicates a more values-driven motivation than the *hierarchical* and *marketized* trajectories might suggest. Similarly, while Regional MAT TSA (Box C) is clearly part of a *hierarchical* MAT structure which requires a largely *exclusive* focus on turning round the challenging schools within the trust, the approach is nonetheless motivated by an underlying set of values which centre on improving the quality of education in deprived communities. We discuss the implications of these complex and overlapping operational models and professional and individual logics in the final section.

Box A: SUCCESS TSA

The principal of a primary school in a small town on the outskirts of Eastern City explained that collaboration had become increasingly essential for school improvement as support from the LA declined after 2010. This meant 'we had to sort our own houses out, really'.

However, he felt that the local cluster, which had historically included 12 local primary schools, had failed to recognize the implications of this shift. The main sticking point was when six of the primary school heads proposed developing a model of peer review, which would involve visiting each others' schools. The other six primaries resisted this proposal, but the proposing group decided to do it anyway:

> Literally, as soon as we mentioned doing inspections (i.e. peer reviews) in each other's schools, the room just divided in two, from 'over my dead body' to those which were, 'fine'… which was why SUCCESS [TSA] formed, because we wanted to move things at a higher pace than some of the other heads. (Principal, primary maintained, Ofsted Good)

One of the schools in the group had subsequently been designated as a Teaching School, with the other five schools taking the role of strategic partners in the SUCCESS Alliance. The peer reviews had been operating for two years at the time of the case study visit and were seen by the participating heads as an important way of sharing ideas and expertise between the schools and of ensuring that they did not become 'complacent', for example, in preparing for an Ofsted inspection (Greany, 2020b). The schools had also developed a range of wider partnership activities, including a common approach to assessing pupil progress; a school business managers group which undertakes some joint procurement; a range of self-initiated subject networks; a middle leaders development programme and some other joint professional development for staff.

However, the principal acknowledged that the development of SUCCESS as a separate entity from the wider cluster had led to a division between what he described as the 'stronger' and 'more vulnerable' schools in the locality. He explained that 'there's a lot more suspicion than there has been in the past. The temperature drops by about 30 degrees as soon as you mention SUCCESS'. The Deputy head explained that whereas, previously, there had been cluster-wide training days, that year there had been only a SUCCESS training day, which only the member schools could attend. In the words of the principal:

> SUCCESS appeared, because we felt we couldn't wait. The world was changing around us, and if we didn't do

> something, we'd be left on our own. I think it's unfortunate that probably the six strongest schools in [the cluster] formed SUCCESS. And that was to our shame, a little bit, I think, that the egalitarianism stopped. And I think that our vulnerable schools within [the cluster], within the locality, are on their own, because they weren't able or willing to join. (Principal, primary maintained, Ofsted Good)

This principal admitted to feeling deeply conflicted by this development but argued that his response was the only option in the context of the government's policy framework:

> I think it's a capitalist model. It's about school-to-school competition, and the government's very hot on that, and for that, there are winners and losers. And right now, I've taken the pragmatic, yet morally dubious position of 'I want to be with the winners', and that means I have to leave out some losers, some people who are vulnerable, on the outside. And we know that they're there. We know that they'd bite our arm off to come and join us. But we can't have lots of voices in the room if we're going to move things on quickly. And that's not fair. (Principal, primary maintained, Ofsted Good)

Box B: Coherence TSA

Coherence TSA had formed about two years before the case study visit, led by a designated primary school. Unlike many alliances, this network had not grown out of a local cluster. Indeed, the Deputy Head of the Teaching School explained that attempts to establish local cluster working in the past had proved frustrating, which he put down to local competition between schools. In his view, the Teaching School model was more effective as it was focussed on addressing real needs, rather than 'geographical for geographical's sake'.

The Executive Head of the primary school was leading the new alliance, often drawing on his own school's staff for capacity and expertise. For example, an experienced maths teacher in the school had been released from class teaching completely, spending half her time supporting other teachers within the school and the other half supporting schools across the wider alliance. In the year of the case study visit, she had worked most closely with an Ofsted 'good' primary school, leading 2 whole-school training days and 12 additional staff meetings, all focussed on deepening subject knowledge. She was also working with the school's maths subject leader to embed this work. Meanwhile, she was trying to ensure that her work reached as many primary schools across the city as possible. For example, she had distributed a monthly maths newsletter to schools, working hard to grow her network so that she reached around 85% of all the maths subject leaders across the city.

The key challenge facing Coherence TSA's Executive Head was how to develop a more sustainable model for the alliance. He was concerned that if he and his staff spent too much time supporting other schools across the city, then the performance of the designated Teaching School itself might suffer (which could lead to the school being de-designated). However, the core government funding for the Teaching School was insufficient to employ a dedicated team, so he was cautious about employing additional staff unless he could be sure how to pay them. Income from one-off government grants for specific pieces of work had proved volatile and hard to predict. The alternative was to generate income by selling services, such as professional development programmes, to other schools, but the challenge there was that he would be in competition with the LA and with other Teaching Schools.

The Executive Head's response was to try to build a series of meta-alliances, with the LA and with other TSAs and groups across the city, arguing the need for a coherent, city-wide approach which could meet the needs of all schools. In practice, this approach had had mixed success, partly due to a perception among some colleague heads that he was 'empire building'. Approaches to two existing partnerships in different parts of the city were rebuffed. He approached a third group of primary schools when he heard that they were applying to become a TSA, persuading them to work with his alliance on a city-wide model. The new bid was successful, bringing in additional funding and capacity, which had enabled the Executive Head to appoint a full-time TSA Manager. However, the principal of the new Teaching School – Reluctant TSA – quickly became concerned by the amount of work involved, fearing that his own school was becoming over-stretched and might decline, so had decided to pull back and focus primarily on his own school.

A further attempt to create coherence had also encountered resistance. The Executive Head sat on the City Primary Heads Group (CPHG), an umbrella group for all primary heads. His vision was that the TSA and CPHG should be linked, with a single subscription covering membership of both groups, but he had not been able to persuade the Chair of CPHG to support this proposal.

The Executive Head's final partnership effort, with Regional MAT TSA on the Maths Hub, was challenging for different reasons, as we explore in the following section.

Box C: Regional MAT TSA

Regional MAT[6] had emerged, prior to 2010, from a single, high-performing secondary school that had taken on responsibility for turning around two of the lowest-performing schools in Eastern City. In the years immediately after 2010, the MAT grew to include 12 schools, half in Eastern City and half across the wider region. The MAT's growth had required a rapid evolution in strategy, not least because the newly joining schools were all in deprived contexts and all required intensive 'turnaround' improvement, which stretched the Trust's limited central capacity.[7]

The creation of Regional MAT TSA was an important step towards increasing the Trust's capacity to manage this 'turnaround' work. The TSA Director, working with a small central team, took on responsibility for coordinating 'school to school support' efforts across the MAT's network of schools and for providing initial teacher training, professional development programmes, subject networks, and a programme of peer reviews between MAT schools.

The TSA's Director was clear that coordinating school-to-school support activities – for example, by seconding staff from higher performing schools in the trust to work in the most challenging, newly joined schools – was his priority. Moving staff around in this way was arguably more feasible for him than for the other TSAs (i.e. because the MAT was the single employer of all staff across the group, whereas in non-MAT Alliances each individual school was the employer). Nevertheless, the TSA Director was dismissive of other TSAs in the city, who he argued had prioritized the easier and more lucrative aspects of their remit – 'the nicer things' – such as professional and leadership development. He argued that school-to-school support should be the core role, even though it is 'the hardest to do', because – in his view – it makes the most direct impact on school improvement.

The focus on intensive turnaround work with schools within the MAT meant that Regional MAT TSA was seen by many other interviewees across Eastern City as internally focussed. One interviewee described it as a 'black hole that sucks everything in'. The TSA Director did argue that 'it's about not being insular' and gave examples of working with schools beyond the MAT but was also clear that he worked for the MAT and was answerable to the MAT's board and CEO, who evaluated his performance.

Finally, Regional MAT TSA was also distinctive in the extent to which it saw itself as a business, meaning that any external work needed to generate income. As the TSA Director put it:

---

[6]A MAT is a non-profit company, with a board and Chief Executive, which operates a number of academies (Greany, 2018; Greany & McGinity, 2020).
[7]See Glazer et al (2022) for a detailed exploration of the MAT's growth challenges and how it responded.

> We are a big business. Don't get me wrong. In terms of commercial work … So, you need to think about how you're going to generate income through work that you do for other schools that is going to make you sustainable into the future.

Mandated Collaboration as a Source of Tension Between TSAs

The nature of inter-TSA collaboration in Eastern City was illuminated further through the development of a government-funded Maths Hub.

Maths Hubs were a government initiative coordinated by a dedicated agency.[8] Hubs received generous funding and were charged with introducing a new pedagogical approach to mathematics teaching in primary schools, modelled on practice in Shanghai and the concept of 'maths mastery' (Boylan et al., 2019). Regional MAT TSA and Coherence TSA both applied to become hubs, but only Regional MAT TSA was successful. However, the government insisted that Regional MAT TSA work with Coherence TSA on the implementation. Working in partnership together in this 'forced marriage' proved challenging because it revealed stark differences in the ethos and approach of the two TSAs: while Regional MAT TSA wanted to focus initially on its own MAT primary schools, Coherence TSA wanted to focus more widely, to reach all primary schools across the city.

The Mathematics Leader in Coherence TSA described the early stage of the partnership as a 'really horrible period, (with) nasty emails flying back and forth about lack of partnership working'. In their view, the issue was that the two TSAs 'had a completely different view of CPD (Continuous Professional Development) and teaching schools'. They characterized these differences as follows:

> Their [i.e. Regional MAT TSA] interpretation of Teaching Schools is – you come and join our trust and we will support you in a really incredible way to turn your failing school around and we're keeping it in this lovely cosy group of 12 schools – and they do nothing to support other schools. And they probably shouldn't need to as they have such an impact on the schools they have … whereas we have a totally different model which is about bits of support here and there and all about going out to other schools … One model is not better than the other, they're just different, but that difference in models caused a really horrible year both for them

---

[8]The National Centre for Excellence in the Teaching of Mathematics (NCETM) coordinates the work of 40 Maths Hubs across England. See https://www.ncetm.org.uk/ (accessed September 1, 2021).

and for us. It's taken a lot of hard work and goodwill on both
sides to get where we are now where there's some common ground.
(Mathematics Lead Teacher, Coherence TSA)

The Director of Regional MAT TSA acknowledged these difficulties – 'we've
normed, formed, stormed, and all of that' – but argued that, ultimately, bringing
the two TSAs together had enhanced the overall approach. Having used the Hub
funding and resources to develop expertise within its own schools, Regional MAT
TSA hoped that these schools could become beacons of good practice for schools
across the wider city to learn from. More recently, the two TSAs had agreed to
consider how other TSAs across the city could develop knowledge of the new
approaches so that this knowledge could be disseminated and embedded before
the Maths Hub funding elapsed.

This brief example adds further depth to the assessment of Coherence and
Regional MAT TSAs. It clearly supports an assessment of Regional MAT TSA
as *exclusive* in its focus on using the resources to benefit its own schools before any
consideration of how the additional funding might benefit schools more widely.
But this *exclusivity* can also be rationalized in terms of equity: in the eyes of
Regional MAT's leaders, the children in these deprived and under-performing
schools deserve additional resources and attention, so this justifies their decision
to focus on these schools initially. By the same token, Coherence TSA rational-
izes its own focus on ensuring that all schools across the city can access the new
pedagogy and resources in terms of equity and fairness, arguing that all schools
and all children should benefit equally. We suggest above that Coherence TSA
could be characterized as combining the *hierarchical* and *marketized* trajectories
in hybrid form, but the example of the Maths Hub work adds further nuance to
this assessment, revealing the extent to which these apparently 'selfish' motives
are bound up with personal and professional logics and values relating to equity,
fairness, and profession-led improvement. As the quotes above indicate, the
resulting tensions can cause significant inter and intra-personal conflict for the
leaders and teachers involved.

In addition, we argue that the Maths Hub example reveals important and still
unresolved differences of opinion around how knowledge and expertise can best
be developed and disseminated across local school systems. Is it better to have
an intensive focus on developing innovative approaches in a small number of
schools and to then use these schools as exemplars for others to learn from (i.e.
the Regional MAT TSA model), or is it better to share resources and encourage adoption across a wider network, in the hopes that new practices will emerge
and spread more organically (i.e. the Coherence TSA model)? These issues are
beyond the immediate scope of this chapter, but we argue that they merit further
investigation.

Conclusion

The evidence presented in this chapter reveals the (often competing) demands
that 'system leader' schools and leaders in England face. They are clearly situated

within, and responding to, hierarchical, market, and network incentives and pressures. They must work simultaneously to i) address the priorities and expectations set by government, ii) secure sufficient income to remain sustainable, and iii) meet the needs and expectations of their alliance members. In addition, they must continue to run their own schools, maintaining high levels of performance, not least in order to retain their Teaching School designation.

We argue above that where governments engage in meta-governance, by seeking to mix hierarchical, market, and network forms of co-ordination to achieve desired outcomes, this can lead to messiness and governance failure and can create tensions and dilemmas for frontline leaders. We see both outcomes here. For example, the schooling landscape across Eastern City is undoubtedly messier as a result of the rollback of the LA and the emergence of new school types and support structures, including MATs and TSAs. It can also be argued that having multiple Teaching Schools across the locality, with each one interpreting its remit in different ways and adopting a different strategy for network improvement, increases the likelihood of governance failure. One example of this is the wasted time and energy expended on agreeing the Maths Hub approach. Equally, we see how these issues can cause tensions and ethical dilemmas for these 'system leaders' and their colleagues. For example, the head teacher involved with SUCCESS TSA clearly feels discomfort at having to take the 'pragmatic, yet morally dubious position of "I want to be with the winners"'. These issues also have important implications for equity, for example, for the six cluster schools who are excluded from the SUCCESS TSA partnership, or the many schools that must wait for support in implementing Maths Mastery.

Greany and Higham (2018) conclude that school 'system leaders', such as the head teachers of TSAs, form part of a 'co-opted elite', who work as part of the managerial state and accrue a range of personal and organizational benefits as a result. At one level, this chapter reinforces that conclusion, showing how Teaching School leaders become the *primus inter pares* in previously equitable clusters and partnerships, in return for implementing government policy. Equally, it adds nuance, by highlighting the extent to which these leaders work – in different ways – to enhance equity and outcomes in line with their individual and collective values. Interestingly, one TSA head teacher in Eastern City argued that, far from increasing her power and elite status, the task of leading across an alliance had actually revealed the limited nature of her authority:

> I think there's a difficulty in trying to help a school-led system where you don't know where the leadership of the school-led system is; I think that's really hard. Because I don't really know where it's supposed to sit. It sits with us, is what we keep being told, but I've got no authority over other principals in the city and they can either listen to me or not, it's up to them. (Executive Head, maintained primary federation, Ofsted Outstanding)

Finally, we have explored the three TSA trajectories outlined by Greany and Higham (2018) – *exclusive, marketized, and hierarchical* – showing how these can be applied in hybrid ways in response to hierarchical, market, and network imperatives. More importantly, we have sought to show how these apparently 'selfish' strategies can be inter-mixed with values-driven approaches which reflect a commitment to equity and systemic improvement, even when such aims might be at odds with the needs and priorities of the designated Teaching School.

Key Implications for Policy and Practice

The data we present through these case studies are illustrative of the complex and turbulent waters that leaders of Teaching Schools and their partners must navigate. Drawing on Hood's model, the data reveal a hybrid approach to collaboration in which school 'system leaders' may be driven by an egalitarian narrative and set of personal values, but this can be in tension with the hierarchical and individualist ways of working that are incentivized by the broader governance and accountability structures in which they operate. As we argue above, these pressures encourage 'selfish' behaviours while increasing the risk of governance and operational failures and of increasing inequality between schools.

Although we see this critique of the Teaching Schools policy and its outcomes as entirely valid, we also recognize its strengths. For example, we note above that perceptions of Teaching Schools among the wider schools we visited were broadly positive. We also recognize that alternative models – including the LA-led model for school improvement in place before 2010 and the MAT-led model that the government now hopes to achieve (Whittaker, 2021) – are not panaceas. The original aspiration for a system in which schools work together and support one another to collectively improve the educational achievement and life chances of children and young people had many strengths, and our findings do include examples of where such networked improvement has added value. The challenge, as we see it, is to address the governance issues so that school-to-school collaboration can develop within a wider context that secures equity and improvement. To this end, we put forward the following recommendations:

1. Purposeful collaboration between schools can be a powerful vehicle for knowledge exchange, innovation, and educational improvement. However, genuine collaboration based on shared values and trust takes time to build and requires sophisticated leadership. The outcomes from such collaboration might include measurable improvements in defined areas, such as school quality and/or pupil achievement, but a narrow focus on these areas can stifle the potential for wider benefits and outcomes. Holding individual schools accountable for performance, with 'high stakes' consequences for 'failure', makes collaboration less likely. Similarly, market incentives which seek to encourage inter-school competition for pupils and/or resources will make collaboration more difficult. We advocate for a fundamental rethink of national and local accountability structures in order to encompass a broader range of outcomes, including both school- and network-level outcomes, and to encourage more ambitious levels of experimentation in how the needs of children and families can best be addressed.

2. Local school systems in England are now remarkably complex and fragmented, with serious implications for equity and sustainable, strategic improvement. There is a need to focus on place-based coherence and collaboration, between schools, academies, MATs, and the various other 'middle tier' groups that exist, including LAs and the new Teaching School Hubs. School 'system leaders' can play a role in helping to shape such local coherence, but they will need to be convened within a common framework that recognizes and addresses existing power imbalances and that places equity at the heart of any new approach.

3. Simply incentivising schools to collaborate, through designations and funding as seen in the Teaching Schools model, is unlikely to work. Rather, schools should be carefully and contextually matched so that they can provide mutual challenge and critical friendship informed by evidence as to their strengths and weaknesses. Furthermore, there is a need to invest in the skills and capacity of school leaders to undertake such network, for example, as seen in the Kāhui Ako|Communities of Learning programme in New Zealand (Greany & Kamp, 2022).

References

Adler, P. (2001). Market, hierarchy and trust: The knowledge economy and the future of capitalism. *Organisation Science, 12*(2), 215–234.

Armstrong, P. W., & Ainscow, M. (2018). School-to-school support within a competitive education system: Views from the inside. *School Effectiveness and School Improvement, 29*(4), 614–633.

Armstrong, P., Brown, C., & Chapman, C. (2020). School-to-School Collaboration in England: A Configurative Review of the Empirical Evidence. *Review of Education, 9*, 391–351.

Ball, S., & Junemann, C. (2012). *Networks, new governance and education.* Policy Press.

Bevir, M. (Ed.). (2011). *The Sage handbook of governance.* Sage.

Boylan, M., Wolstenholme, C., Maxwell, B., Jay, T., Stevens, A., & Demack, S. (2019). *Longitudinal evaluation of the mathematics teacher exchange: China-England.* DfE.

Chapman, C. (2019). From hierarchies to networks: Possibilities and pitfalls for educational reform of the middle tier. *Journal of Educational Administration, 57*(5), 554–570.

Department for Education (DfE). (2010). *The importance of teaching: The schools white paper, Cm 7980.* Department for Education.

Department for Education (DfE). (2016) *Educational excellence everywhere, Cm 9230.* Department for Education.

Exworthy, M., Powell, M., & Mohan, J. (1999, October–December). The NHS: Quasi-market, quasi-hierarchy and quasi-network? *Public Money and Management, 19*, 16–22.

Glazer, J., Greany, T., Duff, M., & Berry, W. (2022). Networked improvement in the US and England: A new role for the middle tier. In D. J. Peurach, J. L. Russell, L. Cohen-Vogel, & W. R. Penuel (Eds.), *Handbook on improvement-focused educational research*, (pp. 165–188). Rowman & Littlefield.

GOV.UK. (2021a). *Ofsted.* Retrieved May 12, 2021, from https://www.gov.uk/government/organisations/ofsted

GOV.UK. (2021b). *Regional school commissioners: About us.* Retrieved May 12, 2021, from https://www.gov.uk/government/organisations/regional-schools-commissioners/about#who-we-are

Greany, T. (2018). *Sustainable improvement in multi-school groups.* Department for Education.

Greany, T. (2020a). Place-based governance and leadership in decentralised school systems: Evidence from England. *Journal of Education Policy, 37*(2), 247–268. https://doi.org/10.1080/02680939.2020.1792554

Greany, T. (2020b). Self-policing or self-improving? Analysing peer reviews between schools in England through the lens of isomorphism. In D. Godfrey (Ed.), *School peer review for educational improvement and accountability: Theory, practice and policy implications* (pp. 71–94). Springer.

Greany, T., & Brown, C. (2015). *Partnerships between teaching schools and universities.* Centre for Leadership in Learning, UCL IOE.

Greany, T., & Higham, R. (2018). *Hierarchy, markets and networks: Analysing the 'self-improving school-led system' agenda in England and the implications for schools.* UCL IOE Press.

Greany, T., & Kamp, A. (2022). *Leading educational networks: Theory, policy and practice.* Bloomsbury.

Greany, T., & McGinity, R. (2021). Structural integration and knowledge exchange in multi-academy trusts: Comparing approaches with evidence and theory from non-educational sectors. *School Leadership and Management.* https://doi.org/10.1080/13632434.2021.1872525

Gu, Q., Rea, S., Smethem, L., Dunford, J., Varley, M., & Sammons, P. (2015). *Teaching schools evaluation: Final report.* Department for Education.

Hood, C. (1991). A public management for all seasons. *Public Administration, 69,* 3–19.

House of Commons Education Committee. (2013). *School partnerships and cooperation: Fourth report of session 2013–14* (Vol. 1).

Newman, J., & Clarke, J. (2009). *Publics, politics and power: Remaking the public in public services.* Sage.

Rhodes, R. (1997). *Understanding governance: Policy networks, governance, reflexivity and accountability.* Open University Press.

Tenbensel, T. (2017). Bridging complexity theory and hierarchies, markets, networks, communities: A "population genetics" framework for understanding institutional change from within. *Public Management Review, 24*(4), 1–20.

West, A., & Wolfe, D. (2018). *Academies, the school system in England and a vision for the future: Executive summary.* Clare Market Papers No. 23. LSE Academic Publishing.

Whittaker, F. (2021). Williamson: Government 'looking at' how to get more schools into multi-academy trusts. *Schools Week.* Retrieved September 1, 20021, from https://schoolsweek.co.uk/williamson-government-looking-at-how-to-get-more-schools-into-multi-academy-trusts/

Index

Note: Page numbers followed by "*n*" indicate notes.